TEMPLES, RELIGION, AND POLITICS
IN THE ROMAN REPUBLIC

TEMPLES, RELIGION, AND POLITICS IN THE ROMAN REPUBLIC

BY

ERIC M. ORLIN

BRILL ACADEMIC PUBLISHERS, INC.
BOSTON • LEIDEN
2002

Library of Congress Cataloging-in-Publication Data

Orlin, Eric M.
    Temples, religion, and politics in the Roman Republic / by Eric M. Orlin.
        p. cm.
    Originally published: Leiden ; New York : E.J. Brill, 1997, in series:
Mnemosyne, bibliotheca classica Batava. Supplementum ; 164.
    Includes bibliographical references and index.
    ISBN 0-391-04132-0
        1. Temples, Roman. 2. Rome—Religious life and customs. 3. Religion and
politics—Rome. I. Title.

    BL805 .O75 2002
    292.07—dc21

                                                                        2002066856

ISBN 0-391-04132-0

PRINTED IN THE UNITED STATES OF AMERICA

To
my mother
and
the memory of my father.

Their love and support
laid the foundation for this accomplishment.

CONTENTS

Acknowledgements ix
Introduction 1

CHAPTER ONE: Origins 11
    I. Theories on Temple Vowing 12
    II. Situations Resulting in New Temples 18
    III. Conclusions 33

CHAPTER TWO: The Vow 35
    I. Vows Undertaken by Magistrates in Rome 36
    II. Vows Undertaken by Magistrates on Campaign 45
    III. The Significance of Temple Vows 66
    IV. Conclusions 74

CHAPTER THREE: The Sibylline Books 76
    I. The Sibylline Books in Roman Religion 76
        I.1   Their Origins and History 76
        I.2   Procedure 81
        I.3   Consultations and Responses 85
    II. The Sibylline Books and the Construction of New
    Temples 97
        II.1   The Cults and Their Origins 97
        II.2   Motivations for the New Temples 105
        II.3   The Sibylline Books as an Authority 113

CHAPTER FOUR: The Construction 116
    I. *Manubiae* 117
        I.1   *Manubiae, Praeda* and Victorious Generals 117
        I.2   Generals' Use of Booty 122
        I.3   Manubial Building of Temples, Reconsidered .. 127
    II. The Construction of New Temples 139
        II.1   Contracts for Public Buildings 140
        II.2   Contracts for Temples 141
        II.3   The Creation and Employment of *Duumviri*
               Aedi Locandae 147

III. Conclusions 159

CHAPTER FIVE: The Dedication 162
    I. The Legal Authority to Dedicate a Temple 163
    II. The Role of *Duumviri Aedi Dedicandae* 172
    III. The Identity of Dedicators 178
    IV. Conclusions 188

Conclusions 190

Appendix One: State Temples Introduced in Rome, 509–55
    B.C.E. 199
Appendix Two: Sibylline Consultations, 509–83, B.C.E. 203
Appendix Three: The Sibylline Oracle Recorded by
    Phlegon 208
Appendix Four: List of Known *Duumviri* 211
Bibliography 212
Index 221

ACKNOWLEDGEMENTS

The project of writing a book involves the efforts of many people, and this one is no exception. The few words expressed here can only begin to repay the debts of gratitude I owe to those who have helped me. The greatest debt is owed to Erich Gruen, who guided this project from its inception as a dissertation through its transformation to the present state. His penetrating eye helped to sharpen the argument and his words of counsel never failed to offer encouragement when roadblocks appeared in the way. Robert Knapp and Anthony Bulloch also kindly served as readers, and guided the project from its infancy to completion and beyond. Jerzy Linderski, Nathan Rosenstein, and Robert Palmer heroically read entire drafts of the work in its various stages and each offered useful insights by bringing his own expertise to bear on these issues. Thanks are also due to Israel Shatzman, who made helpful criticisms of Chapter Four during his sojourn in Berkeley. The suggestions of these scholars served to correct many flaws in the argument, and any mistakes that remain are due to my own stubbornness.

Willem Jongman and Albert Hoffstäedt from E.J. Brill deserve special gratitude, the former for his useful comments and advice on turning the dissertation into a book and the latter for his patience and guidance. I would also like to thank the staff at the Green Library at Stanford University and the Baker Library at Dartmouth College who were very gracious in helping me track down references.

On a personal note, I want to thank several people who have been of invaluable assistance to me. Lisa Zemelman supplied me with much indispensable advice on a wide variety of topics over the past six and a half years. Judy Gaughan and Beth Severy were the perfect colleagues in graduate school, providing companionship and an ideal sounding board for new ideas. Finally, and most importantly, I want to thank my wife Kathleen, whose love, support and encouragement eased this arduous journey and made its completion possible.

INTRODUCTION

The success and smooth functioning of the Roman Republic depended on a careful balancing of the interests of the individual and the interests of the commonwealth.[1] On the one hand, the state depended on the accomplishments of individual Romans to ensure its safety and prosperity. Over the course of four hundred years, Rome expanded from a small city on the banks of the Tiber River to become the dominant state in the entire Mediterranean basin. This feat was made possible through the successes in war of a series of Roman generals, who fought campaigns almost every year to defend and expand Roman territory. In this way the achievements of the state were predicated on the achievements of individual Romans, and it was therefore necessary for the Senate to find ways of rewarding individuals who had helped the state to prosper. On the other hand, in order to ensure that the welfare of the state remained the paramount concern, the Senate needed to keep control over state affairs. It was essential to create mechanisms so that individual generals took actions which served the best interests of the state, and not merely their own best interests. For the system to work properly, the Senate needed to allow sufficient room for the individual initiative and accomplishment on which the state depended while at the same time maintaining overall authority for the direction of affairs in Rome.[2]

The generals who fought on Rome's behalf had their own concerns in addition to merely protecting their homeland; they fought not only to defend and expand Roman territory, but also to enhance their own glory and prestige. The Roman aristocracy was highly competitive, especially in the Middle and Late Republic when our evidence is most abundant.[3] Regardless of whether one views the Romans as fundamentally imperialistic, it is clear that the acquisition

---

[1] As the focus in this study is on Republican Rome, all dates are B.C.E., unless otherwise noted.

[2] Cf. the comments of Brunt (1988), 11–15, on the operation of the Roman government.

[3] Competition and ambition among the Roman aristocracy has been remarked on by many scholars. See recently Wiseman (1985), 3–16, Brunt (1988), esp. 43ff., and Rosenstein, (1990).

of military glory was a primary goal for the vast majority of Roman aristocrats.[4] *Gloria* acquired on military campaigns was the principal means used by members of the ruling elite to distinguish themselves from each other as they strove for a position of preeminence within the state. Victory brought public recognition of their accomplishments and frequently also brought large sums of money to spend in Rome impressing the populace. The latter in particular could be used to improve the individual's standing with the electorate, but victory would also bolster his position within the narrower ruling elite. Roman generals thus needed to achieve military success for their own purposes as much as the state needed them to achieve that success, and these mutually reinforcing needs were the key to the Roman system of government. The interests of the Republic were served by allowing individual generals, within certain limits, to satisfy their own interests.

The danger inherent in this arrangement, that a single man might place his interests above the state and bend the machinery of the state to his own purposes, must have been evident from the outset. The twin principles of collegiality and the yearly tenure of office, the hallmark of Roman magistracies, were clearly intended to reduce the possibility of this occurrence.[5] Collegiality placed a physical limit on magistrates, by assuring that no individual could wield legal powers that were superior to every other member in the state; there would always be at least one other magistrate with equivalent powers to serve as a counterbalance. Yearly tenure placed a temporal limit on magistrates, forcing them to leave office after only a single year in office, presumably before they could accumulate too much power and turn the magistracy to their own personal use. The failure to stick to these principles in the Late Republic reflects the breakdown of this system. The successive consulships of Marius at the end of the second century, the extraordinary commands given to all the leading generals, and the sole consulship given to Pompey in 52 removed one of the primary checks on the power of individuals. When individuals did place their own interests above those of the state, as in

---

[4] See Harris (1979) for the thesis that the Romans were imperialistic by nature. Criticisms of this view can be found in the review of Luttwak in AHR 85 (1980), 606, and the remarks of Eckstein (1987), xiv–xxii. Evidence on the desirability of acquiring military glory is collected by Harris on pp. 11–104.

[5] Cf. Mommsen's remarks on collegiality in *RS* 1.27–61.

88 when Sulla and Marius turned their forces towards controlling
the government in Rome and later in 49 when Pompey and Caesar
did the same, the state was powerless to intervene. The final result
is clearly visible in the fall of the Republic and its eventual replace-
ment by the Principate of Augustus.

The relationship between the Senate and its magistrates during
the first century B.C.E. was therefore largely antagonistic, as the Senate repeatedly sought to control the ambitions of its leading members. The hard-line stance taken in regard to Caesar in 50 and 49
is simply the best known example, but mention may also be made of
the Senate's refusal to ratify Pompey's *acta* in the East in 62 and of
their refusal even earlier to provide land allotments for the veterans
of Marius following the Cimbric wars. Some scholars have been led
to look further backwards in time and to postulate conflict between
the Senate and the leading men even in the Middle Republic.[6] On
this view, although the system did not crack until the Late Republic,
there were frequent stresses and constant tension from an early date,
and the Senate had to continually attempt to rein in its magistrates
who were constantly seeking their own glory even at the expense of
the state. Yet such an approach seems misguided and exaggerates
the amount of tension between the Senate and its magistrates. What
is remarkable is not the strains of the last hundred years of the
Republic, but rather that the system functioned smoothly and with
only minor adjustments for over four hundred years; this fact alone
attests to a high degree of cooperation between the Senate and its
magistrates. That cooperation, rather than any retrojected antago-
nism, deserves to be the focus of study. How did it work? How was
the Senate able to maintain the requisite control of political affairs
while generals were able to obtain a sufficient amount of glory to
satisfy their needs? How was individual initiative reconciled with
corporate supervision to the benefit of both parties? These questions
are essential to a proper understanding of the workings of the Roman
state, but have yet to be thoroughly analyzed.[7]

The present study will attempt to answer these questions through
an investigation of Roman religion, and particularly through an
analysis of the process through which new temples were vowed, built,

---

[6] See Schlag (1968), Carney (1958).
[7] The recent study of A. Eckstein, (1987), has addressed some of these questions
in regard to Roman foreign relations of the third and early second centuries B.C.E.

and dedicated in Republican Rome. The close link between religion and the state in Rome offers one reason for pursuing this line of approach.[8] The principal purpose of the state religion was to safeguard the *pax deum*, the favor of the gods, and thereby to ensure the safety and prosperity of the community. By their very nature, therefore, religious actions had political overtones. The Senate, as *de facto* guardian of the state, exercised a close supervision of religious matters, which included the recognition and handling of prodigies, the resolution of disputes involving sacred matters, and on occasion the introduction or suppression of new cults.[9] Yet in regard to the introduction of new cults and the construction of new temples, the initiative usually lay with the individual; the most common scenario, that of a general on his campaign vowing a temple, will be familiar to any reader of Livy. Previous studies on how the Romans built new temples to their pantheon have made the assumption that a victorious general could complete this project on his own by using his share of the spoils of war, his *manubiae*, and subsequently performing the dedication. The recent work of A. Ziolkowski states this proposition outright: "a single person could vow, locate, and dedicate a public temple of the Roman people without consulting the people or the Senate."[10] This contention leads directly to his conclusion that "a temple could be founded without the state's participation, i.e. entirely beyond the state's control." On this view, the construction of temples played a vital role in the aristocratic competition in Rome, as triumphant generals sought to promote themselves by building monuments of their campaigns. Yet this position implies that, despite

---

[8] The close relationship between religion and the state has been emphasized in many recent studies. See Watson (1992); Beard & North (1990); Morgan (1990); Gruen (1992); Wardman (1982); MacBain (1982); North (1976); Rawson (1974); Schilling (1969).

[9] For prodigies, which the Senate seems to have handled on an annual basis, see Livy, e.g. 22.1.8–20 (217 B.C.E.), 22.36–6–9 (216), 23.31.15 (215). For disputes, note the debate over the shrine of Libertas which Clodius tried to consecrate in Cicero's house. For new cults, consider the introduction of the Magna Mater in 204, and the suppression of the Bacchanalia in 186. See also Beard & North (1990), 30–33, where Beard argues that the Senate was the principal means of controlling human approaches to the divine in Republican Rome, but cf. *contra* the review of Brennan in *BMCR* 2.6 (1991).

[10] Ziolkowski (1992), 235. Other studies have contented themselves with individual aspects of the process of building a new temple, particularly the use of *manubiae* to finance the construction. See in general Bardon (1955); Stambaugh (1978). On *manubiae* and its uses, see Bona (1960); Shatzman (1972); Morgan (1973a); Pietilä-Castrén (1987).

its control over other aspects of Roman religion, the Senate had little or no control over perhaps its most important aspect: the decision of which gods should be publicly worshipped. A general could vow and build a temple to a deity of his choosing, and thus potentially add a new god to the Roman pantheon, without consulting the Senate. The present work questions this thesis by pointing out the active and significant role played by the Senate in the construction of new temples to Rome. The Senate's involvement in this process will force us to modify the picture often given for the significance of this action.

This study will isolate and analyze the normal procedures by which public temples were built in Rome, in order to better understand how the Senate interacted with its magistrates and on occasion with other states. For the purposes of this study, a public temple is considered to be one which is attested as part of the official state religion in Rome, particularly from its appearance on one of the surviving *fasti*, or calendars of the Roman state.[11] It was possible for cults to exist in Rome outside of the official state religion; Festus indicates that rites for which the cost was paid from public money and which were performed on behalf of the *populus* were part of the *sacra publica*, while those performed on behalf of individual men or families were *sacra privata*.[12] Such private cults are attested by epigraphical evidence and included deities, such as Isis, who were not officially welcomed to Rome as part of the state religion but had been brought in by merchants, soldiers, or others who may have spent time overseas. However, since these cults tell us only about the family or group involved with that cult and not about the state, these private cults will not be considered in this discussion. Instead, we will focus on the over eighty public temples which were dedicated in Rome during the Republic.[13]

---

[11] On the *fasti* and the calendar, see especially Degrassi (1963) and Michels (1967).

[12] Festus 245: *Publica sacra quae publico sumptu pro populo fiunt, quae pro montibus, pagis, curiis, sacellis; at privata, quae pro singulis hominibus, familiis, gentibus fiunt.* The distinction between private and public religion is well discussed by Bakker (1994), 1–3, following the earlier work of Wissowa (1909). As Bakker summarizes on p. 2, "Public religion was limited to a fixed number of gods and *feriae publicae*: those approved by the government—representing the *populus*—as state gods and feasts. On the other hand, any god could be worshipped through *feriae privatae*." As Bakker notes, the pontiffs still held jurisdiction over *feriae privatae* through their supervision of the *ius divinum*.

[13] Two temples built towards the end of the Republic, the temple of Venus Victrix built by Pompey in 55 and that to Venus Genetrix built by Julius Caesar in 46, will be treated only at the end of this study; cf. pp. 196–98. The emphasis which these

Details about the construction of these temples vary greatly, from names, dates and circumstances in some cases to nothing except a *terminus ante quem* in others. Much of the evidence for the construction of new temples during the Republic is provided by Livy in his summations of a given year's religious events. While we must be aware of Livian embroidery or misinterpretation in regard to the specifics of any given temple, his use of priestly records usually provides sufficient details to enable us to analyze the circumstances and procedures for the erection of new temples.[14] Furthermore, for the period when Livy's account is usually considered least reliable, the Early Republic, comparatively few temples were built. On the other hand, our reliance on Livy means that our information is notoriously spotty for the years 292–219 and after 167, periods for which Livy's manuscript is lost. These gaps in our knowledge must not be taken to indicate gaps in temple construction, and we must be very careful in drawing conclusions from other periods to fill these gaps. Furthermore, we can not assume that Livy has given a notice for every temple built during the years that his manuscript does cover; he makes no mention of the temple of Ceres, Liber & Libera which was dedicated in 493, nor in a later period does he mention the temple of Hercules Musarum, built by M. Fulvius Nobilior in the 180's or 170's.[15] Nevertheless, Livy's interest in religious matters makes him an invaluable source, if only for the names and dates he provides, names and dates which can be confirmed and supplemented from other sources.

The actual process of constructing a new temple in Rome can be broken down into several distinct phases, and this study will treat each step in order. Before discussing how temples were constructed in Rome, however, we must ask why new temples were felt to be desirable in the first place: why did Rome come to possess over eighty

---

men, and others in the Late Republic, placed on individual accomplishment even at the expense of the state, stands in sharp contrast to the prior four hundred years of the Republic. These two temples have more in common with Imperial temples and Imperial politics than with Republican, and thus can be used to illustrate the transition between Republic and Empire, but not the operation of the Republican system.

[14] See Ziolkowski (1993), 218–219, for a recent defense of Livy's reliability for temple founding.

[15] The temple of Ceres is attested by Dionysios of Halicarnassos (6.17, 6.94), while the temple of Hercules Musarum is not securely dated but seems clearly before 167; it was vowed in 189. This temple is mentioned by Cicero (*Arch.* 27), Pliny (*HN* 35.66), Ovid (*Fasti* 6.797), and Macrobius (1.12.16), among others.

public temples by the end of the Republic? This can not simply be a situation in which more equals better, for if that were true one would expect the number of temples built to be much higher. To say that temples responded to crises or breaches in the *pax deum* does not advance our analysis very far, for many options were available to the Romans to handle such situations. Chapter One first offers a broad analysis of Roman religion and theories which have been offered to explain this phenomenon, and then more narrowly examines the situations in which new temples were vowed. It will become evident that Roman religion was extremely flexible and that political as much as religious factors influenced the decision to build a new temple. This fact serves to underscore the inseparability of politics and religion in Republican Rome, a point which will recur throughout this study.

Our attention then turns to the first step in the process by which new temples came to Rome, the vow, and this leads us directly into a discussion of the relationship between the individual and the community. Two possibilities existed for the vowing of a new temple. As already mentioned, the most common scenario was that of a Roman general on campaign vowing a temple in exchange for military success. In a smaller number of cases, the Senate itself, acting on the advice of the Sibylline Books, directed that a temple should be built to a particular deity. In the former instance, the initiative lay with the individual, even though the construction of a new state temple clearly had implications for the entire community. In the latter, the initiative ostensibly came from a divine source, although the Senate played a significant role in these proceedings. Chapter Two is devoted to an attempt to untangle the lines of authority in the matter of generals' vows and then to a discussion of the significance of those vows. Chapter Three treats the temples built on the authority of the Sibylline Books; the task there is to determine when and why this mechanism was utilized as opposed to the vow of an individual general.

The actual construction of the temple occupied the next stage in the process and thus occupies the next stage in our analysis. This aspect of the introduction of new temples received the least attention from the ancient authors, which may reflect their conception that it was the least important of the three stages. This ancient attitude should warn us not to put too much stress on this aspect of the process, but nevertheless an investigation of who paid for the construction of new temples will further our understanding of the roles played by the

Senate and the individual. Many modern scholars have assumed that
victorious generals used booty from their campaigns, i.e. their *manubiae*, to finance the construction of the temples which they had vowed.
This position implies that temples served as memorials of an individual's accomplishments, and served to further his personal ambition
and electoral career. A reexamination of the evidence for this contention in Chapter Four reveals that this type of manubial building
may be the exception rather than the rule, and that funding may
have often come through the Senate. Although there was some room
for personal advertisement, the close involvement of the Senate causes
a very different picture of the relationship between individual and
state to emerge.

Our study concludes with an exploration of the dedication ceremony, the final step in adding a new temple to the Roman religious system. The dedication was a festive ceremony, performed by
a single man and often accompanied by games, which provided an
excellent opportunity for a Roman aristocrat to publicize his name
and accomplishments. Yet again, the Senate maintained the ability
to select the person who would dedicate a temple, and this process
allows us to draw further conclusions about the nature of the relationship between the Senate as a corporate body and its individual
members. Chapter Five first explores the legal issues surrounding the
dedication, and then analyzes the identity of those men who are known
to have dedicated temples. This will enable us to gain a clear picture
of the relations between Senate and individual, both cooperative and
antagonistic.

The process for the erection of new temples provides a remarkable illustration of the Roman system of government. We will see
that legally defined powers do not exist, but spheres of responsibility
demarcated by custom were understood by all involved. Policy was
often not made by careful forethought; no central organizing principle dictated who should vow a temple, or when, or to which deity.
Rather, such decisions were made on an *ad hoc* basis, responding to
situations as they arose. Vows for new temples were often made
without prior consultation either of the Senate or the priestly colleges, the guardians of Roman religion, despite the fact that the
erection of a new temple could bring an entirely new cult into the
Roman religious system. The Senate allowed magistrates to assume
this initiative for two primary reasons. For one, the Senate through
its active involvement in the construction and dedication of temples

possessed sufficient control over the process. Secondly, and more significantly, complete Senatorial control was not required because of the mutual trust between Senate and magistrates. Magistrates knew what kinds of actions would be acceptable to the Senate and wanted Senatorial approval for those actions to further their own career. In turn, the Senate cooperated in implementing their actions; when the need arose it could still take the initiative itself. The means by which the Romans erected new temples thus sheds important light on the relationship between individual initiative and collective responsibility in Republican Rome.

CHAPTER ONE

ORIGINS

The construction of new temples in Rome presents a tangled series of interrelated questions bearing on Roman religion and Roman politics. On some occasions, a temple was erected in honor of a divinity who was already receiving cult worship in Rome, at an altar in an inaugurated *templum* but without an *aedes*.[1] As the essential religious act of antiquity was the animal sacrifice, which took place at an altar, a temple was not strictly necessary to the performance of cult and its construction was often a secondary development. On other occasions, a temple was erected to a deity who already possessed a sanctuary complete with temple, so that in this case also the erection of a new temple marked another stage in the development of the cult. At other times, however, the decision to erect a temple led to the introduction of a completely new cult, in honor of a divinity who had never previously been worshipped in Rome. The construction of these temples thus had the potential to profoundly alter the religious landscape of Rome, by importing new and/or foreign divinities. One question which will concern us later in this study is whether the same procedures were utilized for the construction of these temples as for temples to recognized deities. Yet before we can begin to analyze the procedures involved in the construction of new temples, we are faced with a more basic question: why did the Romans introduce new temples and new cults to their pantheon in the first place? Studies of Roman religion have frequently noted that the Romans were always prepared to add new cults and practices, yet no satisfactory explanation has been offered for this trait or for the purposes which this practice served. Most scholars have searched for a single theory which would explain all the cults introduced to Rome, yet the cults and the needs to which they responded seem so varied that a single explanation may not be possible. After reviewing several

---

[1] The word *templum* signifies a properly consecrated space in which religious rituals could be performed, while the word *aedes* (less frequently *sacellum* or *fanum*) usually designates the temple as a religious structure. On *templum*, see Catalano (1978), esp. 467–479.

theories which have been offered for the introduction of new cults to
Rome, we will turn to an examination of the circumstances in which
new temples were vowed in an attempt to understand this practice.

I. *Theories on Temple Vowing*

Some scholars have been content to sketch the existence of foreign
gods in Rome without making an attempt to explain their presence.[2]
Most, however, have searched for ways to explain the Romans' tendency to add new gods to their pantheon. Georg Wissowa, the first
great student of Roman religion, argued that this phenomenon was
an integral part of the Roman religious system. In his view, the key
to polytheism's tolerance, as practiced by the Romans, was not to
offend any divine legal claim.[3] He proposed that as the growth in
Rome's hegemony brought the state in contact with other gods and
made their existence known to the Romans, the Romans had to make
an effort to propitiate those gods in addition to their own gods. These
gods had a "right" to worship just as the Roman gods did; in order
to avoid a breach in the *pax deum*, the Romans vowed temples to
foreign deities and accepted their cults in Rome. Some cases do seem
to suit this theory, but the argument runs into a significant difficulty.
The Romans did not recognize the divine claim of every foreign god
they encountered, but rather they were choosy as to whom they
allowed into their religious circle.[4] Alan Watson has recently provided a more apt summation of the Roman options when faced with
a foreign cult:

> One of two official responses was possible. Either the foreign religion
> or ritual was accepted by the state and incorporated as part of the
> official religion, or the foreign performance of the religion itself was
> declared to be criminal, independently even of excesses associated with
> it. Both approaches have a long history at Rome. Which was accepted
> depended on the times and the nature of the religion.[5]

---

[2] E.g. Rose (1949), 88–106; Bailey (1932), 109–142.

[3] Wissowa, *RKR* 38–46.

[4] The repeated injunctions against Isis in the second and first centuries provide
one of the most famous examples of the Romans' rejection and suppression of a
foreign cult they had encountered. An earlier example is the goddess Nortia, who
was not brought to Rome from Volsinii even though the Volsinian god Vortumnus
was. Cf. Taylor (1923), 154–57.

[5] Watson (1992), 58.

Simply encountering a foreign cult was not reason enough to introduce that cult to Rome. Watson's response changes the focus to a
determination of the nature of religions permitted in Rome and the
times which demanded their introduction. This entire line of analysis, however, takes no note of the non-foreign deities who were given
temples in Rome during the Republic, and these are in fact more
numerous than the foreign deities. Any attempt to explain the introduction of new cults in Rome must explain all new gods, and not
merely the foreigners.

Many other scholars have believed that the Romans introduced
new cults out of a feeling of insecurity, that their own gods were no
longer sufficient. W. W. Fowler, in his classic *Religious Experience of the
Roman People*, wrote that the story of Roman religion during the
Republic was

> that of the gradual discovery of the inadequacy of this early formalised
> and organised religion to cope with what we may call new religious
> experience; that is with the difficulties and perils met with by the Roman
> people in their extraordinary advance in the world, and with the new
> ideas of religion and morals which broke in on them in the course of
> their contact with other peoples.[6]

This theory is similar to Wissowa's in that it revolves around the
contact with foreign gods, but it places emphasis on the notion that
such contact revealed weaknesses in the Roman religious system. This
line of reasoning has had a powerful influence in discussions of Roman
religion. Thirty-five years later, J. Bayet wrote in a similar vein that

> if every individual action showed the need to refer oneself to a super-
> natural energy, the social or collective emergencies—always the same,
> wars, plagues, famines, earthquakes; and always insufficiently conjured
> away—required the recourse to new divinities, whose new force propped
> up the more ancient religious routines.[7]

Both Fowler and Bayet, and others as well, argue from the assumption that the Romans introduced new gods from a position of weakness, that the new gods were meant to strengthen a religious system
which was increasingly becoming decrepit.[8] The moralizing tone

---

[6] Fowler, *RERP* 248. For his overall treatment of new cults, cf. 223–269.

[7] Bayet (1969), 120. The first edition of this work was published in 1956.

[8] Cf. also Bardon (1955), 168; Schilling (1969), 461; Toynbee (1965), 2.478. For
a specific application of this principle, cf. Champeaux (1987), 30, who argues that

evident in such analyses, viewing the development of Roman religion as a debasement from a pure and primitive state, formed part
of a progressivist view which explained the rise of Christianity as
responding to a spiritual need which Roman religion no longer met;
such a position can no longer be upheld.[9]

One major problem with this view lies in the fact that the tendency to absorb new cults is inherent in Roman religion and present
from the very beginning.[10] The Romans possessed no cults which
could truly be called their own, excepting perhaps only the Penates
which Aeneas was supposed to have brought with him when fleeing
the sack of Troy. All other cults, including the Capitoline triad of
Jupiter, Juno and Minerva which lay at the heart of the state religion, were taken from neighboring peoples. Even if we make allow-
ances for the Etruscans being the dominant power in early Rome
and so do not count Etruscan divinities as foreign, the first century
of the Republic saw the introduction of two cults which are of Greek
origin: Castor and Pollux who received a temple in 494 and Apollo
who received one in 431. The cult of Hercules, which according to
Livy was celebrated with the Greek rite, apparently goes back even
further; the foundation of the cult at the Ara Maxima was ascribed
to the Arcadian king Evander, supposedly a contemporary of Aeneas.[11]
In view of these very conspicuous examples, it can not be maintained that the introduction of new, foreign gods is a late phenomenon which indicates the increasing poverty of the Roman religious
system. Rather, this process should be considered a token of health,
an indication that Roman religion is functioning normally.

A more recent study of J. A. North has emphasized that in many
cases we should view the introduction of new cults as a sign of strength,
not weakness.[12] The acquisition of new gods parallels an acquisition
of power and of land; just as Rome was strengthened by adding new
territory and new citizens, so too it was strengthened by adding new
gods to the pantheon. Rather than being done out of need to prop

---

the old cults of Fortuna "had become too old to respond still to the needs of the
men of this time" and hence were supplemented by the new cults of Fortuna
Primigenia and Fortuna Equestris.

[9] See the comments of J. A. North (1976), 10, on Toynbee.

[10] Cf. Wardman (1982), 1–21.

[11] Livy 1.7.

[12] North (1976), 11. Palmer in his discussion of Juno in Italy, (1974) 1–56, also
seems to follow this view. Some hints of this view can be detected in certain comments
of earlier writers, including Wissowa, but they are not given full consideration.

up a dying religion, the addition of new gods functioned as a conscious display of Rome's growing power. The establishment of a foreign
cult in Rome served as a mark of Roman domination of the deity's
country of origin; even its gods have been brought to Rome. For
instance, the *evocatio* of Juno Regina in 396, when the Romans installed the Juno of Veii in a new temple on the Aventine hill, put
the final stamp on the Roman eradication of Veii. The capture of
the deity and her establishment in Rome served as a symbol for
Rome's subjugation of the people whom the goddess was supposed
to protect: Rome's domination was so complete that she had even
appropriated Veii's gods. It is significant that the two cities, besides
Veii, which are most often thought to have undergone an *evocatio* are
Volsinii and Carthage, both of which were mortal enemies of Rome,
subdued and completely destroyed only after a long and arduous
struggle.[13] In a similar but less bellicose manner, the erection of the
temple to Diana in Rome, ascribed to Servius Tullius, undoubtedly
was meant to symbolize the transfer of power in the Latin League
from Aricia to Rome.[14] The welcome of these gods to Rome was a
sign of Roman strength in absorbing them, and the communities
which they guarded, into the Roman sphere.

Both of these approaches, the "weakness" model and the "strength"
model, have some validity, as each has several examples to recommend it. Yet both are selective in only explaining a limited number
of new cults, and in their effort to construct a cohesive model, both
have gotten away from the core of Roman religion as the Romans
themselves saw it. The essence of Roman religion was to maintain

---

[13] On Volsinii, cf. Varro *LL* 5.46; Propertius 4.2.3; Fowler *RERP*, 201; Scullard
(1981), 174–75; Wissowa *RKR*, 233–34; Latte *RRG*, 191–92; Basanoff (1947), 56–63.
On Carthage, see Macrobius 3.9.7; Serv. *Ad. Aen.* 12.841; Wissowa *RKR*, 312–13;
Latte *RRG*, 346, n. 4; Basanoff 63–66. I am not convinced by Girard (1989), who
argues, based on Ovid, *Fasti* 3.839–846, that Minerva Capta came from Falerii to
Rome as the result of an *evocatio*. As Dumézil, *ARR* 427, pointed out, the fact the
Minerva possessed this surname is a good reason for believing that this was *not* an
evocatio; see also Basanoff (1947), 50–52. Nor do I believe that the inscription described by Hall (1972) offers evidence of an *evocatio*; even Hall is content to state
that the ceremony was "similar to *evocatio*" and "what this vow involved is unclear."
In general, I believe that the role played by *evocatio* in Roman Republican religion
has been vastly overstated by modern scholars, based on late notices in Pliny the
Elder (*NH* 28.18) and Macrobius (3.9). Only Juno Regina is firmly attested to have
come to Rome in this manner.
[14] Livy 1.45; Val. Max. 7.3.1; Dion. Hal. 4.26. Cf. Wissowa *RKR*, 200–201; Platner
& Ashby, 149–50; Gordon (1934), 10; Latte, *RRG* 173; Palmer, (1974) 62.

the *pax deum*, the favor of the gods.[15] Livy's descriptions of religious rites show clearly that maintaining the *pax deum* was essential to the growth of the Roman state, and on several occasions this link is made explicitly.[16] For instance when the Romans were about to embark on a war against Perseus, the Senate decreed that "the prodigies should be expiated and the peace of the gods sought by prayers."[17] Every rite and ritual in Roman religion was directed at insuring that favor, including the famous Roman need for the punctilious performance of these rites and rituals. The most famous passage about the proper performance of rituals comes from Pliny the Elder:

> We see that the highest magistrates have entreated with fixed prayers and lest any word be omitted or spoken out of place, a reader first dictates, another is appointed guardian who keeps watch, another is appointed who orders a strict silence, and a fluteplayer plays, so that nothing else is heard.[18]

If an error did occur during the performance of the ritual, then the ceremony was repeated in its entirety, a practice known as *instauratio*.[19] The purpose of the *instauratio* was to ensure that the gods were satisfied with the Romans'; offering; Cicero explicitly stated that "the minds of the immortal gods were pleased by the repeated performance of games."[20] Thus the introduction of new cults and the construction of new temples must have responded to this desire in some way and served to maintain the *pax deum*.

One important element of Roman religion to bear in mind is that most actions undertaken by the Romans to cultivate the *pax deum* were capable of two or more interpretations. Most commonly, religious actions served either as a plea for help in the future or as an

---

[15] Cf. e.g. Wissowa, *RKR* 327–29; Latte, *RRG* 40–41; Bayet (1969), 58–60; Schilling (1969), 443; Wardman (1982), 7–8.

[16] See now Linderski (1993), 55–57, who notes that while this theme is very important to Livy, the historian actually uses the term *pax deum* very infrequently: only eleven usages in the entire extant work. As Linderski notes, a full study of this phrase is badly needed.

[17] Livy 42.2.3: *prodigia expiari pacemque deum peti precationibus.* For other examples, cf. Livy 3.5.14; 3.8.1; 7.7.2. See also Cicero, *Rab. Perd.* 5, for a more personal plea for the favor of the gods.

[18] Pliny, *NH* 28.3.11: "*videmusque certis precationibus obsecrasse summos magistratus et ne quod verborum praetereatur aut praeposterum dicatur, de scripto praeire aliquem rursusque alium custodem dari qui adtendat, alium vero praeponi qui favere linguis iubeat, tibicinem canere ne quid aliud exaudiatur.*" On this passage, see Koves-Zulauf (1972), 21–63.

[19] See Cohee (1994) for a recent discussion of this practice.

[20] Cicero, *HR* 11.23: *mentes deorum immortalium ludorum instauratione placantur.*

expression of gratitude for past benefits. The *supplicatio* is a particularly good example of this phenomenon, as on some occasions this ritual was declared as a means to win the gods' favor during a threatening situation, while on other occasions it was declared as a period of thanksgiving following a great victory. To take one early example, in 463 the Senate ordered the people to supplicate the gods on account of a pestilence, while in 449 *supplicationes* were decreed by the Senate to celebrate victories over the Sabines.[21] The vow of a new temple similarly could either mark a plea for help at a critical point in time, or it could express gratitude for the successful resolution of a military or civil crisis. This is particularly true of temples built following a general's vow in battle, for such temples effectively served both purposes; even if the temple had been vowed during a critical moment in the battle, it would not have been built until after the crisis had long passed, so that the construction and dedication would have served as a public thank-offering to the god who had responded to his plea. This dual nature of actions undertaken to preserve the *pax deum* plays a critical role in understanding the situations in which new temples were vowed.

Closely related to the Roman belief in the *pax deum* is their belief that they were the most religious people in the world. Cicero writes "if we wish to compare ourselves with foreign peoples, we will find that in other matters we are equal or even inferior, but in religion, that is in the cult of the gods, we are much superior."[22] He expresses a similar sentiment elsewhere: "in piety and religion we have outstripped all the nations."[23] Nor was Cicero alone in his belief; other Roman authors from Virgil to Livy evince the belief that Rome owed her greatness to her superior cultivation of the favor of the gods.[24] Part of this superior cultivation of the gods may be seen in the number

---

[21] Livy 3.7.7, 3.63.5. Other examples are plentiful, including an instance in 193 where the consul demanded a *supplicatio* in addition to his triumph to thank the gods, while the *decemviri* after consulting the Sibylline books in the same year decreed a *supplicatio* on account of numerous prodigies (Livy 35.8–9). Cf. Halkin (1953), 9–13, who actually divides *supplicationes* into three categories: expiatory, propitiatory, and gratulatory. I make less of a distinction between the first two which, as Halkin himself noted, are very similar, differing only in whether it was celebrated after an "actual" calamity or before an "imminent" one.

[22] Cicero, *ND* 2.3.8: *Et si conferre volumus nostra cum externis, ceteris rebus aut pares aut etiam inferiores reperiemur, religione id est cultu deorum multo superiores.*

[23] Cicero, *HR* 9.19: *pietate ac religione omnes gentes superavimus.*

[24] Livy's view of religion is more complex than this simple statement, but such a belief is part of his view. Cf. Walsh (1961), 46–81 and especially 66–69.

of temples in Rome: having the greatest number of temples is one
indication of being the *religiosissimi* people. In broad terms, this may
help to explain the inherent Roman tendency to introduce new cults,
yet it runs into the same criticisms as the theory of Wissowa; if more
equals better, then why didn't the Romans introduce even more gods?
Why be discriminating at all? There must be other factors at work,
and our task is to draw them out.

The place to begin attacking this problem is to focus on the situations in which new temples were vowed, because the vow invari-
ably brought about the construction of a new temple. It has been
noted that the vow was the critical moment for obtaining the favor
of the gods.[25] At that moment the contract between the gods and the
Romans was created, that if the gods acted in the specified way, the
Romans would perform the specified ritual. The actual performance
of the ritual could come after the gods had come to their aid. The
fulfillment of the vow therefore did not help to obtain the gods'
assistance in an emergency, but it was necessary to maintain good
relations with the gods after the fact. The issue of how far a magistrate's vow put the state under an obligation will be treated in Chapter
Two; here we are concerned with what circumstances led the Romans to vow new temples. One fact will rapidly become evident:
temples were vowed under a wide variety of conditions, but the same
set of conditions at different times did not necessarily produce the
same result, i.e. the construction of a new temple. This state of affairs
reflects the flexibility of Roman religion and once again illustrates
the close relationship between religion and politics at Rome.

II. *Situations Resulting in New Temples*

Of the approximately eighty public temples which were dedicated
between 509 and the mid-first century, we have reports for the vowing of forty-eight, or approximately sixty percent.[26] Evidence for the
foundation of the remaining temples in Rome is lacking, so our
conclusions must remain somewhat tentative. In some cases, an ancient source makes reference to a temple which was clearly standing

---

[25] Cf. Rohde (1932), 11.
[26] See Appendix One for a list of all temples known to have been dedicated in
Rome during the period under discussion.

at the time, but whose foundation is not recorded in any of our sources; for instance, a temple to Luna is mentioned by Livy in connection with the prodigies of 182 and is attested both on the stone *fasti* and by Ovid, yet no record of its founding survives.[27] For such temples, we can not even be sure of the date of the temple's foundation, let alone the circumstances which attended its vowing. For other temples we know something of the circumstances of their foundation, but nothing specifically about the timing of the vow. For instance, five temples were built by aediles out of the fines they collected during their term in office.[28] The exact moment of the vow is often not recorded for these temples, so it is difficult to determine whether these temples should be considered the result of entreaties or thanksgiving, and they are best omitted from this analysis.[29] Nevertheless two facts should give us confidence in conclusions drawn from the information we do have. For one, the missing data is due primarily to the loss of Livy's narrative for the years 292–219 and after 167. Thus it can not be argued that the known cases are known simply because they deviated from normal; in fact many of the reports on new temples are entirely unexceptional. Second, the picture drawn from the surviving evidence is sufficiently clear to allow us to have confidence in the outlines.

The circumstances in which new temples were vowed can be divided into two broad categories. A few were vowed as a response to an internal, civil situation involving only the Romans and their gods;

---

[27] Livy 40.2.1–2; Ovid, *Fasti* 3.883–84. The assumption made by most scholars is that the loss of Livy's history for the years 292–219 is responsible for our lack of knowledge about many of these temples.

[28] The temples include Concordia (Livy 9.46; Pliny, *NH* 33.19), Venus (Livy 10.31.9), Victoria (Livy 10.33.9), Libertas (Livy 24.16.19), and Faunus (Livy 33.42).

[29] In one case our sources give a clear answer: the temple of Concordia, vowed by Cn. Flavius after he alienated the nobility by publishing a legal calendar, was intended to help reconcile the Orders during his year in office (Livy 9.46; Pliny, *NH* 33.19). For the other cases, however, we are left with speculation. The temple of Faunus was built with money collected from the *pecuarii*; it could either thank the patron of the flocks for his help in bringing these shepherds to heel, or it could have been a request for his help when the aediles set out to do so. Similarly, the temple for Venus was erected with money obtained from women who were convicted of *stuprum*. There is a certain irony in this fact, but we can not be sure of its significance, nor indeed whether the equation of the Roman Venus with the Greek Aphrodite had fully taken hold at the time of the temple's construction in 295. There may have been a feeling in this case, like that of Faunus, that the proceeds of the fines should go to the deity to whose jurisdiction those who paid the fines belonged. For the other two aedilician temples, we are not informed about the source of the aediles' fines.

these account for approximately one-fifth of the total, and include such natural phenomena as plagues (two temples), droughts (two temples), and other portents (four temples), as well as internal crises such as a mutiny (two temples). The remaining four-fifths about which we have information were vowed as a response to an external, military situation involving a foreign enemy. This category consists mainly of twenty-six temples (fifty-four percent of the overall total) which were certainly vowed by generals on their campaigns, many at critical points in the battle. For a further eleven temples (twenty-three percent), we know that they were vowed during a particular war, e.g. the First Punic War, but we can not be sure of who made the vow or under what circumstances owing to the loss of the relevant sources. Two other temples (four percent), Mens and Venus Erycina, were vowed on the orders of the Sibylline Books following the defeats at Trebia and Lake Trasimene against Hannibal.[30] All of these situations presented crises that threatened the welfare, or at times the very existence, of the Roman state, and thus the *pax deum* would have been a paramount concern. Yet maintaining good relations with the gods is not a sufficient explanation for the vowing of new temples. Not every similar situation resulted in the vowing of a new temple, but sometimes met with another religious response; the *pax deum* could be assured by a variety of means. An examination of the situations in which new temples were vowed will enable us to offer some suggestions as to why the vow of a new temple was considered the appropriate response on some occasions but not on others.

Temples vowed in response to an internal situation often responded to a prodigy or a sign that there was a rupture in the *pax deum* which needed to be repaired. Four temples arose as a consequence of pestilence or a drought, which the Romans believed came from the gods as punishment for some flaw in their relationship. In these cases, the prodigy itself threatened the health of the Roman state, as a prolonged plague or famine presented one of the gravest threats to ancient cities. In other cases, temples were erected in response to portents which, while causing little actual harm, were considered to portend no less of a threat to the Roman state. For instance, during the war against Pyrrhus in the early third century, the terracotta statue

---

[30] The temple of Tellus, vowed after an earthquake struck during a battle, has been counted under "portents" and under "war", and thus the total exceeds one hundred percent.

of Summanus in the pediment of the temple of Jupiter Optimus Maximus was struck by lightning and hurled from the pediment. The lightning was perceived as a sign that something was not right in the Romans' relations with the gods, a situation which the Romans believed could have dire consequences for their campaign against Pyrrhus, and as a result a temple was erected specifically for Summanus to appease the god of night lightning.[31] Similarly, in 114, a temple was vowed to Venus Verticordia, a Venus who turns hearts from lust to chastity, as part of the expiation following the unchastity of three Vestal Virgins.[32] Such unchastity could be viewed as a sign that the *pax deum* had been shattered, and this temple was meant to correct the flaw and to placate the goddess; it also served as a visible reminder of Roman moral values.[33] These temples all arose from a clearly visible rupture in the *pax deum* which presented a direct threat to the welfare of the state.

Yet repairing a breach in the *pax deum* is not a sufficient explanation for the decision to erect a new temple in Rome; not every internal crisis met with this result. A drought or a plague which resulted in the construction of a new temple in one instance might be handled in a different manner fifty years later. The converse is true as well: prodigies which usually did not lead to the erection of a new temple, such as a shower of stones, did on occasion have that consequence. Furthermore, several temples were vowed not *during* an internal crisis, but only *after* the crisis had already passed. Such temples were clearly not intended to repair a breach in the *pax deum*, and are therefore even more problematic. The matter is thus not as simple as it might seem at first. There must be other factors at work influencing the decision to build a new temple. A closer examination of the circumstances under which new temples were built will make this point clearer, and also shed light on some of these "other" factors.

The Roman reaction to various episodes of pestilence is instructive, since of the numerous episodes of pestilence recorded by Livy only two resulted in the erection of a temple. Rome in the early years following the expulsion of the Tarquins may not have had a god specifically devoted to healing; certainly there was no temple to

---

[31] Ovid, *Fasti* 6.731.

[32] Obs. 37, Val. Max. 8.15.2.

[33] On Venus Verticordia and the problems posed by unchastity among the Vestals, see further Chapter Three, p. 88 and n. 40, pp. 102–3.

a healing deity.[34] According to the literary tradition, the kings of Rome had built temples to the following deities: Jupiter Feretrius, Jupiter Stator, Vesta, Janus, Saturn, Pallor and Pavor, Jupiter Capitolinus, Diana, and Fortuna.[35] The first temple vowed under the Republic was the temple of Castor, which was built in the middle of the Forum, near the Temple of Vesta and the spring of Juturna. Although Castor was introduced as the patron of horsemen following the battle at Lake Regillus, it appears that one element of this temple was a role in healing the sick.[36] For the next sixty years this was the sole temple in Rome, as far as we know, with any aspect devoted to healing. In 436 a pestilence struck Rome, which caused the people to offer up a public prayer (*obsecratio*) under the direction of the *duumviri*.[37] The following year the pestilence was worse, which encouraged the Fidenates to attack Rome itself and caused the appointment of a dictator to meet that threat. Finally in 433 Livy reports that a temple was vowed to Apollo for the health of the people. We see a clear progression here; the original expiation failed to avert the anger of the gods and in fact that anger intensified. Only after three years of plague and the failure of at least one recorded attempt to end the plague was the new temple vowed. Even before the construction of the temple, Apollo seems to have been known in Rome, for Livy speaks of a Senate meeting in 449 which took place in the precinct which "even then they called Apollinar."[38] Although Apollo had many aspects as a god, the temple, his first in Rome, was specifically dedicated to Apollo Medicus.[39] The erection of a temple to Apollo has been taken to indicate that the Romans had

---

[34] A cult of Minerva Medica is attested during the Republic by Cicero, *De Div.* 2.123, and *CIL* 6.10133 and 6.30980. However it is unlikely that the cult dates to the early Republic.

[35] Jupiter Feretrius: Livy 1.10.6, Dion. Hal. 2.34; Jupiter Stator: Livy 10.12, Dion. Hal. 2.50; Vesta: Plut. *Numa* 14.1; Janus: Livy 1.19.2; Saturn: Macrobius 1.8.1; Pallor and Pavor: Livy 1.27.7; Jupiter Capitolinus: Livy 1.38.7, 1.55; Diana: Livy 1.45, Dion. Hal. 4.26; Fortuna: Livy 10.46.14, Dion. Hal. 4.40, Plut. *QR* 74.

[36] On the introduction of Castor and Pollux, see below p. 30. For the healing aspect of the temple of the Dioscuri, see Schilling (1979), 344–47, who bases his case on scholia which indicate incubation or healing in the temple (*Ad Persium* 2.56 [Buechler, p. 20]) and the connection with the spring, whose curative powers both Varro (*LL* 5.71) and Propertius (3.22.6) mention.

[37] For the events of this and the following years, see Livy 4.20–25.

[38] Livy 3.63.7: *iam tum Apollinare appellabant.*

[39] See Livy 40.51 for the surname. According to Asconius (*In Cic. Tog. Cand.,* 80–81), this was the only temple of Apollo in Rome prior to Augustus.

lost faith in the ability of their existing gods to combat the plague, none of whom was really a healing god to begin with. Apollo was therefore approached and given the specific task of being god of healing who could end the misery inflicted on the Romans by this plague.

Almost one hundred and fifty years later a similar series of events led to the introduction of Aesculapius into the Roman circle of gods. In 295, the Roman success in the Samnite war was tempered by a plague which struck the city and by prodigies.[40] The Sibylline Books were consulted, but to no avail, for two years later Livy reports that the pestilence was ravaging both city and country. The devastation caused by the plague was such that in itself it was considered a portent, and once again the Books were consulted. This time, it was discovered that Aesculapius must be brought to Rome from Epidaurus, and, although the consuls were too busy with campaigning to do anything in that year, the god was finally brought to Rome in 291. In the Hellenistic world, Aesculapius was the preeminent healing god, and his sanctuary in Epidaurus was considered the most ancient and true home of the god. Again we see the progression of attempts to end the plague before resorting to the introduction of a new deity. And once again the god introduced is more intimately connected with healing than his predecessor: although Apollo was a healing god he also had many other aspects, while Aesculapius' sole function was as a healer. The Roman pantheon thus underwent further specialization, which appears to make the sequence fit the weakness schema: the older, more general god was no longer considered sufficient in the face of increasing difficulties.

While the desire to have a deity more and more closely devoted to healing may play some role in the successive introductions of Apollo and Aesculapius, it does not tell the whole story. On several other occasions, progressive attempts were made to expiate a pestilence without eventually resorting to the introduction of a new temple or a new god to counter the misery. For instance, a terrible pestilence broke out in 365, which lasted into 364 when a *lectisternium* was held with the object of appeasing the divine wrath.[41] The *ludi scenici* were held for the first time in conjunction with this *lectisternium*, but even

---

[40] For these events, see Livy 10.31.8–9; 10.47.6–7; *Per.* 11. On Aesculapius in Rome, see Roesch, (1982); Musial, (1990).

[41] Livy 7.1.7–2.3.

that failed to remove the pestilence. Finally in 363, "it is said that the elders recollected that a pestilence had once been allayed by the driving of a nail by a dictator."[42] This ancient ceremony, which was also enacted in the cella of Minerva at the temple of Capitoline Jupiter to mark the passage of years, was then performed, and the pestilence apparently ceased, for no more is heard about it. Again we see a three-stage progression, from plague to one attempt to ease it to the final successful appeasement; in this instance however the ultimate step was not the introduction of a new cult, but a return to an ancient ceremony which, according to Livy, only the elders remembered. This same expiation of driving a nail was repeated in 331, after another plague had lasted into a second year, and also in 263.[43] One should also note that no expiation at all was performed for a plague which struck in 412.[44] These examples show clearly that the same problem could lead to very different responses, so that the construction of a new temple can not simply be a response to a breach in the *pax deum*. In the case of Aesculapius, his introduction may be tied to the Roman maneuverings as the Third Samnite War wound down and Roman attention focused more closely on Magna Graecia.[45] This episode provides one instance of how religious decisions could be influenced by non-religious factors.

The Roman response to several droughts presents many similarities and some significant differences to their approach to plagues. During the regal period, there is evidence for several vegetation or harvest deities, including Consus, Ceres, Mars and others; however, none of these deities possessed a temple yet.[46] In 496, however, the Romans were engaged in a war with the Volscians and there was a great fear that food supplies would fail entirely, "because the land had borne no crops and food from the outside could no longer be

---

[42] Livy 7.3.3: *repetitum ex seniorum memoria dicitur pestilentiam quondam clavo ab dictatore fixo sedatam.* This event is also attested in the *fasti Capitolini* which indicate the election of a dictator *causa clavi figendae.*

[43] The ceremony of 331 is attested by Livy 8.18.2 as well as the *fasti Capitolini*, while the ceremony of 263 is attested only in the *fasti.*

[44] Livy 4.52.

[45] This argument is fully developed in Chapter Three, pp. 106–8.

[46] The antiquity of such gods as Consus, Ceres, and Mars is shown by their presence on the so-called "Calendar of Numa" and/or by the existence of a flamen, the most ancient priests of Rome. Mars, who is better known as the god of war, seems to have been a vegetation deity originally. On the calendar, see Michels (1967); on the *flamen*, see now Vanggaard (1988).

imported because of the war."[47] The dictator Postumius ordered the *duumviri* to consult the Sibylline Books, which advised the Romans to propitiate Ceres, Liber and Libera. Therefore, Postumius vowed that if abundance returned to the land, he would build a temple to the triad and institute annual sacrifices. Following the successful conclusion of the war and the return of prosperity to the land, a temple for this triad was built on the Aventine hill, since they were considered responsible for averting the danger from Rome.

Several other droughts or food shortages are recorded in the sources later in the fifth century and down into the fourth and third centuries.[48] Yet none of these famines seems to have resulted in extraordinary religious measures, as for instance a consultation of the Sibylline Books. Only in the midst of a drought in the middle of the third century did the Romans again respond by vowing a temple on the orders of the Sibylline Books, this time to Flora, another vegetation deity.[49] Like Ceres, Flora was an ancient Italian goddess who was already receiving cult worship in Rome prior to the construction of her temple.[50] The question that immediately presents itself is why the Romans chose to honor Ceres with a temple in the early fifth century and then took no similar actions for an additional two hundred fifty years before erecting a temple to Flora. There do not seem to be sufficient differences in the descriptions of the food shortages to account for the different religious responses, which again reminds us that problems with the *pax deum* alone can not explain the decision to erect a new temple.

For these two temples we can point to some factors which may have influenced at least the choice of deity to honor. One suggestion offered for the temple of Ceres is that it was intended to offset the contemporaneous introduction of Castor and Pollux. Ceres was closely connected to the plebs, and so her introduction in 496 would balance out the Dioscuri, who as patrons of horsemen were more connected

---

[47] Dion. Hal. 6.17: πολὺν αὐτοῖς παρέσχον φόβον ὡς ἐπιλείψουσαι, τῆς τε γῆς ἀκάρπου γενομένης καὶ τῆς ἔξωθεν ἀγορᾶς οὐκέτι παρακομιζομένης διὰ τὸν πόλεμον.

[48] See Garnsey (1988), 167–181, for an account of these incidents.

[49] This temple to Flora is usually dated either to 241, following Vell. Pat. 1.14.8, or to 238, following Pliny, *NH* 18.286. See Degrassi (1963), 450–452.

[50] Legend held that Titus Tatius had erected an altar to her in Rome, and she had her own priest, the *flamen Floralis*, which also attests her antiquity (Varro, *LL* 7.45). Furthermore, she received sacrifice from the Arval Brethren in their sacred grove, along with such ancient Roman cults as Janus, Jupiter, Juno and Vesta (Henzen, *Acta Frat. Arv.* 146).

with the wealthier Romans and whose temple had been vowed at Lake Regillus.[51] Another possible explanation is that Flora represented a slightly different domain than Ceres, one that perhaps was less appropriate in 496. A passage in Ovid's *Fasti* about a peculiar rite during the Floralia, when goats and hares were set loose in the Circus Maximus, indicates "that forests were not given to her [Flora], but gardens and fields which were not to be entered by warlike wild beasts."[52] The contrast in this passage is clearly with the areas watched over by Ceres; during the Cerealia foxes were set loose in the Circus and foxes certainly belong in the woods rather than in domestic fields.[53] Perhaps the third century drought particularly affected the domestic fields and gardens, which led to a new temple for the goddess who was responsible for their protection. The loss of Livy's narrative here is particularly crucial here, for we know that the construction of this temple was unique: it was the only temple built on the advice of the Sibylline Books which was erected by aediles.[54] More information about the context in which this temple was built would help shed light on this matter, but it is clear that the mere fact of drought is not sufficient to explain the construction of a temple nor the goddess to whom the temple was dedicated.

Another problem with the notion that temples responded solely to ruptures in the *pax deum* is provided by the vowing of a new temple after a civil crisis had already passed. The temple of Fortuna Muliebris, whose date of dedication is not preserved, provides the clearest example, and the story of its founding deserves close scrutiny.[55] When Coriolanus was marching on Rome with the Volscians, the Roman matrons went out to meet him. The entreaties of his aged mother persuaded Coriolanus not to proceed with his attack on the city, but to turn back. Following this success of the matrons, the Senate met and decided that the women should be praised with a public decree

[51] Schilling (1976), 59–60, who notes that the dictator Postumius played the central role in the introduction of both cults.
[52] Ovid, *Fasti* 5.371-2: *non sibi, respondit, silvas cesisse, sed hortos arvaque pugnaci non adeunda ferae.*
[53] For the celebration of the Cerealia, see Ovid's *Fasti*, especially 4.679-712.
[54] See Chapter Three for the Sibylline Books.
[55] The story of Coriolanus is found in Livy 2.24.7–2.40.12 and 8.1–54. The story of the temple's founding is omitted by Livy, but appears most completely in Dion. Hal. 8.55-56. Elements can also be found in Val. Max. 1.8.4; Festus 282L; and Augustine *CD* 4.19. Champeaux (1982), 335-373, devotes an entire chapter to various aspects of this story, with full bibliography.

and given a gift of their choice. The women asked only for permission to found a temple to Fortuna Muliebris on the spot where they had turned back Coriolanus, and to perform sacrifices on the anniversary of that day. The Senate in response promptly decreed that public funds should be used to buy the land, to erect a temple complete with cult statue and altar, and to perform the sacrifices. The women themselves were to choose the officiant, and they also of their own accord dedicated a second statue of the goddess.

This story is remarkable in a number of ways and, as with anything connected to Coriolanus, can not be accepted uncritically. The story of the temple's founding, since it is so out of keeping with normal practice, might be a late invention to explain the foundation of a temple to this deity. Yet even an anachronistic account maintains a semblance of historical accuracy; it reflects the later understanding of how events might have transpired, for it does no good if the story is patently false. So for instance the matrons did not vow the temple when meeting with Coriolanus, or even after their return to Rome; women did not vow state temples in Rome, and no ancient author could have conceived of such a situation. Only when the Senate, the controlling force in Roman society, decided to honor them did they indicate their wish to erect this temple. This would be a more plausible scenario. Similarly the timing of the decision to build a temple in the story, after the women had turned back the renegade, reflects the fact that temples could be vowed *after* the threat to the state had been averted and not only in the midst of crises.

The construction of a temple following the successful resolution of a crisis can no longer be considered a response to a breach in the *pax deum*, but a symbol of thanks to the gods. In this case, the temple was clearly intended to indicate the gratitude of the Romans towards the tutelary deity of women.[56] Even though the Romans had not specifically prayed to Fortuna Muliebris for help, the building of the temple would recognize the help she had given to Rome in its hour of need and so help maintain the *pax deum*. However, there is a further point to note here in the Senate's close involvement with the details of construction. Had the sole purpose been to honor the goddess,

---

[56] Cf. Champeaux (1982), 349–373, who argues that Fortuna Muliebris actually had two prime functions: a tutelary goddess for Roman matrons, but also a protectrice of the city, especially in view of the location of the temple on the via Latina near the *fossae Cluiliae* at the ancient edge of the *ager Romanus* (368).

the Senate could simply have approved the women's request to build the temple and left the rest of the process to them. The erection of this temple by the matrons of Rome would have acknowledged the divine support which they had received and thus strengthened the *pax deum*. The Senate's decision to provide public sanction for their vow, by setting aside public funds for the temple and annual sacrifices, acknowledged not only that the debt to Fortuna Muliebris was owed by the entire state instead of merely the matrons, but also that the state owed a debt to the matrons themselves. This aspect of the story may be an aetiological embroidery, but it is significant nonetheless. The desire of the state to recognize the role played by women in Roman society can not be considered a religious consideration in our sense of the word, but this message was conveyed through a religious building. The story thus offers one example of how non-religious factors could influence the decision to erect a temple in a specific instance.

The temples considered so far are those vowed in relation to an internal crisis rather than to an external, military threat from one of Rome's enemies. One of the major differences between these two situations lies in the fact that the latter were vowed by individuals acting on their own authority, rather than by the state following the advice of the Sibylline Books as was often the case with the former. Yet some of the same characteristics are encountered in analyzing the circumstances of these vows. Like vows made in response to an internal crisis, vows made during the course of a military campaign could either serve as a plea for help at a time of crisis or as a token of thanks following a successful encounter. Furthermore the same variety of responses seen in internal situations is evident in generals' actions; some generals vowed temples, while others vowed different objects and many generals made no vows at all. Again let us examine a few examples.

The most common scenario, repeated many times in the text of Livy, was for a general, in the heat of battle and unsure of the outcome, to vow a temple if the gods granted him the victory. This attitude is explicit in the vow of Appius Claudius Caecus recorded by Livy at a critical moment in a battle against the Etruscans and the Samnites in 296: "Bellona, if today you grant victory to us, then I vow to you a temple."[57] Other generals made similar vows for the

---

[57] Livy 10.19: *Bellona, si hodie nobis victoriam duis, ast ego tibi templum voveo.* Even if

same reason just before the battle began, rather than waiting until a critical moment.[58] Such vows seem to originate from a position of weakness, in that the consul expressed concern that his forces were not strong enough to defeat the enemy without additional divine support. Note, however, that it is the general's perceived weakness of his own position, and not the perceived weakness of the Roman national gods in dealing with this crisis, that is at issue here. In fact, almost none of the divinities who received temples as the result of a battlefield vow can be considered foreign.[59] In the case just cited, Bellona, the personification of war (*bellum*), can hardly be considered a foreign deity, although she may not have been recognized by the state until this vow of Appius Claudius. The divinity, in exchange for a temple and continual worship in Rome, is asked to shore up any potential deficiencies in the battle plan and ensure the victory for the general. There is no sense that the Roman gods were not sufficient to meet the threat without the help of foreign gods, but that Appius was not able to meet the threat without the help of a Roman god.

In other instances the outcome of the battle was already decided when the general vowed a new temple, so the point of his vow can not be to guarantee victory. The clearest example comes from a battle in Spain fought against the Celtiberians in 180. This battle was very hard-fought, and the Celtiberians nearly succeeded in breaking the Roman line until the commander Fulvius Flaccus ordered the cavalry into the center of the fray. Livy reports the subsequent events as follows:

> Then indeed all the Celtiberians were turned to flight and the Roman commander, gazing upon the backs of the enemy, vowed a temple to Fortuna Equestris and games to Jupiter Optimus Maximus.[60]

The temple to Jupiter Victor was similarly vowed at Sentinum in 295 as the consul pressed on to the enemy's camp after their line had been broken; in this battle the favor of the gods had already

---

Livy has put these intentionally archaizing words in Appius' mouth, they reflect his understanding of the sentiment behind such vows.

[58] E.g. the temple to Fortuna Primigenia (Livy 29.36.8) and the temple to Juno Sospita (Livy 32.30.10).

[59] A notable exception is Juno Regina, who came to Rome as the result of the *evocatio* performed by Camillus at the siege of Veii in 396. See pp. 62–3.

[60] Livy 40.40.10: *Tunc vero Celtiberi omnes in fugam effunduntur et imperator Romanus aversos hostes contemplatus aedem Fortunae Equestri Iovique optimo maximo ludos vovit.*

been obtained by the *devotio* of Decius Mus.[61] Likewise the dictator
Postumius vowed a temple to Castor after his troops had broken
through the Latin line at Lake Regillus in 496 and were pursuing to
the enemy's camp.[62] These vows were not intended to provide the
margin of victory but as a reward for the gods, just as the booty
from the enemy's camp was to be a reward to the soldiers.[63] Such
vows have a different flavor from those made in a moment of danger and seem more designed to give thanks to a deity who had helped
propel the Romans to victory. Fortuna Equestris and Castor were
patrons of the cavalry, which played a critical role in those two battles,
while Jupiter Victor's role as patron of victory is self-evident. There
is no sense of weakness evident anywhere in these types of vows.
Thus, vows made by generals on campaign can not be attributed to
weakness, the heat of battle or uncertainty about the outcome.

Furthermore, as with internal crises, it was not necessary for a
general to vow a new temple in order to insure the favor of heaven.
Generals could and did make other vows, ranging from burning the
spoils of the enemy to giving a tithe of the booty to Apollo to celebrating games.[64] The most unusual vow of this type occurred in
293, and is worth reporting in full:

> in that very moment of danger, in which it was the custom for temples
> to be vowed to the immortal gods, he had vowed a little cup of mead
> to Jupiter Victor before he drank wine, if he routed the legions of the
> enemy.[65]

Livy himself recognized that this was the normal moment to vow
temples, and yet the consul, L. Papirius Cursor, vowed only a liba-

---

[61] Livy 10.29.14.

[62] Livy 2.20.11–12. It is worth noting that Livy chooses to report this version of
the story rather than the variant offered by Dionysius of Halicarnassus (6.13), that
two supernatural horsemen appeared at the critical moment in battle to provide the
victory, and later that same day were seen watering their horses in the spring of
Juturna and announcing the victory. While Dionysius offers an aetiological explanation for the location of the temple, Livy's version is more in keeping with his conception of how new temples were built, i.e. following a general's vow in battle.

[63] In the case of Postumius's vow, his promises may have served a dual purpose:
a reward for past successes, but also to offer a further incentive to sack the enemy's
camp. The propitiatory and gratulatory aspects could thus be represented in a single
vow.

[64] For the games, see those vowed by the Scipiones below, plus one by military
tribunes (Livy 4.35.3) and one by a dictator (Livy 4.27.2). For burning the spoils,
see Livy 23.46. For the tithe, promised by Camillus at Veii, see Livy 5.23.8.

[65] Livy 10.42.7: *in ipso discrimine quo templa deis immortalibus voveri mos erat Iovi Victori,*
si legiones hostium fudisset, pocillum mulsi priusquam temetum biberet . . .

tion, a vow not recorded anywhere else. No reason is given for his decision to make this unusual vow rather than the more normal temple, although Papirius was likely aware of that tradition: after his campaign his colleague Sp. Carvilius let the contract for a temple to Fors Fortuna, which had presumably been vowed at some point during his campaign.[66] According to Livy the libation vow had the same effect as a temple vow normally did, that is, it made Papirius confident in the successful outcome when the auspices indicated the vow had been pleasing to the gods. This incident provides proof that vowing a temple, as opposed to another object, was not necessary to win the favor of the gods: vowing a temple certainly addressed a religious need, but that same religious need could be addressed by other means as well.

This point brings up one more similarity between vows made by generals on military campaigns and vows made during internal crises: not every campaign resulted in a vow to build a new temple in Rome. In fact, the large majority of campaigns resulted in no recorded vow at all. During the period under discussion, from 509 to 100 B.C.E., Rome elected approximately eight hundred consuls. Balancing out the dictators and praetors who led armies on Rome's behalf with those consuls who did not lead armies on campaign, this means that approximately nine out of ten generals did *not* vow a new temple while on campaign. It is difficult, if not impossible, to establish a single theory to explain why some generals but not others vowed temples, as an exhaustive review of the temples vowed by generals on campaign shows.[67] The nature of the war or the nature of the enemy seems to have made no difference; temples were vowed during important campaigns and insignificant campaigns, against mortal enemies and against minor tribes, against Greeks and against "barbarians". Critical battles or campaigns are no more likely to result in temple vows than other battles or campaigns; while there does seem to be increased activity at certain periods of stress, i.e. when Rome was engaged in important campaigns whose outcome was in serious doubt, the Second Punic War, surely one of the most stressful periods in Roman history, did not result in a greatly increased number of temples. Nor can individual characteristics provide a defining

---

[66] Livy 10.46. Curiously, the vow for the temple is not reported by Livy. Perhaps the historian or his source only recorded the more unusual of the two vows. On this temple, see further Chapter Four, pp. 123–24, 135.

[67] Cf. the list of temples vowed in Appendix One.

feature, since all sorts of generals vowed temples: plebeian and patrician, *novus homo* and *nobilis*, established statesman and relative neo-
phytes.[68]

One factor we must consider is one which we can not even hope
to isolate: the different personalities of the individual generals. The
temples of Tellus and Pales provide the clearest illustration of the
importance of personal predilections and the difficulty in searching
for common factors as an explanation for temple vows. These two
temples were vowed in consecutive years, 268 and 267, years in which
both consuls were given the same *provincia*.[69] Although in each year
both consuls celebrated triumphs, these campaigns do not seem particularly important or distinguished by critical battles, and in each
year only one of the consuls vowed a temple. P. Sempronius Sophus
vowed the temple to Tellus in 268 during the campaign against the
Picenes.[70] It is recorded that an earthquake struck during this battle,
which, although other propitiatory offerings were possible, provides
an obvious motivation for the vowing of a temple to the goddess
Earth. Yet for the temple of Pales no such aetiology is provided; we
simply know that M. Atilius Regulus vowed this temple during the
campaign against the Sallentini.[71] There is no reason to think that
he encountered any situations drastically different from that of his
colleague: they fought the same enemy with the same results. Yet
Atilius chose to meet that situation with a different response; he chose
to vow a temple.[72] This decision is difficult to explain on the basis
of anything other than the personal characteristics of the general
involved.

As with temples built as a response to an internal state of affairs,
temples vowed on campaigns were always an appropriate religious
reaction to the circumstances, but we can not assume that the vow
of a new temple was the highest religious vow a Roman could make.

---

[68] Pietilä-Castrén (1987) has done a remarkable job of cataloguing the evidence
for the victory monuments, mostly temples, built during the period of the Punic
Wars. Yet she makes no attempt to determine why the generals in her survey vowed
monuments while others did not, and it is clear from her summary that there is no
single factor held in common by all the generals who did build victory monuments.
[69] In 268 both consuls dealt with the Picene rebellion, while in 267 both consuls
fought the Sallentini.
[70] Florus 1.14.2, Val. Max. 6.3.1b.
[71] Florus 1.15.20, Ovid, *Fasti* 4.721.
[72] In a similar fashion, Sempronius' colleague may have felt the earthquake, but
elected to meet the crisis without vowing a temple.

Rather, as with the former category, political, social and cultural considerations factored into the final decision on whether to vow a temple. Yet in order to understand those considerations, we need to have a clear understanding of the process by which new temples were vowed, built and dedicated in Rome. The process itself reveals many of these factors at work, and thus offers insight into the motivations both of the individuals who vowed the temples and of the society which expanded its pantheon in this fashion. Thus, only after examining the details of this process can we return to a contemplation of the significance of this act.

III. *Conclusions*

The varied responses to crisis situations, potential or actual breaches in the *pax deum*, illustrate one of the essential strengths of Roman religion: its flexibility. It is not possible to speak of a certain situation as "demanding" a given religious response from the Romans; a variety of equally valid responses were available. We can not attempt to create a hierarchy of religious responses in order to state that the erection of a new temple was the greatest vow that the community could undertake, nor can we claim that such actions imply that other religious attempts at expiation had been deemed insufficient. Prodigies, plagues, and the uncertainties of the battlefield served as necessary preconditions for the erection of a new temple, but they were not sufficient causes. It is this very flexibility of response which made it possible for religious actions to have political implications; the decision to build a new temple becomes significant only if it was one choice out of many, and not a predetermined response. The common thread is the restoration of the *pax deum*, but the Romans were able to choose the means by which to placate the gods from a variety of options; each option had social and political as well as religious ramifications.

One of the great virtues of this flexibility was that it both provided continuity with the past and also allowed innovations to be introduced. Rome underwent a great transformation as she evolved from a small city into an imperial power, and her needs changed accordingly. Her territorial expansion around the Mediterranean basin is paralleled by the expansion of her pantheon and the construction of new temples. These included temples for foreign deities as well as for existing deities and for personified abstractions of Roman values. Rather than looking solely at the foreigners and focusing on the poverty of the Roman gods, we should appreciate that this process represented an affirmation of Rome's own traditions as well as an recognition of the city's expanded cultural horizons. These two poles are demonstrated superbly in the Roman responses to pestilence outlined above. In 363 and again in 331, the Romans had recourse to the ancient ceremony of driving a nail into the wall of the temple. This conservatism may indicate the desire of the Romans at that time to reaffirm their self-sufficiency and their own traditions as they consolidated their hold on central Italy. On the other hand, the introduction of Aesculapius in 293 may be related to the Romans putting the Samnite Wars behind them and looking ahead to entering the new cultural world of Greek southern Italy. The erection of a new temple, whether to a new or an old deity, needs to be seen in its historical, political, and social context in order to be properly understood.

CHAPTER TWO

THE VOW

As noted in the previous chapter, the most common procedure for the construction of a new temple in Rome was for a magistrate with *imperium* to vow a temple while on his campaign. The temple was duly built following the successful completion of his campaign and his return to Rome. Roman vows were conditional, almost contractual; the vow of Appius Claudius Caecus discussed in the previous chapter is typical.[1] If the campaign was unsuccessful, then no temple was built; the gods had not fulfilled their side of the contract, so the general was not obligated to fulfill his side either. Obviously, a general on campaign could not consult with the Senate before undertaking a vow; if he needed the assistance of the gods at some moment in the campaign, and particularly in the heat of battle, he had no time to dispatch an envoy to Rome and wait for a reply. This consideration raises the question of whether the vow of a magistrate with *imperium* was binding on the entire Roman state, or simply on the individual. Upon this point hinges the essential power of the individual to effect changes in Roman state religion. If the state was powerless to block the construction of a new temple once vowed, then theoretically a Roman commander could introduce any deity into Rome simply by vowing a temple while on campaign. The state would have no options but to accept the new deity, no matter how inimical to the best interests of the state it was felt to be; failure to fulfill a vow would have grave consequences for the *pax deum*. If, on

---

[1] Cf. pp. 28–29 and also below, pp. 48–49 and n. 48. The standard conception of the Roman vow as a bargain with the gods appears in Wissowa, *RKR* 319–20, Fowler, *RERP* 200–206, and Latte, *RRG* 46, but has also come under attack, notably by Turlan (1955) and Schilling (1969). Schilling, 444–45, argues, with special reference to the *devotio*, that a vow could often be "an unconditional appeal to divine benevolence" and goes on to state that "the unconditional *votum* recurs often in Roman history, for example, when promises were made to raise a temple." Versnel (1976) in his discussion of *devotio* defends the contractual model, especially on pp. 367–68. Recently Watson (1992), 39–43, has elucidated many parallels between the *votum* and the *stipulatio*. See also Hickson (1993), 91–93, for the language of vows in Livy. The form of numerous vows recorded by Livy has convinced me that temple vows must be regarded as conditional and quasi-contractual.

the other hand, the state maintained control over the vow in some
manner, the authority of the individual was limited in proportion to
the amount of state control. Determining the respective spheres of
competence for the individual and the Senate is thus of the highest
significance for a study of Roman religion.

As a starting point we must note several different categories of
vows in Roman religion, for the type of vow had a direct bearing on
whether the vow was binding on the state. Vows undertaken by private
citizens would obviously be binding only on that citizen and its performance or non-performance would have repercussions for that
individual and his family only. On the other hand, *vota publica*, vows
on behalf of the state, involved the welfare of the whole community,
and so are usually considered to be binding on the state. The question before us is to examine the status of vows made by magistrates
cum imperio: should they be considered vows made by an individual,
binding on him alone, or should he be seen as the representative of
the *res publica*, and the vows thus binding on the state? In this regard, we must observe that a magistrate might undertake several
different types of vows during his term in office: in Rome and/or in
his province, on the direct order of the Senate and/or on his own
initiative. These factors are significant in determining which vows
were binding on the state, and it is to them that we must now direct
our attention.

I. *Vows Undertaken by Magistrates in Rome*

The sources indicate that there were two different types of vows which
a Roman consul would undertake before he ever left Rome. Standard Roman practice called for the consuls and praetors to ascend
the Capitoline hill on the day they assumed office in order to sacrifice
and make vows to the gods.[2] Although we do not know the specific
content of these vows, nor whether the Senate dictated the terms of
the vow or the individual himself made that decision, the purpose of
these vows was apparently to ensure the general success of the magistrate during his term of office. Rather than praying for the success
of a specific undertaking, the magistrate attempted to provide for the

---

[2] Ovid, *Ex ponto* 4.4, describes the ceremony on the day the consuls entered office,
including the vows (line 30).

continued safety of the state by asking in advance for the assistance of the gods in whatever as yet unforeseen crises might arise during the coming year, be it plague, drought, or battle. A tradition has grown up in modern scholarship that the sacrifice by the consuls on the Capitoline on their first day in office fulfilled the vows which had been made by the consuls of the previous year, and that the new consuls then made vows for the following year which would be discharged by their successors.[3] Yet the purpose of these sacrifices seems to be to obtain favorable auspices for the coming year rather than to perform the *solutio* of the previous consuls' vows.[4]

These annual vows of the consuls have often been compared to the quinquennial vows offered by the censors, for the censors made sacrifices and offered vows at the *lustrum* which closed their term in office.[5] For the censors at least, we possess a purported text of these vows, from an episode reported by Valerius Maximus.[6] When Scipio Aemilianus was censor, the scribe began to dictate the words of the prayer to him from the public records, that the immortal gods should make the affairs of the Roman people better and bigger. Scipio

---

[3] See Mommsen, *RS* 1.616; Marquardt (1881–85), 3.266; Fowler, *RERP* 203; Bouché-Leclerq (1931), 59; Latte, *RRG* 152–3; Schilling (1969), 474; and Hickson (1993), 94. While the ancient evidence cited for support (Cicero, *Leg. Agr.* 2.93 and *De Div.* 2.39, and Ovid, *Fasti* 1.79f.) is not conclusive, J. Scheid (1990), 300–330, has recently argued, based on the preserved records of the Arval Brethren, that the sacrifice at the beginning of the year did in fact represent the *solutio* of the previous year's vows, followed by the *nuncupatio* of vows for the coming year. There are two problems with equating the vows of the Arval Brethren with those of the consuls on their entrance to office: the former represents the situation under the Empire, and they represent the vows of a group which remained largely unchanged from year to year, while Republican magistrates rotated annually. Thus the Arval Brethren would be fulfilling vows which they had made the previous year, while magistrates would have to fulfill vows made by a completely different set of individuals.

[4] Cf. the episode reported by Livy in 176 (41.14.7–15.4), when the incoming consul Q. Petilius had to report to the Senate not once but twice that he was unable to obtain favorable omens, because no head to the liver was found on the cattle he was sacrificing. The Senate ordered him to continue sacrificing until favorable omens were obtained.

[5] Cf. Mommsen, *RS* 2.406; Fowler, *RERP* 203; Hickson (1993), 94. Suetonius, *Aug.* 97, in his description of these vows does imply that the same individual who made the vow as censor was supposed fulfill it five years later, but this practice is probably a function of Augustus' extraordinary position and can not be read back into the Republic.

[6] Val. Max. 4.1.10: *scriba ex publicis tabulis sollemne ei precationis carmen praeiret, quo di immortales ut populi Romani res meliores amplioresque facerent rogabantur. "Satis", inquit, "bonae et magnae sunt: itaque precor ut eas perpetuo incolumes servent," ac protinus in publicis tabulis ad hunc modem carmen emendari iussit. Qua votorum verecundia deinceps censores in condendis lustris usi sunt.*

interrupted, saying that the state was sufficiently large and well-off, and that therefore he was going to pray that the gods should always keep them safe; from that point forward the censors used this new formula. While doubts have been cast on the authenticity of the story, for our purposes the accuracy of the details may be less relevant than some of the fundamental facts revealed by the anecdote.[7] If the basic thrust of the vows can be taken as reliable, it confirms that these regular vows of magistrates were indeed more concerned with the general welfare of the state than with requests for aid on specific occasions, and also shows that there was a set formula for these recurring vows.[8] However, it does not help us solve the question as to whether the sacrifices at the *lustrum* served an augural purpose, to ascertain that the gods approved of the censors' actions during their term in office, or whether they served as the *solutio* of the previous censors' vows.

Consuls and praetors also made vows on the Capitoline upon setting out for their provinces. Festus defines these vows as *vota nuncupata* and indicates that they were made in the presence of many witnesses and registered on tablets.[9] The best description of this practice derives from a speech which Livy recorded during a debate over granting a triumph in 167:

> A consul or a praetor setting out for his province and for war, with his lictors in military dress, announces his vows on the Capitoline; having achieved victory in that war, he returns triumphant to the Capitoline, bearing the well-deserved gifts to those gods, to whom he announced his vows.[10]

---

[7] For the most recent discussion of the authenticity of this story, see Astin (1967), 325–31, with references to previous studies. Certainly the story can not be true in all its details, for, as everyone has recognized, it is unthinkable that Scipio could have executed a change in the vow on his own authority, without consulting the Senate or the college of pontiffs; cf. e.g. Astin, 327–28.

[8] It may also show that these vows could be modified to suit a new political and/or historical context, but as indicated in the previous note, such a change must have involved the Senate and the pontiffs.

[9] Festus, 176L: *vota nuncupata dicuntur, quae consules praetores cum in provinciam proficiscuntur faciunt; ea in tabulas praesentibus multis referentur.* Writing down the vows may have been intended to prevent the magistrate from attempting to shirk the fulfillment of the vow after his term expired. It may also have served as a reminder to insure that the vows were properly fulfilled, or perhaps more simply to underscore the solemnity of the vow.

[10] Livy 45.39.12: *Consul proficiscens praetorve paludatis lictoribus in provinciam et ad bellum vota in Capitolio nuncupat; victor perpetrato bello eodem in Capitolium triumphans eosdem deos, quibus vota nuncupavit, merita dona portans redit.* The speech is undoubtedly fictional, but

Again the exact nature of the vows and of the gifts brought to the Capitoline upon successful conclusion of the campaign remain a mystery. The gift seems to have been some token of victory, although it was probably not a tithe from the spoils.[11] According to Livy's descriptions, these vows were discharged by the general himself, probably as part of the triumph if he had been granted one.[12]

There is some question as to whether the vows taken before departing for one's province should be distinguished from the vows taken upon entering office, especially as both were taken on the Capitoline. The situation in 217, when C. Flaminius neglected to make any vows on the Capitoline before the battle at Lake Trasimene, provides the most useful piece of evidence on this issue. Livy reports that the Senate, angry at the behavior of Flaminius, laid the following accusations against him:

> he fled the accustomed pronouncement of vows (*sollemnem votorum nuncupationem*), that he might not approach the temple of Jupiter Optimus Maximus on the day of entering office, that he might not see and consult the Senate, which he hated and which hated him alone, that he might not proclaim the Latin festival and perform the accustomed sacrifice to Jupiter Latiaris on the [Alban] mount, that he might not proceed to the Capitol after taking the auspices in order to pronounce his vows (*ad vota nuncupanda*) in the general's cloak and thence go to his province accompanied by lictors.[13]

These events are listed in the order in which they customarily took place. On the first day in office occurred sacrifices to Jupiter on the Capitoline hill and usually also the convening of the Senate for the

---

other references make it clear that Livy is referring to an actual established practice. For other attestations of vows made upon departing for one's province, see Livy 22.1.6, 38.48.16, 42.49.1; Cicero, *Verr.* 5.34; Caesar, *BC* 1.6. For modern discussions, see Mommsen, *RS* 1.63–64; Wissowa, *RKR* 320–21; Latte, *RRG* 152–53; Keaveney (1982), 161–64; Hickson (1993), 91–94.

[11] Although there is some speculation that Roman generals tithed a part of their spoils, the practice is usually associated with Hercules rather than with the Capitoline triad, and even the evidence for Hercules is not convincing. See further Marquardt (1881), 361; De Sanctis (1907–1923), 4.2.1.260–62; and Bona (1960), 151 and n. 116.

[12] Note that Livy uses the word *triumphans* in his description. The connection between these vows and the triumph is noted by Latte, *RRG* 153, following Lacquer (1909).

[13] Livy 21.63.7–9: *sollemnem votorum nuncupationem fugisse, ne die initi magistratus Iovis optimi maximi templum adiret, ne senatum invisus ipse et sibi uni invisum videret consuleretque, ne Latinas indiceret Iovique Latiari sollemne sacrum in monte faceret, ne auspicato profectus in Capitolium ad vota nuncupanda paludatus inde cum lictoribus in provinciam iret.*

first time under the new magistrates. The proclamation of the Latin festival and the actual performance of the Latin festival took place subsequent to that first day in office, but prior to the general's departure from the city on his campaign.[14] Thus we must envision two separate sets of vows; one was made on the first day in office and the other was made when leaving Rome, on whatever day that happened to be.[15] For the second set of vows, Livy usually describes the consul as dressed in his military cloak (*paludamentum*) and accompanied by lictors, and the ceremony as occurring just before the consul set out for his province, confirming that these were separate from those taken on assuming office.[16]

Of the two types of vows, it appears that the latter were binding on the general himself to fulfill, while the status of the former is more difficult to determine. Many analyses of this issue, including the present one, depend in part on the question of who bore the financial responsibility for fulfilling a vow. If the state provided the means with which to fulfill the vows made by magistrates, then it seems logical to conclude that the state took the responsibility for these vows and that the magistrates were merely acting as its agents both in making the vows and in fulfilling them. On the other hand, if the magistrate himself was expected to pay for the vow, then it would seem to take on more of the character of a private vow, which would have direct consequences for the individual involved.[17] If the

---

[14] Cf. Livy 25.12.1–2, where the Latin festival was completed on the 26th of April, and immediately afterward the consuls set out for their provinces.

[15] Wissowa, *RKR* 320, Latte, *RRG* 152–53, and Keaveney (1982), 161–64 all recognize that these were two separate types of vows. Latte believes that the sacrifice on the first day of the year fulfilled the vow made on that day by the previous year's consuls, while the offering on the Capitoline at the conclusion of the triumph fulfilled the vow made when leaving Rome for one's campaign. Hence he draws a distinction between these vows. Wissowa aligns the vows made on departing Rome closely with those made on the battlefield, since both were undertaken to meet a special circumstance, while those on the first day in office were for the general welfare of the state. The present analysis draws a distinction between all three types of vows; such is also the opinion of Mommsen, *RS* 1.616, n. 6, and Hickson (1993), 94. This third group, of vows made on the field of battle, is the one which frequently resulted in the erection of new temples; it is discussed more fully below in Section II.

[16] See the instances cited in n. 10 above.

[17] If this were the case, the practice seems similar to the liturgical system which developed in Greece, where magistrates were expected to erect public buildings or undertake other services to the state. The nature of this work was left to the magistrate's discretion, but the money often came from his pocket because the city did not have the funds to pay for these works. On this system, cf. Jones (1966);

magistrate was remiss in the fulfillment of such a vow, it might affect the state indirectly, but not on the same scale as if the *comitia* had undertaken a vow. Thus, as vows made by consuls when departing for their provinces were often discharged by the general as part of the triumph, they seem to be more in the nature of individual vows than *vota publica*.[18] Unfortunately we are not informed about the fulfilling of the vows made upon entering office, unless we assume that the sacrifice on the Capitoline was indeed the *solutio* of the previous year's vows.[19] Without knowing how these vows were fulfilled, it is difficult to know on whom these vows were binding.

A third category of vows is evident on other occasions, when the Senate ordered a magistrate to make a particular vow before departing for his campaign. In such cases, it seems clear that the state did assume responsibility for fulfilling these vows, although it is not clear whether these vows were in addition to the magistrate's own vows or instead of them. In some instances, the orders came at the instigation of the Sibylline Books, but the Senate also gave such orders without consulting the Books, i.e. on its own initiative.[20] In 396 and again in 360, the dictator appointed by the Senate was ordered to vow *ludi magni* to Jupiter before leaving the city for his campaign.[21] In 208 the Senate, in an effort to combat a plague, ordered the urban praetor to propose a bill making the *Ludi Apollinares* an annual celebration, and the praetor himself was the first to vow them on those terms.[22] Eight years later the Senate ordered a consul to vow

---

Veyne (1990), 71–94. In Rome, the games offered by the aediles seem very much like a liturgy, inasmuch as aediles tried to outdo one another and to reap political benefits from staging more and more elaborate games. See for example Caelius' repeated requests to Cicero to bring him panthers and other exotic animals so that he might outshine, or at least compete with, Curio (Cicero, *Ad Fam* 8.2, 8.4, 8.8, 8.9). Note however that these games were not vowed from year to year, but simply appeared on the annual religious calendar.

[18] Cf. above, pp. 50–51.

[19] If this were the case, then these vows were similar to the extraordinary vows made by magistrates on the direct order of the Senate, such as that of M'. Acilius Glabrio in 191. These vows are discussed in the ensuing pages. Note that the argument that only vows made on the direct orders of the Senate were binding on the state is strengthened if in fact the vows undertaken by one set of consuls were fulfilled by the subsequent pair, the implication being that the office, and hence the state, rather than the individual was responsible for the vow.

[20] On the Sibylline Books, see Chapter Three.

[21] Livy 5.19.6, 7.11.5.

[22] Livy 27.23.7. As Livy notes, the games had first been celebrated in 212, but their purpose at that time was military, not healing, and they had been renewed on an *ad hoc* basis. Cf Gagé, (1955).

ludi magni before setting out for his province. In this instance a controversy arose only because a definite amount of money was not set
aside prior to the campaign; the *pontifex maximus* originally ruled that
a vow for an indefinite sum was not allowable, but he was overruled
by the entire college of pontiffs.[23] After this, games of an indetermi-
nate sum of money were vowed on the order of the Senate in 191
and again in 172.[24] That the Senate determined how much to spend
on these games at the appropriate time implies that the Senate provided the requisite funds from the state treasury and thus took
responsibility for discharging this obligation.[25]

The games of 191 provide a particularly good opportunity to analyze these state-sponsored vows, because Livy has given us an actual
text for this vow. In that year, a *senatus consultum* was passed to the
effect that the consuls should order a *supplicatio* for the sake of this
undertaking, and that the consul M'. Acilius Glabrio, who had been
assigned the war against Antiochus, should vow *ludi magni* to Jupiter
and gifts to all the *pulvinaria*.[26] The vow of Acilius is recorded, following the formula dictated by the *pontifex maximus*:

> If the war which the people has ordered to be undertaken with King
> Antiochus shall have been finished to the satisfaction of the Senate
> and the Roman people, then to you, Jupiter, the Roman people will
> perform the Great Games for ten consecutive days, and gifts will be
> given at all the *pulvinaria*, of however much value the Senate shall decree.
> Whatever magistrate shall celebrate those games, whenever and wher-
> ever he does so, let these games be considered as celebrated properly
> and the gifts as offered properly.[27]

---

[23] Livy 31.9.

[24] Livy 36.2, 42.28.

[25] Similarly, for annual *ludi* which the aediles were responsible for staging, the
Senate regularly supplied a fixed sum of money, which the aediles could supplement
with other funds if they desired to curry favor with the electorate; cf. Cohee (1994).
The Senate eventually established limits on how much aediles could spend on these
games following the aedileship of Tiberius Gracchus the Elder (Livy 40.44.10–12).

[26] Livy 36.2.2.

[27] Livy 36.2.5: *Si duellum quod cum rege Antiocho sumi populus iussit, id ex sententia senatus
populique Romani confectum erit, tum tibi, Iuppiter, populus Romanus ludos magnos dies decem
continuos faciet, donaque ad omnia pulvinaria dabuntur de pecunia, quantam senatus decreverit.
Quisquis magistratus eos ludos quando ubique faxit, hi ludi recte facti donaque data recte sunto.*
We must of course recognize the very real possibility that Livy's purported text of
the vow may bear little resemblance to the actual vow. Nonetheless, the manner in
which Livy words the vow reveals an educated Roman's perception of its key com-
ponents. As such, we may at least take it as a reasonable approximation of this type
of vow.

This vow was made at the beginning of the year, after the allotment of provinces and before Acilius departed the city for Greece on May 3.[28]

In this case, the text of the vow clearly indicates that the state would have to fulfill this vow, even though an individual spoke the words. Acilius is clearly making the vow as the representative of the state, and not as an individual; he vowed that "the Roman people" will perform the *ludi magni*, not that he himself would be responsible for their celebration. This is perfectly understandable, especially since the Senate ordered him to make the vow and the *pontifex maximus* dictated the words of the vow. The second sentence of the vow is also significant and confirms this interpretation. The vow will be considered fulfilled if any representative of the state celebrates the *ludi magni*; it does not have to be the *same* representative of the state. Acilius, as the magistrate who made the vow, is not to be held personally responsible for discharging the vow. Note also that the Senate is to decide on the value of the gifts, confirming that a Senatorial determination on the amount spent means that the Senate will provide the money. Thus, in those instances where the Senate ordered a magistrate to vow *ludi*, especially in those cases where the amount of money was not specified, it is clear that the Senate must have been the source of funds for the celebration.

It is important to recognize that there is not a single attested instance of the Senate's expenditure of private monies without the approval of the individual affected. The *ver sacrum* vowed following the advice of the Sibylline Books in 217 provides a clear example of Roman practice in this regard.[29] This vow, which called for all the livestock born in the designated spring to be sacrificed to Jupiter, would have affected anyone who owned livestock; each citizen would have to offer up a share of his property to the god. However, when the praetor M. Aemilius, as directed by the Senate, consulted the college of pontiffs about how to put this vow into effect, the Pontifex Maximus declared that "it [the Sacred Spring] could not be vowed without the authorization of the people."[30] Thus, authorization from those whose property would be affected by the *ver sacrum* needed to be obtained before the vow could be undertaken. This incident points

---

[28] Livy 36.3.14.
[29] Livy 22.10.2–6.
[30] Livy 22.10.1: *iniussu populi voveri non posse.*

toward the conclusion that the fulfillment of a vow undertaken at
the direction of the Senate could not involve the use of private funds,
unless specific approval to that end was granted.

These considerations of the *ver sacrum* and of vows for *ludi* made at
the behest of the Senate help us to understand temple vows as well.
We possess several examples of temples, rather than games, being
vowed by generals before leaving Rome for their campaigns. In
496, following a consultation of the Sibylline Books, the dictator
A. Postumius Albus vowed to build a temple to Ceres, Liber and
Libera "when he was about to lead out his army."[31] Although there
are some notable differences between the vow of Acilius in 191 and
that of Postumius in 496, notably that the latter came in response to
a consultation of the Sibylline Books and thus served as a response
to a prodigy, there are some striking similarities as well. Postumius,
like Acilius, made his vow on the direct orders of the Senate, and
like Acilius he made the vow before leaving the city and not on the
field of battle. Dionysius is explicit that the vow was undertaken on
behalf of the state, reporting that Postumius vowed "to dedicate it to
the gods on behalf of the city."[32] To underline further that this was
a civic vow, Dionysius goes on to state that the Senate voted which
funds should be used for the construction of the temple.[33] This incident provides a close parallel to that of Acilius and the *ludi magni*,
and as in that episode, it includes the detail that the Senate arranged
for underwriting the cost of the vow.[34]

The dictator M. Furius Camillus undertook a similar vow as part
of the preparation for his campaign against Veii in 396. Livy reports
as follows:

> With everything already sufficiently prepared for this war, he vowed,
> in accord with a *senatus consultum*, that once Veii was captured he would

---

[31] Dion. Hal. 6.17.3.

[32] Dion. Hal. 6.94.3.

[33] That the Senate directed that booty from Postumius' campaign be used to
build the temple does not detract from the basic significance of the Senate taking
the responsibility to earmark funds for construction.

[34] Two other temples were vowed according to a directive from the Sibylline
Books prior to the general's departure from the city: Venus Erycina and Mens in
217 (Livy 22.10.10–22.11). In this instance Livy does not explicitly indicate that the
Senate designated funds for the construction of the temples, but it may fairly be
inferred from the involvement of the Sibylline Books and the importance which
these temples held for the state's survival at this critical moment in the Second
Punic War. These temples are treated in detail, pp. 175–76.

celebrate *ludi magni* and that he would dedicate the rebuilt temple of Mater Matuta . . .[35]

In Livy's account, Camillus then marched out from the city immediately after taking these vows. This vow is even more similar to the vow of Acilius, for the *senatus consultum* that prompted it was apparently not provoked by a prodigy and the Sibylline Books played no role here. Again it was undertaken by the general in obedience to a Senatorial decree before leaving the city. The vow to celebrate games and to dedicate a temple merely confirms the parallel between these two items that was noted above. In this instance, Camillus personally performed the dedication of the reconstructed temple of Mater Matuta, but he did not have to provide any of his own money; the actual process of rebuilding was a matter of state concern. These examples, from Camillus to Acilius, clearly illustrate that the key elements of vows made on the direct order of the state remained largely unchanged for most of the Republic. They were made before the general departed Rome for his campaign, and they were largely binding on the state to fulfill, and not necessarily the individual.

II. *Vows Undertaken by Magistrates on Campaign*

As we have noted, vows made by generals on campaign are the most frequent means by which new temples were built in Rome, and are therefore the most significant for our study. In these cases, the sources give no indication that the magistrate had been specifically authorized or directed to make the vow by the Senate or by one of the religious colleges.[36] The assumption that the magistrate made these vows on his own authority simply by virtue of his office is therefore an appropriate place to start. The crux of the problem was outlined at the beginning of this chapter: were these vows, made

---

[35] Livy 5.19.6: *satis iam omnibus ad id bellum paratis ludos magnos ex senatus consulto vovit Veiis captis se facturum aedemque Matutae Matris refectam dedicaturum . . .*

[36] The suggestion of R. D. Weigel, (1982–83), 188 and n. 40, that the pontiffs or the decemvirs may have suggested "appropriate deities who needed special recognition" is without basis in the ancient sources. Furthermore, as we have seen these two bodies were essentially consultative, and any action suggested by them needed to be ratified by the Senate. Again there is no trace of such a procedure in the sources.

by magistrates *cum imperio* while on their campaigns, legally binding on the state?

Modern authorities have had a difficult time answering this question. Mommsen argued against this position, believing that the burden lay with the individual and that the state treasury took no responsibility for vows made without the approval of the state.[37] Despite the magistrate's office, he was empowered to make sacred contracts only on his own behalf, and not on behalf of the state. The vow is meant to help him to win the battle; that the state also profits is in a sense incidental. However, most scholars have favored the opposite position, that any vows made by a magistrate *cum imperio* were binding on the state, even if the general later did not want to fulfill the vow or if he had no money available.[38] According to this view, the magistrate is seen as the representative of the state, and whatever actions he might take therefore involved the entire state. These scholars occasionally find instances where the Senate played a more significant role or note that the Senate might have desired to play such a role, but they all make the claim that the state was bound by the vow of the magistrate.[39]

A recent study by A. Ziolkowski has attempted to resolve this problem by reference to the term *vota nuncupata*. He argues that "all solemn vows made by the magistrates *cum imperio* on behalf of the Roman state were *vota nuncupata*" and that "the binding character of these vows for the whole community in whose name they were pronounced seems obvious."[40] Yet both claims are questionable. The

---

[37] Mommsen, *RS* 3.1062. Cf. 1.246.

[38] Bardon (1955), 169; Daremberg-Saglio, 977–78; *RE*, Suppl. 14, cols. 964–973. The position of Willems (1878–1883), 320 and n. 5, is difficult to understand: on the one hand, the Senate's authorization was not necessary for such vows, but on the other hand, the Senate would not help financially if it did not authorize the vow. This would seem to result in a situation in which new public temples could be built and new state cults added as long as no state money was involved. Wissowa *RKR*, 319–22, associated temple vows with *vota publica*, thereby implying that such vows did involve the state and were thus paid for by the state. Latte *RRG*, 46–7, noted that the state regularly discharged the vows of magistrates in good times and bad, without actually addressing the question of whether it was forced to do so. Bleicken (1975), 111, also straddles this issue, arguing that the approval of the *comitia* was necessary when the whole people was to be bound by a vow, but then goes on to say that in practice vows and dedications were accomplished without comitial approval.

[39] Many analyses of this issue, including the present one, depend in part on who bore the financial responsibility for the fulfillment of a given vow, a topic that will be treated in Chapter Four.

[40] Ziolkowski (1992), 195–198.

ancient sources are extremely loose in their use of this word. We have already seen that Festus defined *vota nuncupata* as those vows undertaken by magistrates departing from the city, not necessarily all those made by magistrates *cum imperio*. On the other hand, a ceremony known as the *Nuncupatio Votorum* appears on the calendars of the Arval Brethren on the third of January; this imperial celebration seems to be derived from the vows made on the first day in office rather than from vows made upon setting out on campaign.[41] Furthermore, Livy uses forms of the word *nuncupare* in three separate situations: both to describe the vows made on assuming office and the vows made on leaving Rome, and also to describe vows pronounced to repair the *pax deum*, including some made on the orders of the Sibylline Books.[42] Thus, one can hardly narrow the definition of *nuncupare vota* beyond "to publicly pronounce vows." Even Ziolkowski cites "*nuncupationes* made by private persons", but then remarks that "for clarity's sake it would be better to limit the use of the term to *vota* made by magistrates."[43] But that is precisely the problem: the ancient sources did not limit their usage in this way, and we can not artificially create clarity for the sake of our own arguments. Without such a definition of *vota nuncupata*, it becomes impossible to state that all such vows were binding on the state. On the contrary, the evidence marshaled so far indicates that the *vota nuncupata* of Festus' definition were binding on the individual alone. Other *vota nuncupata* were binding on the state, especially those made at the behest of the Sibylline Books, but the evidence is too mixed to draw any general conclusions from the use of this term.

The example of M'. Acilius Glabrio highlights the complexities surrounding vows made by generals. As noted above, Acilius vowed *ludi magni* at the behest of the Senate before leaving Rome for Greece in 191; here he was unquestionably the representative of the state and the vow clearly a state responsibility.[44] Later that year, at the

---

[41] *CIL* 6.2028. Cf. commentary at *CIL* I², p. 305, Henzen *Acta Frat. Arv.*, 89–99, and most recently the work of J. Scheid (1990), especially the section on vows, 290–356.

[42] Cf. Livy 22.10.8: *votis rite nuncupatis* in reference to the *ver sacrum* and the *ludi Magni* ordered by the Books (Livy 22.9.9–10), as well as sacrifices to many other gods which had not been explicitly ordered by the Books. Cf. Packard (1968) for Livy's use of *nuncupare*. Unfortunately the study of Hickson (1993) does not cover the word *nuncupare*.

[43] Ziolkowski (1992), 195–6, n. 10.

[44] Livy 36.2. See above, pp. 55–56.

critical battle of Thermopylae, he vowed a temple to Pietas, which was dedicated ten years later in the Forum Holitorium.[45] In his description of Acilius' preparations for his campaign and of his religious activities before leaving the city, Livy says nothing about obtaining permission to vow a temple, again leading to the assumption that the vow was made on his own authority.[46] Modern scholars have been unable to come up with a suitable explanation for why Acilius vowed a temple to Pietas, a god who has no obvious connection to success in battle.[47] Yet when Acilius returned to Rome and brought the question of his vow before the Senate, the Senate raised no objections but appointed Acilius to let the contract for the temple. Acilius thus made one vow before leaving Rome on the orders of the Senate, and another while on campaign which was only afterwards approved by the Senate. The former was undeniably binding on the state, but the same can not be said of the latter before its approval by the Senate.

The form of the vow made in the heat of battle differs sharply from that made on the Senate's orders before leaving Rome, and gives no indication that such vows were thought to be binding on the community. In this context it is instructive to compare the vow which Acilius made in Rome with a vow which Appius Claudius Caecus made in battle against the Etruscans and Samnites in 296: "Bellona, if today you grant to us the victory, then I vow to you a temple."[48] The wording of the vow strongly implies that this is an obligation that Appius personally has undertaken, as he stresses *ego voveo*, even though the Roman people as a whole, *nobis*, will benefit.

---

[45] Livy 40.34.4.

[46] Livy 36.2–3.

[47] Wissowa (*RKR*), 331, argued that some act of filial piety occurred during the battle, since it was Acilius' son who dedicated the temple. However there is no evidence for such an act, and sons were frequently made *duumviri* for the purpose of dedicating temples vowed by their fathers. Galinsky (1969), 179–186, tried to connect Pietas with Venus Erycina, since both temples were dedicated in the same year. However, as Schilling (1954), 254–62, points out, the connection between these two temples is not that close; the second temple to Venus Erycina was not vowed until 184, so it can hardly explain the vow to Pietas in 191. The connection between these two temples is only that they were dedicated in the same year, which may merely be coincidental.

[48] Livy 10.19.17: *Bellona, si hodie nobis victoriam duis, ast ego tibi templum voveo*. As with Acilius' vow, we can certainly be skeptical as to whether Livy is merely putting words into Appius' mouth, but those words would not be created out of whole cloth. The vow, if invented by Livy, would be worded in a way consistent with his understanding of Roman generals' vows.

In contrast, the vow made by Acilius specifically stated that the "Roman people" would perform the vowed ritual, and that any magistrate could fulfill the obligation. The vow to Ceres by Postumius was similarly undertaken "on behalf of the city."[49] Appius' vow mentions no one other than himself, and thus we may not assume that he placed an obligation on anyone other than himself.

On the other hand, the Senate clearly took an interest in the vows made by the consuls. The failure of a magistrate to fulfill the religious obligations of his office could have disastrous consequences for the state. The behavior of C. Flaminius in 217 offers the best model for this belief; Flaminius failed to offer the customary vows and sacrifices before assuming his command, and later Roman tradition ascribed his subsequent defeat and death at Lake Trasimene to this act of impiety.[50] The Senate also maintained an interest in the vows undertaken by generals while on their campaigns; although the person who vowed the temple generally performed the dedication, the Senate on occasion appointed another person to this task.[51] This points to the fact that these vows were not treated simply as private vows, which could only be discharged by the individual, but that there was a public interest in seeing that these vows were fulfilled. The line between public actions and private actions was not always clearly demarcated in Rome.

The major problem in analyzing the legal authority of magistrates *cum imperio* lies in the lack of ancient testimony on this question. Not a single ancient source refers to any law or *senatus consultum* which might throw some light on whether the vow of a magistrate *cum imperio* was binding upon the state. This fact in itself should immediately force us to question whether the Romans had ever formulated the problem in this way or attempted to define the legal authority of magistrates as moderns have.[52] The Roman system of government had no written Constitution such as exists in the United States which outlined the powers and limitations of the various organs of government. Rather, it was much more fluid, as magistrates acted in accord

---

[49] Dion. Hal. 6.94.3. See above, p. 56.

[50] Livy 21.63.7. Flaminius' offense probably lay more in his failure to be properly inaugurated and to celebrate the *feriae Latinae* than in his failure to offer the vows on the Capitoline, but the vows were clearly an integral part of this ceremony.

[51] See Chapter Five for a discussion of the *duumviri aedi dedicandae*.

[52] W. Eisenhut, in his article on *votum* in *RE* (Suppl. 14, col. 967), noted the difficulty which Mommsen faced in trying to answer this question on a strictly constitutional basis, a difficulty which anyone making such an attempt would face.

with what they considered to be their powers, and the notions of those powers were derived from custom, i.e. the *mos maiorum*. Limitations on those powers, which certainly existed, were often not legal or constitutional, but social and political. The Senate might step in to reassert its authority or curtail that of the magistrates on an *ad hoc* basis, when a majority of senators felt that a particular action exceeded the bounds of what they were willing to grant as the magistrate's prerogative. Because the Senate was composed of many former magistrates, the assumption of excess power by one magistrate could adversely affect the position of the others who had already held that office: he had been able to do something that no one else had, and that gave him an unfair advantage as members of the aristocracy jockeyed for primacy. It might also set an unwelcome precedent for the future in terms of the powers arrogated by individuals as opposed to the collective will of the Senate. In these situations, it is often difficult to decide whether the resulting *senatus consultum* laid down a permanent law for all subsequent magistrates, or whether it was more narrowly aimed at the individual magistrate who had aroused the Senate's ire.[53] Compounding the problem is the fact that different incidents occurring in different periods lend themselves to different conclusions, forcing us to conclude that the same principle did not operate at all times, or even that no single principle existed which guided policy in this area. The Romans may never have formulated a principle which defined the position of the magistrate in regard to his ability to make vows which would be considered binding on the state.

A comparison of the process by which the Roman state made treaties may provide the best illustration of how vows were regarded by the Senate. The comparison is especially apt because in the Roman system of *do ut des*, a vow functioned as a sacred contract, i.e. a treaty between a human and a divine entity stipulating that if the divine provided timely assistance, the human would respond with a specified honor.[54] Roman generals possessed a great deal of latitude

---

[53] As a parallel we might consider United States Supreme Court decisions, which may be broadly written to strike down a whole range of laws, or narrowly written to focus on the specific circumstances of the individual case. Supreme Court decisions, however, are elaborate documents which explain the reasoning behind the decision, and so make it clear whether a broad or narrow interpretation is intended. With Roman *senatus consulta*, however, we have no such exegesis; we have only the decision.

[54] On this contractual nature of vows, cf. above p. 35 and n. 1. The language of

to conduct affairs in their province as they saw fit, waging the campaign and concluding peace treaties according to their own assessment of the situation. However, all peace treaties, and indeed all the *acta* of a general, had to be ratified by the Senate to be effective.[55] Failure to obtain Senatorial approval would deprive a treaty of its validity. Even Eckstein, who argues that generals played the major role in formulating Roman policy, admits that "legally any decisions made by the generals in the field remained preliminary and transitory until explicitly approved by the Senate."[56] While it was not common for the Senate to reject ratification of a peace treaty, it did happen on occasion, with the result that the treaty was annulled and the war resumed.[57] Although treaties often invoked the gods as guarantors of good faith, the rejection of a treaty was not held to constitute a breach of faith; rather the general who had agreed to the terms could be sent back to the enemy, thus removing the religious liability from the state. This interpretation is made explicit in the speech which Livy puts in the mouth of Postumius, urging rejection of the Caudine Forks peace:

> I bound myself by a disgraceful or perhaps a necessary pledge (*sponsio*); by which nevertheless the Roman people is not bound, because it was

---

vows is often similar to that of legal contracts. Imperial inscriptions are marked V.S.L.M. for *votum solvit libens merito*, just as *solvo* is used with debts. Furthermore, *reus* is used both for one who binds himself to the gods by a vow and for the debtor in *stipulatio*. Cf. Watson (1992), 43, and Hickson (1993), 92–93 and 100–102 (on the phrase *reus voti*).

[55] Cf. Mommsen, *RS* 3.1158–1173. Roman history provides plentiful examples of the ratification of peace treaties or other *acta*. To cite only a few, see M. Claudius Marcellus after his campaigns in Sicily (Livy 26.31–32), Flamininus and Sparta (Livy 34.43.1–2, Diod. 28.13), and Cato the Elder and Spain (Plut. *Cato* 11). Several such ratifications caused very heated debate in the Senate, which proves that Senatorial approval was not merely a rubber stamp. On these and other cases, see Eckstein (1987), *passim*.

[56] Eckstein (1987), xiii. In his analysis of specific situations throughout the book, Eckstein repeats similar sentiments, e.g. "Legally the Senate could have modified, or even rejected any of Flamininus's Greek decisions" (312–13).

[57] For examples, cf. the treaty with the Samnites following the Caudine Forks disaster (Livy 9.8, Cicero, *De inv.* 2.91, Eutropius 2.9), the treaty ending the First Punic War (Polyb. 1.62.8–63.7), a treaty ending the Second Punic War (Livy 30.23), the treaty of Q. Pompeius (App. *Ib.* 79, Vell. 2.90.3, Livy, *Per.* 55) and another treaty of C. Mancinus with the Numantines (App. *Ib.* 80, Plut. *Tib. Gr.* 5), and a treaty with Jugurtha (Sall. *Iug.* 39.3, Livy, *Per.* 64, Eutropius 4.26). Some of these may be apocryphal (such as the Caudine Forks) or mistaken (such as Livy's account of the treaty of 203/2 with Carthage), but even in such cases it is clear that such action on the part of the Senate or the *comitia* was possible. Cf. in general Mommsen, *RS* 3.1166–68.

made without the authorization of the people, nor is anything owed to the Samnites by its terms other than our bodies. Let us be handed over, bound and stripped, by the fetiales; let us absolve the people of their religious obligation, if we have involved them in any such obligation . . .[58]

Postumius denies that there was any legal obligation created by his oaths and questions whether or not there was any religious obligation; even if there were, he says that he himself can discharge this religious burden. Again the distinction between public and private is blurred, but the principle is clearly expressed that the state can not be bound, either legally or religiously, by the actions of an individual.[59]

Another incident from Livy's history indicates that the state had the ability to distance itself not only from an action taken by an individual in regards to other men, but to the gods as well; the same principle applies in both cases. At Aquilonia in 293 a *pullarius* falsely reported that auspices from the *tripudium* were favorable, and this falsification was eventually reported to the consul prior to the battle. The consul, Lucius Papirius, declared however that "he who assists at the auspices, if he reports anything false draws down the ritual pollution on himself; for me a *tripudium* was reported, and it is an excellent auspice for the Roman people and the army."[60] Thus the consul considered that the pollution created by an individual, even though he was acting on behalf of the state, did not taint the entire army. Rather the sign was still considered valid, and the *pullarius* alone was responsible for his impiety; when he was stationed in the front ranks and struck by a random javelin before the battle even commenced, the interpretation of Papirius was confirmed.[61] Although this example does not concern vows, it indicates that a religious burden incurred by an individual acting on behalf of the state did not

---

[58] Livy 9.8–10: *me seu turpi seu necessaria sponsione obstrinxi; qua tamen, quando iniussu populi facta est, non tenetur populus Romanus, nec quicquam ex ea praetereaquam corpora nostra debentur Samnitibus. Dedamur per fetiales nudi vinctique; exsolvamus religione populum, si qua obligavimus . . .*

[59] The historicity of Livy's account of the Caudine Forks incident may be doubted, especially as variant versions survived, including one which denied that the treaty had been abrogated. Yet a similar incident occurred in more historical times, when the treaty of C. Mancinus with the Numantines in 137 was repudiated and Mancinus was handed over to the enemy by the fetiales. For a thorough discussion of this incident, including the legal and religious implications, see Rosenstein (1986).

[60] Livy 10.40: *Ceterum qui auspicio adest si quid falsi nuntiat, in semet ipsum religionem recipit: mihi quidem tripudium nuntiatum; populo Romano exercituique egregium auspicium est.*

[61] For a more extended discussion of this incident, see Linderski (1993), 60–61.

necessarily involve the entire community. In this instance, as with the treaty of the Caudine Forks, there was a religious liability to be discharged, and while the state was concerned that the liability be discharged, it did not assume that liability itself.

Just as the Senate did not often exercise its power to reject treaties, so we should not envision that the Senate often exercised its power to remove itself from the religious obligations incurred by its generals. We will see that only one general is known to have had his vow rejected, and that vow was only for games and not for a temple. Eckstein has strongly argued that "in practice, such original decisions on the part of Roman commanders exerted enormous influence over the later creation of policy at Rome. Indeed, as a result of Senatorial ratification, most of these magisterial decisions became official Roman policy."[62] Substituting "vow" for "decision", and "religion" for "policy", both here and in the sentence quoted earlier, offers us a better chance at understanding the position of vows made by generals in the field. The vows made by Roman generals, when ratified by the Senate, led to the erection of temples and/or the introduction of deities which became part of the official state religion. An examination of the individual incidents in which the Senate responded to these vows will illuminate the respective roles which individual magistrates and the Senate played in the development of Roman religion.

The sack of Veii by the dictator M. Furius Camillus provides one telling incident from the early, quasi-mythical period of the Republic. In the Roman camp just before the final assault, Camillus vowed a tenth part of the spoils of Veii to Apollo and a temple to the Juno that dwelled in Veii.[63] At the sack of the city, individual Romans gathered booty for themselves, as had been decided in advance, so that on the return to Rome, the booty was already scattered into the hands of the people.[64] This naturally raised a problem when it came time to pay the tithe to Apollo:

> The pontiffs decided that the people must discharge this obligation . . . They resorted to what seemed the least oppressive plan, that whoever wished to acquit himself and his household of the obligation, when he

---

[62] Eckstein (1987), xiii. Eckstein makes these remarks immediately after noting the superior legal authority of the Senate.
[63] Livy 5.21.2.
[64] Livy 5.20, 5.21.14.

had estimated his share of the spoils, he should pay a tenth part to the public treasury, so that from this a gift of gold could be made . . .[65]

This vow stands apart from the vow to Mater Matuta which Camillus had made on the orders of the Senate, which we examined earlier.[66] Camillus made this second vow in the camps, just prior to battle, apparently on his own authority, but the decision of the pontiffs clearly indicates that the fulfillment of the vow was considered a matter of state concern. It was decided that the obligation was binding on the state, a decision which caused much grumbling among the populace and made Camillus very unpopular.[67] That Camillus neglected to collect the tithe before allowing Veii to be plundered undoubtedly contributed to the fact that the burden was transferred to the state, but the pontiffs also had to be willing to accept this burden on behalf of the state. Having accepted the obligation, the pontiffs subsequently had to decide how to fulfill this vow, and in deciding that each man should contribute one-tenth of his share of the booty they transferred the liability from the state back to the individual citizens. Regardless of whether the sum actually comprised one-tenth of the spoils from Veii, by making a gift of this amount the state considered its obligations fulfilled, as a complaint by Camillus in the following year makes clear: "in this regard each man had bound himself as an individual, and the *populus* was freed."[68] It might have been more correct to say that each individual had been bound by the pontiffs' decision, but the end result of this episode was that the vow which Camillus had made while on campaign, but neglected to fulfill, was discharged not by him personally, but through the organs of the

---

[65] Livy 5.23.8–11: *pontifices solvendum religione populum censerent . . . Tandem eo quod lenissimum videbatur decursum est, ut qui se domumque religione exsolvere vellet, cum sibimet ipse praedam aestimasset suam, decimae pretium partis in publicum deferret, ut ex eo donum aureum . . . fieret.*

[66] See above pp. 44–45.

[67] It is noteworthy that Camillus fulfilled his vow to build a new temple for Juno, as well as his vow to Mater Matuta, before he resigned the dictatorship, but did not attempt to act on the tithe until after his resignation (5.23.7). The manner in which the vows were fulfilled would seem more appropriate if the tithe to Apollo was the state-sponsored vow rather than the temple for Mater Matuta, since the state assumed responsibility for the former while Camillus himself fulfilled the latter obligation.

[68] Livy 5.25.5: *ea se quisque privatim obligaverit, liberatus sit populus. Populus* in this sentence could refer either to the state or only to those who had served on the campaign, as in 5.23. In either situation, the crucial factor is that the decision of the pontiffs removed the obligation from Camillus personally and distributed it to others.

state. His vow, though made solely on his own authority, nevertheless had implications for the welfare of the state, and the pontiffs and Senate acted to ensure the *pax deum.*

A second example, from a slightly later period, reveals the same attitude, that a vow made by a magistrate on campaign involved the entire state. In 294, in the course of a battle at Luceria in the Samnite War

> a temple was vowed to Jupiter Stator, as Romulus had vowed one earlier; but so far there was only a *fanum,* that is a place set apart as a sacred precinct. However, in that year, religious scruples demanded that the Senate should order that the temple be built, since the state had been obligated twice by the same vow.[69]

The crucial phrase for our investigation appears at the very end: *bis eiusdem voti damnata re publica. Damnata* is a term borrowed from legal terminology where it denotes conviction of a crime or legal liability; by extension here it refers to the liability for the fulfillment of a vow.[70] The Senate thus explicitly declared that the state had been made liable twice for the temple of Jupiter Stator, once by Romulus and a second time by M. Atilius Regulus against the Samnites. The right of kings to make vows on behalf of the state is not surprising, since during the regal period the kings essentially were the government.[71] That the state considered the vow of Regulus to have placed it under an obligation indicates that this prerogative in some fashion passed to the consuls during the Republic. The phrase *in religionem venit* shows that the fulfillment of the vow was a matter of state concern. As with Camillus, religious scruples demanded that the state should become involved; in order to maintain the *pax deum,* they had to ensure that the magistrate's vow was fulfilled.

However, an incident from the following century demonstrates that the Senate was not always willing to allow the state to be bound by the vows of an individual magistrate.[72] During a battle in Spain against

---

[69] Livy 10.37.15–16: *inque ea pugna Iovis Statoris aedem votam, ut Romulus ante voverat; sed fanum tantum, id est locus templo effatus, fuerat. Ceterum hoc demum anno ut aedem etiam fieri senatus iuberet bis eiusdem voti damnata re publica in religionem venit.*

[70] Cf. *TLL,* s.v. *damno.*

[71] Cf. H. Bardon (1955), 166–68; Magdelain (1978), 71–72; Ziolkowski, (1992), 195.

[72] This example involves games rather than a temple, but the religious force of a vow for games should be no less than that for a temple. For the parallel between the two types of vows, cf. the vows for both made by Fulvius Flaccus and the Senate's response in 179 (Livy 40.44.8–12). This issue is discussed in more detail in Chapter Four, pp. 155–58.

the Lusitanians in 194, the propraetor P. Cornelius Scipio Nasica
vowed games to Jupiter if he should rout and slaughter the enemy.[73]
Following his election in 191 as consul for the following year, he
asked the Senate to grant him money to celebrate the games and
fulfill his vow. Livy reports the reaction of the Senate:

> He seemed to demand something new and unjustified; therefore they
> decided that whatever games he had vowed on his own sole initiative,
> without consulting the Senate, he should celebrate them either from
> the *manubiae*, if he had reserved any money for that purpose, or from
> his own pocket."[74]

This response clearly indicates that the Senate did not feel itself bound
to fulfill the vow, but that the individual who had made the vow was
obligated to discharge it.[75] A parallel decision in the case of Camillus,
for instance, would be that Camillus himself had to pay the tithe
vowed to Apollo. The example of Nasica thus points in the other
direction, toward the position that the state was not legally bound by
the vows of its magistrates. Nevertheless this episode also shows that
the Senate maintained a strong interest in seeing that the vow was
fulfilled to ensure the *pax deum*.

This incident presents several difficulties of interpretation which
bear directly on the issue of a magistrate's vows. The Senate decided
that Nasica's request was *novum atque iniquum*, apparently because the
vow had been made on his own authority, *inconsulto senatu*. Livy
emphasized this point by writing not merely *ex sua sententia*, but *ex sua
unius sententia*. Yet the situation could hardly have been otherwise; it
would have been impossible for Nasica to pause in the midst of battle,
quickly return to Rome to consult the Senate, then return to Spain
and resume the battle. No general could possibly have received authorization once the battle began, and we have seen that the Senate
accepted other vows made by generals out on the battlefield as placing the state under an obligation. Consultation of the Senate hardly
seems an adequate means of distinguishing between those vows which
the Senate would help fulfill and those vows it would not.[76]

---

[73] Livy 35.1.8.

[74] Livy 36.36.2: *Novum atque iniquum postulare est visus; censuerunt ergo, quos ludos inconsulto
senatu ex sua unius sententia vovisset, eos vel de manubiis, si quam pecuniam ad id reservasset,
vel sua ipse impensa facerent.*

[75] Cf. the treatment of this passage by Bardon (1955), 173.

[76] One could hypothesize that generals were expected to consult the Senate and
obtain its authorization *before* they left Rome for any vows which they might make

It may be significant that, of the many vows undertaken by generals in the midst of battle, Nasica's is the only reported case in which the Senate refused public funding. One may therefore speculate whether the resolution was influenced by political factors, i.e. that this *senatus consultum* was the first strike in the attack against the Scipios which was to be launched more fully in 187.[77] If this were the case, one should be very careful about attempting to discern a rule which would apply to all generals from this attack against an individual politician. Yet attacking Nasica in this way would be a very indirect blow to Africanus, the main target of the later attacks, and the attacks of the 180's left Nasica largely unscathed. We can also point to several other incidents which suggest that Nasica's family ties were not the primary reason for the treatment he received from the Senate.

In 186, shortly after the initial attack on the Scipios, Lucius Scipio, who had nominally been the target of that attack, celebrated games which he said he had vowed during the war with Antiochus.[78] Livy cites Valerius Antias as his source for an embassy on which Lucius was sent and that "finally, after the embassy, action was taken in the Senate about those games, of which he had made no mention after the war, in which he said that they had been vowed."[79] Apparently on his return from the campaign against Antiochus, Lucius had not mentioned any vows which he had made during the campaign; only later did he say that he had undertaken such a vow. This would have been the perfect opportunity for the Senate to deny permission for celebrating games to a person much more central to the Scipionic controversy. They could argue that the vow was entirely fictitious,

---

while on campaign, and that Nasica's failure to do so led to this incident. Such a scenario would certainly emphasize the dominant role of the Senate, both in deciding when new temples would be built and to which deity. However, there are numerous implausibilities involved in a hypothesis of advance authorizations: this type of conditional approval runs completely counter to the Roman style of government, and it presupposes that the Senate could foresee what situations might arise on the campaign or which deities might be the most important to entreat. Furthermore, there is absolutely no evidence to support it, and we have little hope of arriving at an accurate understanding of the Roman government if we move into the realm of speculation.

[77] This is the position taken by Champeaux (1987), 139 n. 37: "the first skirmishes which provide a prelude to the trials of the Scipios; rather than attacking Africanus directly, one takes on his entourage."

[78] Livy 39.22.8.

[79] Livy 39.22.10: *quorum ludorum post bellum, in quo votos diceret, mentionem non fecisset, de iis post legationem demum in senatu actum.*

since Lucius should have mentioned it when he first returned from the East. If the vow had never been made, there could be no breach of contract which might adversely affect the *pax deum*. Instead, the Senate explicitly decided to permit Lucius to celebrate his games; we are specifically informed that the Senate took action concerning these games, and since the games were celebrated, the action must have been at least to allow the games to proceed.[80] The attack on the Scipios personally thus seems an inadequate explanation for the Senate's treatment of Scipio Nasica in 191.

Some scholars have therefore been led to conclude that what was "new and unjustified" about Nasica's situation was not that he made a vow, but that he asked the Senate to help pay for it.[81] Yet fifteen years earlier the Senate had encountered a similar situation with another member of the Scipionic family, Scipio Africanus. As proconsul, Africanus had vowed games during a mutiny of soldiers in Spain; later in Rome,

> the question being raised by P. Scipio, a *senatus consultum* was passed to the effect that whatever games he had vowed during the mutiny in Spain, he should celebrate from that money which he himself had brought into the treasury.[82]

The Senate here voted to aid Africanus in the fulfillment of his vow, directing that money should be used from the state treasury to this end. While it is not insignificant that the Senate directed that Africanus should use the money which he himself had brought into the treasury, his situation differs from that of Nasica because this money was already a part of the state treasury; the *manubiae* which Nasica was told to use were equated with money which came from his own pocket (*sua impensa*).[83] Yet there may be a significant distinction between the situations of Africanus and Nasica. Nasica apparently did

---

[80] It is true that Lucius paid for his games with money collected specifically for that purpose; the Senate was not asked to provide money. Yet the Senate clearly had jurisdiction over such money collected from the kings and cities of the East, as other episodes illustrate. Cf. Livy 39.5.7–10; 40.44.9–12.

[81] Briscoe (1981), 274, following the commentary of Weissenborn and Müller (1880–1911), 8.147. Bardon (1955) makes no attempt to explain the significance of this phrase.

[82] Livy 28.38: *Ibi referente P. Scipione senatus consultum factum est ut, quos ludos inter seditionem militarem in Hispania vovisset, ex ea pecunia quam ipse in aerarium detulisset faceret.*

[83] On the vexed question of what exactly was meant by the term *manubiae* and how this money might be used, see Chapter Four, pp. 117–122.

not turn any money at all from his campaign into the state treasury; after allowing the citizens of Ilipa to reclaim lost possessions from the Lusitani, he sold the rest of the spoils and divided the proceeds among the soldiers.[84] Thus, what was *novum et iniquum* about Nasica's request was perhaps not that he asked the Senate to pay for his vow, but that he had not contributed anything to the state treasury. The Senate may have felt that Nasica was hoarding his spoils, or that he had been too generous in his donative to the soldiers, and thus declined to assume liability for his vow. Whatever the explanation, the implications of the incident are clear: the Senate did not feel itself bound by the religious obligations incurred by a magistrate *cum imperio*.

The rejection of Nasica's request, especially if it was justified by his failure to deposit any of his spoils in the state treasury, places it within a larger Senatorial effort to exercise more control over its magistrates and the money passing through their hands. It will suffice to sketch the outline of this hypothesis here, as it will be discussed in greater detail in a subsequent chapter.[85] The early second century saw the most rapid growth in the amount of territory which the Romans controlled, and Roman generals vied with one another in the amount of booty they brought back from their campaigns and in the lavishness of their triumphs.[86] The Senate's reaction to Nasica may have served to indicate the Senate's displeasure with such displays and to reduce the amount of money available to the general; either they would deposit more money in the treasury or they would be forced to fulfill vows from their spoils or their own pocket.[87] Indeed, over the course of the next decade the Senate continued to place restrictions on the money used to celebrate games, both on the manner in which the money was collected and on the amount expended.[88]

---

[84] Livy 35.1.12. I am grateful to Nate Rosenstein for bringing this detail to my attention.

[85] See Chapter Five, pp. 185–87 and the sources cited there.

[86] Of course Nasica himself did not celebrate a triumph for his victory over the Lusitani, but many other triumphs of this period were notable: e.g. Flamininus in 194, Acilius Glabrio in 190, Scipio Asiaticus in 189, Manlius Vulso in 187.

[87] Again, this is the point of distinction between Nasica and Africanus; because the latter had already deposited his booty in the treasury, he could no longer use it without Senatorial approval, whereas the former was free to use his booty however he chose.

[88] These restrictions on games culminated in a *senatus consultum* of 182, whose content is unknown, but which was passed in response to the lavish expenditure of the aedile Ti. Sempronius and hence must have concerned itself with controlling

At the outset, the Senate contented itself with making Nasica pay for
his own games, but because of the huge sums of booty controlled by
victorious generals, that strategy proved futile in restraining expenditures, and stronger measures had to be taken. The rejection of Nasica's
request should be viewed as part of this campaign and hence as an
extraordinary event; it may in fact have been the Senate's action
that was *novum atque iniquum*, but one that was perhaps felt to be
necessary in order to reassert its collective authority.

It should not be overlooked that the Senate recognized that Nasica's
vow had created a religious obligation which could have affected the
pax deum. At the same time as the Senate declared Nasica's vow to
be not binding on the state, they insisted that the games themselves
must be celebrated. Nor did Nasica challenge their authority on this
point; Livy reports the celebration of Nasica's games in the very next
sentence.[89] This situation repeats what we saw earlier in regard to
the Caudine Forks treaty and the falsified auspices; while the Senate
denied that the state had any responsibility to help a magistrate fulfill his vows, both the Senate and the individuals involved recognized
that there was an obligation to be fulfilled. The *pax deum* always acted
as an overriding consideration, both for the Senate and for the individual who had incurred the liability. Vows of magistrates *cum imperio*,
as evidenced by the experience of Nasica, may thus be seen as an
unusual combination of public and private vows.

One further incident recorded by Livy in the early second century
confirms this view of such vows. In 179, the new consul Q. Fulvius
Flaccus said that "before he brought up any state business, he wished
to free himself and the state of a religious obligation by fulfilling his
vows."[90] Fulvius then described his vows of games and a temple and
the Senate voted that the vows should be fulfilled. The language
used by Livy in his description of this episode supports the interpretation outlined above. Fulvius recognized that by making a vow he
had placed himself personally (*se*) under an obligation, but that as a
magistrate of the state the vow also affected the state (*rem publicam*).
He thus brought the matter to the attention of the Senate, which, as
in the case of Nasica, voted on the manner in which the fulfillment

---

such expenditures (Livy 40.44.10–12). Monetary limits are attested as early as 187
(Livy 39.5.7).

[89] Livy 36.36.2.

[90] Livy 40.44.8: *Q. Fulvius consul priusquam ullam rem publicam ageret, liberare se et rem
publicam religione votis solvendis dixit velle.*

of the vows should proceed.[91] Although the decision of the Senate might differ from case to case, as evidenced by the very different treatment of Fulvius and Nasica, in every instance the Senate appears as the final arbiter on vows made by magistrates in the field.

From these incidents we see that vows made by magistrates *cum imperio* can not be categorized simply as public or private vows, and that no sharp distinction can be made between these two in this regard; these vows were both public and private at the same time. As vows made by state officials, their non-performance had implications for the relations between the state and the gods; as vows made without state authorization, their performance rested largely on the shoulders of the individual who made the vow. The Senate could choose to offer assistance, but it could not be forced to do so, and thus it maintained a collective authority over the process of introducing new cults to Rome. If a general made a temple vow for which the Senate declined to assume the obligation, the general might have to build a private shrine in order to fulfill the vow; such a temple would not be part of the state religious system and its impact could be minimized. That the Senate usually decided to back the vows of its magistrates, however, allowed those individuals to exert great influence on the direction of Roman religion. The temples vowed by individuals on campaign generally became part of the state religion.

In fact, the most remarkable feature concerning vows made by generals during their campaigns is precisely that so few of them were rejected. Roman generals understood that the state maintained the authority to reject their vows, but they also understood the parameters within which they could make vows which would not be rejected. To the best of our knowledge, no Roman general ever tried to single-handedly introduce a deity which he had reason to believe would not be acceptable in Rome. Reviewing the list of temples constructed in Rome during the Republic, it becomes evident that temples to foreign, clearly non-Roman deities were almost always introduced through the initiative of the Senate.[92] Aesculapius from

---

[91] A significant difference in the case of Flaccus was that he had collected money from Spain to be used in the celebration of games, while as discussed above Nasica did not. However, that does not explain the Senate's decision to appoint *duumviri* for the construction of the temple, a point that will be discussed more fully in Chapter Four, pp. 155–57.

[92] Again see Appendix One for the list of temples vowed during the Republic. Of course, the great difficulty here lies in determining exactly which deities should count

Greece, Venus from Mount Eryx, Cybele from Phrygia all came to
Rome on the Senate's invitation following a consultation of the
Sibylline Books.[93] With few exceptions, the deities to whom individual
magistrates vowed temples were already known and publicly recognized in Rome, such as Jupiter Victor, or they were abstract deities,
concepts such as Fides or Virtus.[94] No legal barrier prevented generals from vowing temples to foreign deities, although we may suspect
that if such a vow had been made to a deity which the Senate deemed
undesirable, the Senate would decline to add that deity to the official state pantheon and make its rites part of the *sacra publica*. But
generals did not make such vows; they recognized that the introduction of foreign cults was the prerogative of the Senate, and that such
cult introduction would be handled through the medium of the
Sibylline Books.[95]

One instance stands out as an apparent exception to this rule: the
introduction of Juno Regina by Camillus in 396 following her *evocatio*
from Veii. Camillus, outside the gates of Veii, vowed to build a temple
to this goddess if she left her city and came to Rome.[96] Camillus
subsequently let the contract for this temple, which was erected on

---

as "foreign" deities. I suggest that the Romans' conception of what counted as foreign may have been very different from our own. For instance, some deities from
neighboring Italic towns might be counted as "foreign" while others from similar
towns were not so counted, and Greek gods which came to Rome through Italic
intermediaries also may not have been treated as "foreign". Some of these examples
will be treated on the following pages, but one obvious example is the temple to
Castor and Pollux. Vowed by the dictator A. Postumius in 496 at the battle of Lake
Regillus, at first sight it appears to have introduced the worship of a foreign (i.e.
Greek) god to Rome. Yet its location in the heart of the city inside the *pomerium*
and the discovery that the Dioscuri were worshipped in Lanuvium (see below, pp.
104–5) should make us question whether the Romans considered this twosome to
be "foreign." On the "pomerial rule" as a marker for foreign and non-foreign cults,
see Schilling (1979), 94–102.

[93] While it is debatable whether the first temple to Apollo in Rome arose following a directive of the Sibylline Books, this temple certainly did not introduce Apollo
to Rome. As discussed below (p. 98), worship of Apollo is attested eighteen years
prior to the construction of this temple; apart from these references, nothing further
is known about how or when Apollo made his first appearance in Rome.

[94] Although a general might introduce a new cult by vowing a temple to an
abstract concept, he can not be said to initiate major changes in the nature of
Roman religion by doing so, for both the concepts deified and the very notion of
deifying them were thoroughly Roman. On the deification of abstract notions in
Rome, see Axtell (1907); Fears (1981).

[95] The cults introduced by the Sibylline Books and the significance of the Books
as a method for introducing new cults will be discussed in the next chapter.

[96] Livy 5.21.2.

the Aventine hill. This is clearly an exception to the notion that individuals should not introduce foreign gods, and yet it may be explainable by the extraordinary nature of the *evocatio* ritual. Furthermore, there are circumstances which may have mitigated the "foreign" nature of this goddess. As the Etruscan Uni and protectress of Rome's enemy, she would indeed have been a foreigner, but the *evocatio* and the temple in Rome were dedicated to Juno Regina, a goddess who had been worshipped as part of the Capitoline triad for over a hundred years already.[97] One should also note that Camillus undertook a number of other religious actions during his campaign, several of them on the direct orders of the Senate. It would not be surprising if the decision to perform an *evocatio* was not made by the general on the spur of the moment, but by the Senate after due consideration back in Rome.[98] The fact that this is the only instance recorded by the annalists of an *evocatio* hampers our ability to understand the nature of that ritual and how it might affect the procedures for introducing a new cult to Rome.

Several other examples at first glance might appear to be exceptions to the notion that the Senate should introduce foreign deities, but on closer inspection they prove to uphold this rule. In 197, the consul C. Cornelius Cethegus vowed a temple to Juno Sospita if his army should put the Gauls to flight; following the successful conclusion of the battle, the temple was dedicated in 194 in the Forum Holitorium.[99] In one sense Juno Sospita was a foreign goddess,

---

[97] The fact that the Capitoline temple was supposedly built by the Tarquins, i.e. during the Etruscan domination of Rome, can only have further reduced the foreign nature of this goddess: the Juno Regina of the Capitoline triad may have also been an Uni originally.

[98] Again, it may be noteworthy that the two cities besides Veii which are most often thought to have undergone an *evocatio*, Volsinii and Carthage, were both mortal enemies of Rome defeated after a lengthy siege. The length of the siege operations would surely have provided time to consider whether an *evocatio* was appropriate or necessary to the purposes at hand. While there is no evidence to support a hypothesis of this nature, at the very least it argues against a impulsive decision made in the heat of battle.

[99] Livy 32.30; 34.53. Livy (or a copyist) has made an error in reporting the dedication of the temple, where the name of the goddess is given as Juno Matuta. However, the *fasti* know only of Juno Sospita. Further problems are caused by Ovid's statement (*Fasti*, 2.55–58) that the temple of Juno Sospita was a neighbor of the Magna Mater, which would place the shrine on the Palatine. Livy's problem may have been confusion with the temple of Mater Matuta, which did in fact stand in the Forum Holitorium, and the difficulty for both authors would have been compounded by the fact that only ruins of this temple remained in their day. Cf. Scullard (1981), 70–71.

worshipped primarily by the town of Lanuvium. But a more important factor to consider is that when Rome granted citizenship to the
Lanuvians in 338 following the defeat of the Latin League, she stipu-
lated that "the shrine and grove of Juno Sospita should be held in
common by the citizens of Lanuvium and the Roman people."[100]
Cicero indicates that even in his day the consuls still made an annual
visit to Lanuvium to offer sacrifice there.[101] The Romans thus had a
long-standing relationship with this goddess, so that even though she
came from outside the city and the territory of Rome, the Romans
did not consider her to be "foreign". Cethegus' vow is thus perfectly
comprehensible as a vow to deity already worshipped by the Romans, and so did not involve the introduction of foreign elements.

Two other examples show that it was possible for an individual
to make some innovations in the Roman religious system, but only
by recognizing the limits on such innovation. In 204, the consul
P. Sempronius Tuditanus vowed a temple to Fortuna Primigenia just
prior to a successful engagement with Hannibal near Croton, and
the temple was dedicated ten years later by the *duumvir* Q. Marcius
Ralla.[102] This goddess was evidently the same as the famous goddess
of Praeneste, where she had an oracular shrine. As recently as 241,
the Senate had indicated that they considered this to be a foreign
cult, despite its proximity to Rome, for they prevented the consul
Q. Lutatius Cerco from consulting the oracle there: "they judged it
was proper for the affairs of the state to be administered with the
ancestral *auspicia*, and not with foreign-born."[103] The real objection
in 241 seems to have been the use of a foreign oracle, and hence
one uncontrolled by the Senate, rather than a particular hostility to
the goddess of Praeneste. Furthermore, Fortuna herself had a long
and illustrious history in Rome; legend held that Servius Tullius had
founded at least two temples to Fortuna, including one in the Forum
Boarium and one across the Tiber, and Spurius Carvilius built one
in 293.[104] The fact that Fortuna had been worshipped at Rome for

---

[100] Livy 8.14.2: *aedes lucusque Sospitae Iunonis communis Lanuvinis municipibus cum populo Romano esset.*

[101] Cicero *Mur.* 90; cf. also *CIL* 5.7814.

[102] Livy 29.36; 34.53.

[103] Val. Max. 1.3.2: *Lutatius Cerco, qui primum Punicum bellum confecit, a senatu prohibitus est sortes Fortunae Praenestinae adire; auspiciis enim patriis, non alienigenis rem publicam administrari iudicabant oportere.* Cf. Pietilä-Castrén (1987), 65.

[104] Plutarch, *De Fort. Rom.* 10 and *QR* 74, records numerous temples dedicated to various forms of Fortuna by Tullius, including one to Fortuna Primigenia. However,

a long time would have helped to smooth over any hesitancy based on the alien nature of this particular incarnation of the goddess: she could be presented as a new aspect of an old deity, like Jupiter Victor, and Praeneste had long been part of the Roman sphere. This temple thus indicates how an individual could make an innovation and yet remain within the context of allowable behavior and the *mos maiorum*.

The temple built by M. Fulvius Nobilior offers a more striking instance of individual innovation in the Roman pantheon. At some point during his campaigns against the Ambraciots in 187, he apparently vowed a temple to Hercules Musarum; although Livy does not record this vow, the temple was built and dedicated, probably in 179.[105] Unfortunately the most complete source for the origins of this cult comes from Eumenius in the third century C.E.[106] Nevertheless, it seems clear that the focus of this cult was on the Muses, rather then Hercules. Nobilior set up statues of the nine Muses in the temple, and Nobilior's literary interests and his friendship with the poet Ennius also point in this direction.[107] Even more than temple to Fortuna Primigenia, this cult represents an innovation, and with its predilection for Hellenic culture quite possibly a controversial one as well. It is therefore all the more significant that Nobilior vowed his temple to Hercules Musarum; Nobilior claimed that the temple was modeled on the cult of Hercules Musagetes, which he had encountered in Greece and to whom he had vowed a temple during the campaign. Curiously, however, no cult of Hercules Musagetes has been attested in Greece as yet, although there are other similar cults, such as for Apollo Musagetes.[108] It is quite possible that Nobilior fabricated this

---

only the two mentioned above find any sort of confirmation in other sources, so the remainder should not be considered as actual historical foundations. For Carvilius' temple, see Livy 10.46.

[105] Livy's silence on this temple is perplexing and provides a cautionary note: for all the temple foundings which Livy does report, he clearly omitted others which are therefore lost to our view unless preserved by a chance reference in another source.

[106] Eumenius, *Pro Instaur. Sch.* 7–8. Other sources who indicate an awareness of this temple and its furnishings include Cicero, *Arch.* 27; Pliny, *NH* 35.66; Ovid, *Fasti* 6.797; Varro, *LL* 6.33; Servius, *Ad Aen.* 1.8; and Macrobius, 1.12.16.

[107] The statuary is mentioned by Pliny, Ovid, and Servius, while the relationship with Ennius is noted by Cicero in the passage mentioned in the previous note as well as in *Tusc.* 1.3. Cicero's *Brutus*, 79, makes further mention of Nobilior's literary interests. See also Richardson (1977) and Martina (1981) for further discussion of the dominant position of the Muses in this cult.

[108] For this point, I am indebted to M. Pelikan, who discusses this issue in her forthcoming dissertation.

detail in order to provide a lineage for his cult and thus distance it from the appearance of innovation as much as he could. Hercules was one of the oldest and most established of the Roman cults, and the Romans continued to recognize its Greek roots by sacrificing with bare head at the Ara Maxima.[109] Thus Nobilior could claim he was not instituting major changes, but following an age-old practice: vowing a temple on his campaign to a new aspect of a deity already worshipped in Rome, and one who had helped him during his campaign. This sequence of events serves to underscore that innovation was possible for the individual only within limited boundaries, and such maneuvering on the part of Nobilior shows that Roman generals were fully aware of those boundaries. The Senate had certain expectations concerning the actions of generals in his sphere, but generals had certain expectations of the Senate as well; if they acted within the accepted limits, they expected their vows to be approved.

III. *The Significance of Temple Vows*

These considerations help to shed new light on the significance of vowing new temples in Rome. The active involvement of the Senate in this process provides a richer context for this religio-political act which actually strengthens its importance in the aristocratic competition in Rome. Rather than going it alone and engaging in grand exercises of self-aggrandizement, Roman generals sought approval of their actions by the Senate. Such approval served as a collective endorsement of a general's actions, and thus offered more *gloria* than was available to an individual who tried to claim it for himself. In this respect, one might consider the celebration of an official triumph granted by the Senate as opposed to the celebration of a triumph *in monte Albano* by an individual: while one could celebrate the latter on one's own initiative, it was a secondary option, celebrated only by those who had been denied triumphs in Rome. The former brought greater prestige to the general, not only because the celebration took place in the center of Rome itself but also because the honor had been approved by a vote of his peers.[110] An episode

---

[109] Livy 1.7.3, Varro, apud Macrobius 3.6.17.
[110] The frequency of acrimonious debates over the right to triumph in the early

described by Livy in 197 makes this abundantly clear; in that year
the consul C. Cornelius celebrated a triumph "with the consent of
all (*omnium consensu*)", while his colleague Q. Minucius celebrated a
triumph on the Alban Mount.[111] Livy remarks that "this triumph
was less regarded, because of the place and the talk of his deeds,
and because everyone knew that [the money to pay for] it had been
taken from the treasury and not voted out."[112] Minucius had not
won approval from the Senate, and was thus forced to appropriate
money from the treasury in order to cover the cost of his celebration; this had the effect of tarnishing his *gloria*.[113] Similarly a victorious general might act on his own to fulfill a temple vow made on
his campaign, but without Senatorial action it would remain a private family shrine. The Senatorial decision to assume responsibility
for the construction of the temple which an individual had vowed
made that temple part of the state religious system and also served
as official approval of his conduct on campaign, just as the triumph
did. It thus added more luster to a general's name than could be
attained by an individual who insisted on building a monument on
his own.

Building a new temple in cooperation with the Senate could bring
direct political advantage in another way. Since vowing a temple
served the best interests of the state, generals who made such vows
could create the image of an individual who placed the best interests
of the state above his own.[114] Even today this remains an effective
form of political propaganda and is actively sought by politicians of
all stripes. Among Roman politicians, Cato the Elder stands out in
this regard. Cato built his reputation, as well as his political career,

---

second century is one indication of how highly Roman generals coveted this honor.
Even if a triumph was eventually granted, the public and noisy debate would have
the effect of tarnishing somewhat the luster of the moment, by showing that the
victorious general did not have the unanimous support of his fellow Senators.

[111] Livy 33.23.

[112] Livy 33.23.8: *Is triumphus, ut loco et fama rerum gestarum et quod sumptum non erogatum
ex aerario omnes sciebant, inhonoratior fuit.*

[113] Cf. the comments of Wallace-Hadrill (1990), 160–161. This episode provides
another example of the shadowy or non-existent lines between public and private
monies in Rome. To modern legalistic minds, it is unfathomable that Minucius
could have used money from the state treasury without having it voted to him, but
he was clearly able to do so even after his formal motion for a triumph had been
rejected.

[114] Cf. the remarks of Brunt (1988), 49–50, on the need for Roman politicians to
profess that they were acting in the public good.

on the perception of placing the interests of the state above all other interests. It can hardly be coincidence that Cato vowed a temple during his consulship in Spain in 195; this action fit perfectly into the image that Cato wished to portray. Nor can it be coincidence that Cato dedicated this temple himself several years later despite the tendency at this time for the Senate to rein in its generals by having other individuals perform the dedication.[115] Cato's stance was successful in convincing the Senate that he was not overly interested in personal aggrandizement, and thus he was permitted to perform the dedication and reap the extra *gloria* provided by that action. Building a new temple was still an effective form of political maneuvering, but the meaning of this action is different from what has been commonly proposed.

The significance thus attached to the construction of new temples helps to explain why more individuals did not vow temples. If erecting a new temple in Rome brought only benefits the individual who made the vow, then the actions of the approximately seven hundred consuls who did *not* vow temples become inexplicable. These generals must have felt that vowing a temple had some undesirable consequences which outweighed the potential benefit to themselves and to the state. I suggest that while vowing a temple held the promise of benefit by aligning oneself with the interests of the state and the Senate, it came at the cost of emphasizing the role of the gods instead of oneself in the victory. It has recently been argued that the Romans habitually ascribed defeat in battle to a breach in the *pax deum*, in order to shield defeated generals from political repercussions in Rome.[116] The individual general could not be held responsible for the defeat, because he had entered battle without the support of the gods due to some previously unsuspected flaw in the *pax deum*. This principle works in the other direction as well: making a vow in battle affirmed that victory must be ascribed to the favor of the gods, but doing so diminished the human role in securing the victory.[117] Although the Romans did not necessarily expect their military leaders

---

[115] See the discussion in Chapter Five, pp. 185–87.

[116] Rosenstein (1990), 54–91.

[117] Champeaux (1987), 138, argues to the contrary in the specific case of Fortuna Equestris; according to her interpretation, the fact that the vow was made *after* the battle had been won indicates that Fulvius Flaccus wished "to affirm the primacy of the human action." This incident is discussed above in Chapter One, pp. 29–30.

to be tactical geniuses, they did expect them to possess certain quali-
ties, e.g. *virtus*, which might lead the troops to victory. Victory in
battle might be ascribed to a number of different factors, including
the gods, the commander, and the troops themselves. Construction
of a temple would have had the effect of focusing the attention of
the populace on the deity rather than on the individual and his role.
While most Roman generals would have accepted the general proposition that success in war was due to the favor of the gods, fewer
would have wanted to publicly acknowledge this fact in a monumental fashion. Just as not all Romans chose to build their political careers in the same fashion as Cato, so not all generals would have
wanted to share the credit and glory for their victory with the gods
and the Senate.

This point becomes clearer when one compares the actions of Cato
with those of the Scipios, who as in so many other ways provide an
appropriate counterpoint for each other in the late third and early
second centuries. Members of the Scipionic family made several
vows during this period, but significantly none was for a temple; rather
each was for the celebration of *ludi*. In 206 Scipio Africanus vowed
games in Spain while quelling a mutiny, and again in 205 he vowed
games while in Africa.[118] Later, Scipio Nasica vowed games during his campaign in Spain against the Lusitanians in 193.[119] Finally,
L. Scipio Asiaticus claimed that he had vowed to celebrate *ludi* in his
campaign against Antiochus in 190.[120] These decisions not to vow
temples seem impossible to explain on the basis of individual characteristics or the nature of the campaign. To take the last instance as
an example, Asiaticus was a patrician, a member of the most prominent military family in Rome at the time, fighting the most important
campaign of his day, and yet he chose to vow games rather than a
temple. However in the light of the behavior of his clansmen, he
may have been following a Scipionic family tradition.[121] It is difficult

---

[118] Livy 28.38.14, 31.49.5. Livy's report of the latter vow presents some problems, for he indicates that Scipio made the vow as consul in Africa, although Africanus
did not reach Africa until 204 when he was proconsul. However, it seems that this
vow must be distinct from his first vow for *ludi*, for Scipio was neither consul nor
in Africa when he made that vow.

[119] Livy 35.1.9. This is the famous incident where the Senate refused to pay for
the games which Nasica had vowed. See further above, pp. 55–60.

[120] Livy 39.22.8.

[121] Only L. Cornelius Scipio seventy years earlier, caught at sea in a storm during his Corsican campaign, vowed a temple, to the Tempestates.

to see why the Scipios would have been averse to vowing temples if
such vows would merely add to their *gloria*. Yet if such vows also
raised the possibility of deflecting attention away from their glorious
achievements, their actions become more understandable; the decision to vow *ludi* would have kept the spotlight firmly trained on the
individual. Scipio Africanus followed a different path than Cato to a
position of preeminence in the state, a difference symbolized by Cato's
decision to vow a temple and Scipio's decision to vow games.

   In this regard, the celebration of *ludi* seems to be a more effective
means for publicizing the name of an individual than the erection of
a temple, even if this "monument" was only a short-term event. The
importance which aediles attached to staging elaborate *ludi* in preparation for future electoral campaigns in the Late Republic is well-
known from Cicero's correspondence with Marcus Caelius as well as
from other sources.[122] Games were an especially effective means to
promote one's popularity, since they could be mounted on short notice,
while a temple would take a number of years to complete, even if it
provided more long-term *gloria*. Furthermore, although *ludi* also honored the gods, they were associated more closely than temples with
the individual who staged them, and thus provided an better opportunity for making an impression on the populace. While people associated the celebration of spectacular games with an individual, I
suggest that in passing a temple they would think first of the deity
involved, even if the architrave contained an elaborate inscription
honoring the person who made the vow. For instance, one might
think first of "the temple to Lares Permarini" and only secondarily
of L. Aemilius Regillus; the detailed recounting of the latter's deeds
on the architrave found its true audience in Livy and the other
antiquarians.[123] The significance of *ludi* is borne out by several generals who vowed both a temple and *ludi* in the early second century,
and by the frequent celebration of *ludi* in connection with a new
temple.[124] The construction of a new state temple thus had its draw-

---

[122] See Cicero *Ad Fam.* 8.2.2, 8.4.5, 8.6.5, 8.8.10, et al. For a modern discussion
of the importance of games, cf. Nicolet (1980), 361–373.
[123] If the literacy rate in Rome was as low as 15 percent, as Harris (1989) has
argued, then the majority of the populace would not even be able to read the
inscription and credit the founder. Although a number of scholars have disputed
this figure, it seems clear that the value of such inscriptions in electoral politics at
Rome was limited.
[124] *Ludi* were celebrated at the dedication of several temples, e.g. Juventas in 191
(Livy 36.36.7); Diana and Juno Regina in 179 (Livy 40.52.3); and Fortuna Equestris

backs as a means of advertising one's prowess and obtaining immediate *gloria*, and a general had to make a conscious decision about
the statement and the direction he wished to take.

As a corollary to the choice between temples and *ludi*, generals
who did engage in acts of personal self-aggrandizement in the construction of public buildings in Rome often built monuments which
were not religious in nature. For instance, L. Stertinius followed up
his successful campaigns in Spain in 199 by erecting two *fornices* in
the Forum Boarium and another in the Circus Maximus.[125] These
were the first such *fornices* in Rome, barrel-vaulted arches on which
statues could be placed which seem to have been the forerunner of
the later Imperial arches. This monument had no implications for
the Romans' relations with the gods, and so could be erected without the close supervision of the Senate.[126] Furthermore, by making
no reference to the gods, it left the focus squarely on the victorious
general himself; service to the state is implied only by the construction of a building which beautified the city and enhanced its dignity
and amenities. These arches therefore provided a much better vehicle
for advertising the prowess of an individual than a temple, particularly here since Stertinius introduced a new architectural form. The
personal aspect of this type of monument is again underscored by a
Scipio: in 190, Scipio Africanus constructed a *fornix* on the Capitoline
hill before he even departed the city as a legate with his brother's
expedition against Antiochus.[127] F. Coarelli has suggested that this
was a very personal monument, with the seven bronze statues representing Scipio's ancestors.[128] Other generals also built secular monuments following their campaigns, such as the *columna rostrata* of
C. Duilius following his naval victory at Mylae in 260, or the *porticus
Octavia* of Cn. Octavius after his naval victories in the Third Macedonian War.[129] These monuments, in part because they were *not*

---

in 173 (Livy 42.10.5). *Ludi* were also occasionally celebrated at the *locatio*, e.g. Hercules
Musarum in 187 (Livy 39.22.1–2).

[125] Livy 33.27.4. On this monument and the *fornix* of Scipio discussed below, see
Calabi Limentani (1982).

[126] Wallace-Hadrill (1990), 146, also notes how the *fornix* might be erected without input from the Senate and how it served as an effective means of self-advertise-
ment.

[127] Livy 37.3.7.

[128] Coarelli (1972), 71. See also Pietilä-Castrén (1987), 71–74. Wallace-Hadrill
(1990), 162–165, discusses the erection of statues as a means of glorifying one's
name, and again makes particular reference to the Scipios (161–162 and n. 61).

[129] For Duilius, Pliny, *NH* 34.20–21, and Quintilian, *Inst.* 1.7.12 only report one

religious structures, did offer the opportunity to leave a lasting monument which could proudly trumpet the accomplishments of an individual both to their contemporaries and to posterity.

This interpretation of the significance of the construction of new temples helps us to understand a few instances which fall outside the normal patterns of temple construction and which therefore have defied explanation. Perhaps the most conspicuous example concerns M. Aemilius Lepidus, who is the only commander known to have vowed two separate temples during the course of a single campaign. The problem in explaining his action has been compounded by the fact that his campaign was otherwise undistinguished; Lepidus spent his tenure in office in 187 pacifying the Ligurians and building the Via Aemilia.[130] His campaign did not involve any major pitched battles, it did not bring the war against the Ligurians to a successful conclusion and quite properly he was not granted a triumph for his activities. Nevertheless, Lepidus vowed a temple to Diana and another to Juno Regina at separate points during the year. Further complicating the issue, both of the deities to whom he vowed temples already had temples which had stood in Rome for over two hundred years.[131]

The entire sequence of events has defied explanation. Although it seems unlikely, we can not entirely discount the possibility that Lepidus felt genuinely threatened during his pitched battles with the Ligurians, so that his vows were motivated solely by his desire for divine assistance.[132] The fact that he vowed two temples, however, eliminates the simplest overall explanation for generals' vows: that the more "religious" generals vowed temples to the deity to whom he felt a special connection or a special debt of gratitude. One scholar has suggested that Lepidus was so incensed at being sent to Liguria while commanders in the East were being prorogued that "he wanted to per-

---

column, but Servius, *Georg.* 3.29, indicates that there were two which could still be seen in his day, one in the Forum and one near the Circus Maximus. For the *porticus Octavia*, cf. Pliny, *NH* 34.13.

[130] Livy 39.2.7–11.

[131] The article of R. D. Weigel (1982–83) fails to come to grips with the religious implications of having several cult centers ostensibly for the same goddess. He raises the questions in a brief seven lines at the end of his discussion on p. 191. This point is worth a more detailed examination.

[132] Livy's account does not give any hint that Lepidus was in any danger, but his account is very cursory and the important point is how Lepidus reacted. Lepidus' idea of an appropriate religious response may not be the same as Livy's, nor ours for that matter.

petuate his mediocre campaign in a dramatic fashion."[133] Another
has speculated that the temple to Juno Regina was meant as a com-
panion temple to the recently constructed temple of Jupiter Stator,
and that in fact the temple for Juno Regina should have been vowed
prior to that of Diana.[134] A third suggestion contends that Lepidus,
as pontiff, was carrying out a directive from his college or the *decemviri*
in regard to whom he should vow a temple should the occasion arise.[135]

Yet none of these arguments is satisfactory. In the first place, one
should not assume that Lepidus was attempting to arrogate *gloria* to
himself that he had failed to win on the battlefield; such a suggestion
runs counter to the weight of the evidence presented above. The
latter two theories both acknowledge that Lepidus provided a service
to the state by vowing the two temples, but they allege a far greater
degree of centralized planning for the construction of new temples
than our evidence warrants. It is more beneficial to focus on Lepidus
himself; given the relatively unglamorous operations he was assigned
for his consulship, he seems to have made a conscious decision to
present himself as one who aligned himself closely with the needs of
the state. Thus during his year in office he busied himself with essential tasks, and also came to the aid of the Cenomani, who had
been needlessly provoked by the praetor Marcus Furius.[136] To drive
home the point he vowed the two temples. This was indeed a dramatic statement, but one which called attention to the gods, to the
state, and to Lepidus' position in relation to them, and only after
that to his own personal accomplishments. Such would be the implications of engaging in the construction of public temples in Rome.

[133] Pietilä-Castrén (1987), 104.
[134] Richardson (1992), 216. Richardson explains the Diana temple as more appropriate to the nature of Lepidus' campaign, fighting in mountainous woodland territory, and the second as dictated by the "natural sequence" in Rome. This argument
is tenuous on several grounds, not least that it postulates a greater degree of planning in the order of Roman temples than our evidence permits; can we speak of a
"natural sequence" for deities to whom temples were built? It also involves assuming that the temple of Jupiter Stator was built prior to that of Juno Regina, for
which Richardson resorts to circular reasoning. Unfortunately, this temple can not
be securely dated. Cf. Boyd (1953) for another discussion of these temples.
[135] Weigel (1982–83), 188–89. Weigel also links the temple of Juno Regina with
Jupiter Stator, and argues that it may have been a common practice for a pontiff
to supply the commander with the names of deities who needed special recognition
in Rome. As he notes, this would account for temple vowed to deities with whom
the general, enemy, location, terrain, etc. had no connection, but there is no evidence at all in the sources for this hypothesis.
[136] Livy 39.3.1–3.

IV. *Conclusions*

It has been argued throughout this chapter that the concept of whether a vow was "technically binding" on the state seems foreign to the Roman style of government. The alternative model proposed here would allow for a more fluid approach to the whole issue. The only hard and fast rule was that vows represented an obligation to the gods which had to be discharged, while the manner in which the obligation was discharged could vary from case to case. With the tithe vowed by Camillus, the decision was first taken that the vow needed to be discharged by the state, then a decision was taken on how to accomplish the vow. The eventual decision did not necessarily result in a tenth of the booty being turned over to Apollo, as an early "honor system" was used to encourage individuals to return the necessary money. Nevertheless, from a state perspective, the obligation was considered paid, until Camillus pointed out that the vow should have included Veientine land as well as movable property. A further decision of the pontiffs supported this claim of Camillus, and the Senate thus took further action to provide enough money for the dedication to Apollo.[137] At each step, a decision was made as to whether the state would regard the vow as binding and what the vow entailed, and then afterward a second decision had to be made as to the practical means of fulfilling the vow.

A similar decision-making process is visible with many other vows made by magistrates on campaign. The Senate or the pontiffs could have determined that the *fanum* for Jupiter Stator was sufficient to fulfill at least one of the vows made to him, or conversely that two temples should be erected because two vows had been made. Again, a decision was made that the state had been bound by the vow, and further the Senate directed that a single building should be erected which would suffice to discharge both vows. We hear of no general debate as to whether magistrate's vows should always be considered binding or non-binding, not even in the case of Nasica. Rather, the Senate's decision there referred to his specific vow, the games which he had vowed on his own authority. In most cases, the Senate agreed to help with the fulfillment of the particular vow in question, without specifically remarking that they considered the vow binding on the state, thus leaving us to grapple with a question which they never

---

[137] Livy 5.25.4–10.

formally answered. This process reflects a general principle of Roman government; decisions were made on an *ad hoc* basis, and while precedents could be cited in support of a position, they were not decisive.

Thus, the vowing of new temples in Rome reflects important elements in the functioning of the Roman system of government. This process illustrates the fundamental concord which existed between the individuals who comprised the Senate and the collective Senate itself. The fundamental ethos of the aristocracy valued service to the community, a point that was recognized on all sides and repeatedly put into practice. The Senate, itself composed of men who were former or future generals, continued to support the custom of generals making vows in the midst of battle because the generals, who were themselves members of the Senatorial aristocracy, continued to make vows which they knew would be acceptable to a majority of senators.[138] Likewise generals made these kinds of vows because approval was all but certain and offered a kind of *gloria* that could not be obtained by other means. This process, in which both sides participated and both sides benefited, perfectly exemplifies the tradition of mutually reinforcing trust and dependence which allowed the classical Roman Republic to operate. We will encounter this feature again and again as we examine the construction of new temples in Rome.

---

[138] Cf. the remarks of Eckstein (1987) concerning the political actions of generals, xiii and 319–24.

CHAPTER THREE

THE SIBYLLINE BOOKS

The previous chapter noted that a large majority of new temples were built in Rome by means of a vow made by an individual, usually a Roman commander on campaign. For some new cults, however, the first steps toward bringing them to Rome were taken not by an individual, but by the collective Roman state through the medium of the Sibylline Books. The Sibylline Books were a collection of scrolls that were stored in the temple of Jupiter Optimus Maximus on the Capitoline hill until Augustus moved them into the temple of Apollo. To focus solely on the new cults introduced by the Books, however, would constitute a serious misrepresentation, for the Books played a much larger role in the development of Roman religion than just the introduction of the occasional new cult. In order to understand the significance of these new cults introduced by the Sibylline Books, we need to see those introductions in the context of the other actions undertaken at the behest of the oracular scrolls. The first task in this chapter is therefore to gain a clear understanding of the Sibylline Books themselves: their origins and history in Rome, the procedure used for consulting them, the reasons for which they were consulted, and the responses they gave. Only after laying out this background will it be possible to focus on the issue of most interest to this study: the Sibylline Books and the construction of new temples.

I. *The Sibylline Books in Roman Religion*

I.1 *Their Origins and History*

Roman legend placed the introduction of the Sibylline Books in the regal period. According to the tradition, preserved in several sources, an unknown old woman offered nine rolls of prophecies to Tarquinius Superbus at an inordinate price.[1] When Tarquinius scoffed at her

---

[1] The story, with some variations, can be found in Dion. Hal. 4.62; Aulus Gellius

and refused to buy, she burned three rolls and offered him the remaining rolls at the same price. When Tarquinius again refused, she burned three more rolls and offered him the final three rolls, still at the original price. At this point Tarquinius decided to buy the remaining books, either at the bidding of the augurs or because he himself recognized that such persistence must be well-founded. Rome thus became the possessor of three rolls of Sibylline oracles, written in Greek hexameter verse. When the temple of Jupiter Optimus Maximus was completed, the rolls were stored in the temple underground in a stone chest.

This story clearly possesses many folkloric elements, and yet can not be exactly paralleled anywhere in the Mediterranean world. The tale is exclusively Roman, meant to explain Rome's exclusive possession of these scrolls, and is thus demanding of an explanation. It is no accident that the Books were purchased; no one could dispute that they were Roman property, and the Romans had paid up front for them, so they had no continuing obligations. The sudden appearance and disappearance of the anonymous old woman are obvious folktale tricks to imply that she was divine, although the story never says so. Tarquinius was undoubtedly chosen as the purchaser for a number of reasons. He was an Etruscan, and as Etruscans were supposed to be the most knowledgeable in matters of divination, he could be trusted to have bought legitimate divine oracles. As a king, no one could doubt his authority to buy the Books for Rome, and yet as a member of a family which was expelled from Rome, no subsequent Roman could claim to have a special connection to the Books or a special ability to interpret them. And obviously, the burning of the scrolls taught not only Tarquin but all subsequent Romans their true value; in fact, the very scarcity of scrolls made them that much more valuable.

1.19.1; Lactantius, *Div. Inst.* 1.6.10–11; Servius, *Ad Aen.* 6.72; Zonaras 7.11.1; Tzetzes, on Lycophron, 1279. Lactantius identifies Tarquinius as Priscus, but the other sources are agreed in naming Superbus. Much ink has been spilled, both in antiquity and in modern times, trying to ascertain the identity of the woman and the origin of the Books. When the ancient sources give the old woman a name, they usually call her Amalthea and identify her as one of the nine Sibyls, either from Cumae or Erythrae. Modern scholars have been no less eager to assign the Books an origin, either from Greece or Etruria. See Wissowa, *RKR* 461–69; Hoffmann (1933); Dumézil, *ARR* 601–2; Latte, *RRG* 160–61. The issue of origins seems impossible to settle conclusively and because it is not particularly relevant to our discussion here of how and why the Books were used, we will leave it to one side.

One important feature missing from the story of the Sibylline Books'
arrival in Rome needs special attention: no source connects the Books
in any way with the god Apollo. Modern scholars have often wanted
to see this connection, because Apollo was the Greek god most closely
associated with prophecy.[2] The Books have even been used as evidence for a cult of Apollo in Rome from the time of their introduction. Yet Apollo had no overt connection to the Books until Augustus
moved the scrolls into the newly built temple of Apollo on the Palatine in 28 B.C.E.[3] Considering Augustus' adoption of Apollo, this
act should be seen as part of his program to emphasize Apollo and
part of his attempt to bring prophetic oracles more tightly under his
control, not as the long lost repatriation of the oracles.[4] We should
note that Apollo's first temple in Rome was directed to his aspect as
the god of healing and not the god of prophesy.[5] That the scrolls
were kept in the temple of Capitoline Jupiter, the most important
cult in the state, confirms that their connection is not with Apollo,
but with the state religion.

While the legend concerning the arrival of the Sibylline Books in
Rome may not be literally true, the date is plausible. The first recorded consultation of the Books took place in 496 B.C.E., when the
dictator A. Postumius Albus had the Books consulted because a
drought and the current war against the Volscians threatened to bring
Rome to a state of starvation.[6] One may doubt the veracity of this
notice, especially as Livy says nothing about this consultation and

---

[2] See e.g. Wissowa, *RKR* 239–40; Bailey (1932), 122–23, De Sanctis *SdR*, 2.503–
504, and particularly Gagé (1955), 26–38 and 196–204. The lone scholar holding
out against this view is Dumézil *ARR*, 441–443.

[3] Livy does put a speech in the mouth of Decius Mus during the debate over the
lex Ogulnia in 300 in which Decius mentions that the *decemviri* were "overseers of
Apollo's rites" (Livy 10.8.2: *antistites Apollinaris sacri*), but this is of dubious value for
establishing a connection between Apollo and the Books in the early Republic. Similarly, a reference in Julius Obsequens (47) to the *decemviri* performing a sacrifice in
the temple of Apollo in 98 does little to prove that Apollo was the patron god of
the Books throughout the Republic.

[4] The dedication of the temple of Apollo in 28 is described by Dio (53.1.3).
Suetonius (*Aug.* 31) puts the transfer of the Books together with the assumption of
the pontificate and Augustus' edict on prophesies in 12 B.C.E., but other references
make it appear that the Books had been moved before then. See also Tac., *Ann.*
6.12, for Augustus' order that all prophetic books be surrendered to the urban praetor.
Cf. Parke (1988), 149 n. 11. On Augustus' connection to Apollo, see Kienast (1982),
192ff.

[5] See below, p. 98.

[6] Dion. Hal. 6.17.

several other fifth-century consultations do seem spurious, particularly those putting the introduction of the *ludi saeculares* back into the
fifth century.[7] Yet there is nothing implausible about the situation
leading to the consultation in 496, and a few spurious examples
involving the tangled origins of the *ludi saeculares* do not warrant discarding the remaining fifth- and fourth-century consultations. The
oracles certainly continued to be consulted during periods when our
evidence is more complete and reliable, and it would be impossible
for us to draw an arbitrary line at which the consultations should
begin to be considered genuine. Over fifty consultations are recorded
by the ancient sources from the fifth century down to the end of the
second century.[8]

In 83 B.C.E., during Sulla's fighting in Italy, a fire destroyed the
temple of Capitoline Jove and with it the supposed original rolls of
Sibylline oracles.[9] A Senatorial commission was appointed in 76 to
collect a new set of oracles, and this commission began its search in
Erythrae.[10] However, only one thousand verses were found there,
perhaps equivalent to a single book, and so the commission continued to collect verses deriving from other reputed homes of the Sibyl.
Eventually, the collection was turned over to the *quindecemviri* in charge
of the oracles, who edited out whatever seemed to them to be an
interpolation. This new set of Sibylline oracles was consulted at least
by 56 B.C.E., when they produced the famous response concerning

---

[7] Cf. Zon. 2.3.3; Plut., *Publ.* 21. I agree with Parke (1988), 193, that the consultation of 461, found in Livy (3.10.7) and Dion. Hal. (10.2.5, 10.9.1), is "part of the
fictional dressing up of the story" of the seizure of the Capitol by Appius Herdonius
and hence not likely to be genuine.

[8] See Appendix Two. I have omitted the instance mentioned in the previous
note as an obviously late invention. On the other hand, I have included those cases
where the sources do not explicitly mention the Sibylline Books, but state only that
a particular action was undertaken according to a decree of the *decemviri*, e.g. Livy
38.36, 38.44. Because the *decemviri*, as far as we know, did not give orders without
consulting the Books and the approval of the Senate, I assume that the phrase *ex
decreto decemvirorum* is shorthand for "by a decree of the Senate approving the actions
recommended by the *decemviri* following a consultation of the Sibylline Books." For
this procedure for consulting the Books, see below pp. 81–85.

[9] Dion. Hal. 4.62.6; Tac. *Ann.* 6.12.

[10] For the collecting of new oracles, see Lact., *Div. Inst.* 1.6.14; Dion. Hal. (following Varro) 4.62.6; Tac., *Ann.* 6.12. That the commission went first to Erythrae
may indicate that the Senate accepted the version that the old woman was the
Erythraean Sibyl, rather than the Cumaean. However, some sources report that the
Cumaean Sibyl had actually migrated from Erythrae, so this distinction may not be
very significant.

the restoration of Ptolemy Auletes.[11] The burning and subsequent reassembling of a new set of oracles indicate clearly that the story of Tarquinius and the old woman is not essential to the validity of the oracles. There is no hint in our sources that the Senatorial commission was trying to find exact duplicates of the oracles which had been lost; rather it was searching for genuine Sibylline utterances. By the first century, it was the divine source, the Sibyl, which gave the scrolls their legitimacy, and not the particular hand of the old woman who had visited Tarquinius Superbus. That set could be, and was, supplemented or replaced by any set of oracles which the Senate deemed to be authentically Sibylline.

One test which the *quindecemviri* used to determine that a given oracle was genuine actually makes it evident to us, with the benefit of hindsight and modern literary analysis, that the old woman of legend could not in fact have been responsible for that particular oracle. Both Cicero and Varro noted that an acrostic pattern was an essential feature of a Sibylline oracle, and the *quindecemviri* had expunged certain verses on the grounds that they did not fit this pattern.[12] Modern scholars, following the lead of Hermann Diels over a century ago, have noted that we have no known examples of acrostics before the Hellenistic period, when they come into vogue.[13] Our sole surviving purported text of a Sibylline oracle apparently dates to 125 B.C.E. and fits this acrostic pattern, which indicates that this test antedates the first-century restoration of the collection.[14] The Romans may not have been aware that the use of acrostics in the sixth century is highly unlikely, so this point would not have diminished the authority of the Sibyl for them in any way.[15] It does confirm for

---

[11] Dio 39.15–16; Cic. *Fam.* 1.1.3.

[12] Cicero, *De Div.* 2.54.112; Varro, *apud* Dion. Hal. 4.62.6.

[13] Diels, (1890), passim. See also Parke (1988), 139.

[14] The oracle, which is reproduced in Appendix Three and can also be found in *FGH* 257 f 36 X, is preserved in a book on marvels by Phlegon of Tralles, composed in the second century C.E. Most modern scholars are willing to accept this as a genuine oracle published around 125 B.C.E., as Phlegon claims. Cf. Diels (1890); Hoffmann (1933); Parke (1988), 137–39. Diels argued that this oracle was actually stitched together from two oracles originally produced towards the end of the Second Punic War, but does not dispute that the oracle as we have it is authentically Sibylline.

[15] Cicero, for instance, uses the detail of the acrostics only to prove that the Sibyl could not have been in an ecstatic trance when she gave her prophecies, because she could not have composed acrostics in such a state.

us, however, either that the entire collection has nothing to do with
the old woman and dates from the Hellenistic period, or that even
before 83 new oracles, which the Senate had accepted as genuine,
had found their way into the original collection.

I.2 *Procedure*

The foregoing discussion has already disclosed a trait which is essential to an understanding of the Sibylline Books and leads directly to
an examination of the procedure used for consulting the Books: during
the Republic, the Senate always maintained the ultimate authority
over the oracles. When the Books were first deposited in the temple
of Jupiter Optimus Maximus, two men were appointed to have charge
of them, the *duumviri sacris faciundis*.[16] This number was raised to ten
in 367, half plebeian and half patrician, and again to fifteen some-
time in the first half of the first century B.C.E.[17] These men, like
members of the other religious colleges, were drawn from the ruling
class, although it was rare for a man to serve on more than one of
these priesthoods. As magistrates or senators, they might be absent
from the city for extended periods of time, and so the full comple-
ment of the college need not have been present to consult the Books.
Only these men, however, were allowed to consult the Books and
then only when the Senate ordered them to do so, not on their own
initiative. Roman legend recorded that one of the first guardians of
the Sibylline Books, M. Atilius (or Acilius) was found to have secretly
copied some of the verses, and suffered the same penalty as for a

---

[16] Their full title suggests that these men were involved with performing sacrifices,
but in what capacity is unknown. As G. Szemler (1972), 27 recognized, to the best
of our knowledge the primary duties of the *decemviri* consisted of guarding, consulting, and interpreting the Sibylline Books. Many modern authorities have written
that the responsibilities of the *decemviri* included the supervision of foreign cults as
well as the guardianship of the Sibylline Books; cf. most recently Beard (1990), Table 1
on pp. 20–21. Yet direct evidence for this supervision of foreign rites is lacking; the
assumption seems based primarily on the supposed connection between the *libri Sibyllini*
and the introduction of Greek cults. The ensuing argument will show that this
connection is more apparent than real.

[17] The change to ten is recorded in Livy 6.37.12 and 6.42.2, but because it appears
as part of the patrician-plebeian skirmishing, the date may not be completely historical. The change to fifteen is usually ascribed to Sulla, based on a passage in
Servius (*Aen.* 6.73), but is first attested in a letter of Caelius to Cicero dated to 51
(*Fam.* 8.4.1). Cf. Parke (1988), 206. For the purposes of this study the board will be
referred to as *decemviri*, since for most of the period under discussion the board
consisted of ten members.

parricide: he was sewn into a sack and thrown into the sea.[18] This tale was probably invented as a cautionary tale for the *decemviri*, a reminder that the state controlled the Sibylline Books.

On those occasions when the Senate ordered a consultation of the Sibylline Books, the *decemviri* did so alone. The means by which they arrived at their prescription remain a complete mystery, and the possibilities are seemingly endless.[19] For instance, we do not know whether all ten members of the board approached the Books, or whether one or two were appointed, by the Senate or by the other *decemviri* to do so. It is difficult to believe that the original three rolls accurately foresaw all the different prodigies which at one point or another were reported in Rome. Thus the *decemviri* might have had to read through the entire three rolls in order to select the oracle which best seemed to match the current situation. Or they may have created an index of sorts, listing where to look in case of famine, plague, the birth of a hermaphrodite, et al., and matched up the expiations as best they could. Or perhaps they spread out the rolls and chose a passage at random, allowing fate or the will of the gods to choose the remedy to be applied.[20] The *decemviri* did have public slaves at their disposal, but it is difficult to believe that slaves could have played a significant role in the consultation of the Books, despite Varro's assertion to the contrary.[21] It is entirely conceivable that the Senate, its leading members, or the magistrates in office might have strongly hinted or explicitly told the *decemviri* what sort of response they wanted from the Books. The *decemviri*, as members of the Senate themselves, might even have known without being told what sort of response was desired. The *decemviri* might then have

---

[18] Zonaras 7.11.1; Tzetzes, on Lycophron, 1279.

[19] Cf. Parke (1988), 191.

[20] This seems the least satisfactory conjecture for the consultation of the Books, since certain prodigies seem normally to have had a regular expiation. For instance, showers of stones were normally followed by a *novemdiale sacrum*, and the appearance of hermaphrodites also led to a performance of a fairly standardized set of rituals. On the latter, see MacBain (1982).

[21] The existence of the slaves is proved by *CIL* 6.2312 which refers to a *publicus a commentari[i]s XVvir[orum] s.f.* Yet as his title indicates, the slave's job was to keep records of previous Sibylline consultations, perhaps including the date, the prodigy, and the outcome. For Varro's assertion that no consultation could proceed without their presence, see Dion. Hal. 4.62. Zonaras (7.11) claims that Tarquinius brought two interpreters from Greece to help the *duumviri* with the inspection of the Books, but no other source mentions these men. Zonaras may be referring to the public slaves and projecting their origins back to arrival of the Books in Rome. On these matters, cf. Wissowa, *RKR* 461-2.

approached the Books with a specific idea of the response they wanted. As the consultation was done by the *decemviri* alone, attended by only a few slaves, it would have been easy to manage the process in order to achieve a desired result. This type of "manipulation" was by no means unusual in Roman religion, and did not in any way lessen the impact of the Sibylline advice.[22]

Finding an appropriate passage in the Sibylline scrolls was only half the battle; the passage still had to be interpreted. Different interpretations of the same oracle could lead to vastly different courses of action, as was true of most Greek oracles.[23] After the *decemviri* completed their consultation, they reported back to the Senate, and it was the Senate's responsibility to decide how an oracle should be applied to a particular situation. There was thus a great deal of latitude available both in finding an appropriate response and in interpreting that response. If the Senate had already settled on a course of action, they could usually proceed with at least the appearance of divine approbation; if the oracle itself did not explicitly recommend that action, the interpretation could be fashioned to suit the Senate's purposes, if it so desired. This is not to say that the Senate regularly manipulated consultations of the Sibylline Books; in most cases the Senate allowed itself to be guided by the *decemviri* in the interpretation of Sibylline oracles. Furthermore, the Senate was not bound to accept the advice of the Sibyl, as the following example shows.

In 143, the Senate allowed construction of the Aqua Marcia to continue despite Sibylline opposition. Frontinus provides the most complete account of this incident in his account of the aqueducts of Rome:

> At that time, the *decemviri*, when they were inspecting the Sibylline Books on other grounds, are said to have discovered that it was not right for the Aqua Marcia, or rather the Anio—for more regularly the tradition speaks about this—to be brought to the Capitol. It was debated in the

---

[22] For instance, similar manipulation of omens did not affect their efficacy. Starving the sacred chickens so that they would eat greedily enough to drop some food on the ground did not lessen the impact of this omen (Cicero, *De Div.* 1.15.28, 2.34.72). The significance was merely that the omen occurred, not how it occurred. Along the same lines, the consul Marcellus is reported to haven ridden about in his carriage with the blinds drawn, so that he would not see unfavorable omens (Cicero, *De Div.* 2.36.77): a portent was not a portent unless it was recognized as such. This again highlights that humans could have some control over omens without affecting their religious significance.

[23] One need only think of the famous "wooden walls" oracle to the Athenians reported by Herodotus, 7.141–43.

Senate about this matter ... and again three years later, but on both
occasions the influence of Marcius Rex was victorious, and thus the
water was brought to the Capitol.[24]

Thus after a highly contentious debate, Marcius was able to build
his aqueduct despite the opposition of the Sibyl. It would be extremely helpful to know some of the arguments used by his supporters to discount the force of the Sibylline authority. Perhaps because
the *decemviri* were consulting the Books "on other grounds" they were
able to argue that this pronouncement should carry less weight, or
perhaps they argued that this bit of advice was invented by Marcius'
political enemies. Whatever the case, the incident certainly demonstrates that the advice of the Sibyl was not automatically implemented,
but was subject to a debate which could be highly contentious and
that the advice could eventually be rejected. By reserving the right
to make the final decision, the Senate maintained the ultimate authority over the Books.

Following the Senate's interpretation, the contents of the Sibylline
oracle were then made known to the populace, either by a Senatorial decree authorizing the recommended actions, or by a publication of the *decemviri* themselves. The Senate was responsible for
finding the money to pay for whatever rites were required, but the
decemviri themselves or other assigned magistrates oversaw the actual
fulfillment of the Sibylline mandate.[25] In most instances only the actions suggested by the Sibyl and not the entire text of the oracle
were made known; for example in 173 "announcement was made
by the *decemviri* both to which gods and with what victims sacrifice
should be made ... accordingly sacrifice was made in the manner

---

[24] Front., *de Aqua.* 7: *Eo tempore decemviri, dum aliis ex causis libros Sibyllinos inspiciunt,
invenisse dicuntur, non esse fas aquam Marciam seu potius Anionem—de hoc enim constantius
traditur—in Capitolium perduci, deque ea re in senatu M. Lepido pro collegio verba faciente
actum Appio Claudio Q. Caecilio consulibus, eandemque post annum tertium a Lucio Lentulo
retractam C. Laelio Q. Servilio consulibus, sed utroque tempore vicisse gratiam Marci Regis; atque
ita in Capitolium esse aquam perductam.* The outline of this acount is confirmed by a
notice in Livy, *Ep. Oxy.* 54. The Mss. actually read *collega* instead of *collegio*, but
emendation may make better sense here; Lepidus is not otherwise attested as a
magistrate for 143, and to speak of him as "colleague" with the propraetor Marcius
would be stretching. Lepidus and Lentulus thus would presumably be members of
the decemviral college, although such membership is not otherwise attested. Cf.
Broughton *MRR*, 1.472–473 and n. 1. The solution to this problem does not affect
the argument that the Senate could reject Sibylline advice.

[25] In 493, the Senate decreed that the money should come from the booty of the
victorious general (Dion. Hal. 6.17, 6.94). For *decemviri*, see e.g. Livy 5.13.6, 37.3.
For magistrates assigned tasks, see e.g. Livy 22.9.8, 36.37.5, 43.13.7.

which the *decemviri* had published in writing."[26] Publication of actual Sibylline verses was supposedly allowed only by order of the Senate, although in 56 the tribune Caius Cato was able to force the *decemviri* to read the oracle concerning the restoration of Ptolemy Auletes before the Senate had given its permission.[27] Such publication was intended to convince the populace that the Books had actually been consulted, and that the proposed action was indeed in accord with the Sibyl's advice. No doubt due in part to this restriction on publication, only one text of a purported Sibylline oracle from the Books survives.[28] Most of our information on the Sibylline responses therefore comes from the reports of Livy, who also describes the situations in which the Books were consulted. It is time to turn our attention to these topics.

I.3 *Consultations and Responses*

Because Livy is our primary source for Sibylline consultations, we must be wary of drawing conclusions about the historical periods in which the Romans most frequently consulted the Books. A glance at Appendix Two shows that the Books were consulted only sporadically until the beginning of the Second Punic War. The next fifty years saw a huge upsurge in the number of recorded consultations, followed by a dropoff in the mid-second century. Over half of the recorded consultations took place between 218 and 165, and the immediate assumption is that the pressure of Hannibal's invasion resulted in an increased tendency to seek divine aid, which took many years after the conclusion of that war to disappear. Yet these figures are more likely an accident of preservation than indicative of any real trends. Livy's text survives basically intact for the years 218–167, during which period he records an average of one consultation every two years. For the period from 292–218 and for the period after 167 we have only *periochae*, which are hardly even summaries of Livy's text, and the rate of recorded consultations reflects this state of affairs.[29]

---

[26] Livy 42.2.6–7: *editumque ab decemviris est et quibus diis quibusque hostiis sacrificaretur . . . Itaque sacrificatum est ut decemviri scriptum ediderant.*

[27] Dio 39.15: οὐ γὰρ ἐξῆν οὐδὲν τῶν Σιβυλλείων, εἰ μὴ ἡ βουλὴ ψηφίσαιτο, ἐς τὸ πλῆθος ἐξαγγέλλεσθαι.

[28] Cf. note 14 above.

[29] For the period before 292, Livy does record several consultations, but obviously his sources for that period were less complete than for the later period. There

We should not assume that the Second Punic War marks a watershed in the Senate's use of the Sibylline Books.

Turning to the reasons for consulting the Sibylline Books, the ancient sources reveal that the Books were normally consulted to repair a breach in the *pax deum*. This rupture could be made manifest in numerous ways. Dionysius of Halicarnassus gives the most straightforward analysis:

> They consult them [the Books], by order of the Senate, when the state is in the grip of party strife or some great misfortune has happened to them in war, or some important prodigies and apparitions have been seen which are difficult of interpretation, as has often happened.[30]

The circumstances of the actual consultations confirms the substance of this analysis. However, the first of these reasons was essentially a product of the Late Republic, when civil strife was at its highest, and even these consultations were usually justified by reference to prodigies. For instance, the consultation following the violent death of Tiberius Gracchus was prompted by prodigies which indicated that danger threatened the state.[31] Consultations which were prompted by a disaster in battle also used prodigies as a pretext, as after the disastrous encounter with Hannibal at Trebia; the official reason given for that consultation was the numerous prodigies reported that winter.[32] Thus we may reduce the three categories of Dionysius down to a single statement: consultation of the Sibylline Books followed the announcement of prodigies.

Two exceptions do exist to this rule, which are not overly significant in themselves but are important in indicating that the Sibylline Books could play another role. In 390, after the Gauls had sacked Rome, Camillus obtained a decree from the Senate that the Sibylline Books should be consulted as to the proper rites for restoring and cleansing the shrines in the city.[33] This consultation is unique in the recorded history of the Books: no prodigy prompted it, but rather a question concerning proper rites for purification, which would nor-

---

may have been more consultations during these years than we know about, even though we have Livy's text for this period.

[30] Dion. Hal. 4.62.5: Χρῶνται δ᾽ αὐτοῖς, ὅταν ἡ βουλὴ ψηφίσηται, στάσεως καταλαβούσης τὴν πόλιν ἢ δυστυχίας τινὸς μεγάλης συμπεσούσης κατὰ πόλεμον ἢ τεράτων τινῶν καὶ φαντασμάτων μεγάλων καὶ δυσευρέτων αὐτοῖς φανέντων, οἷα πολλάκις συνέβη.

[31] Cicero *Verr.* 2.4.108.

[32] Livy 21.62.

[33] Livy 5.50.

mally be the province of the pontiffs. This incident is so out of character with what we know of the Sibyl that one is tempted to dismiss it as part of the fictional tales surrounding Camillus, except that it is hard to imagine the invention a detail which everyone would recognize as patently false. If a Roman historian could believe this use of the Books, then we should not be so quick to discard it as a possibility. Perhaps the sack of the city by the Gauls was in itself considered a prodigy; certainly it provided concrete evidence that the *pax deum* was no longer functioning. In the early fourth century the traditions concerning when to consult the Books may not have been as firmly established, and the Books were known to contain remedies for restoring the Romans' relations with their gods. In these circumstances consultation of the Sibylline Books may have seemed the logical first step towards the restoration of Rome.

The second exceptional consultation of the Sibylline Books took place in 212, after the verses of a certain Marcius recommended the celebration of *ludi* in honor of Apollo.[34] The Senate ordered the *decemviri* to consult the Books in regard to the celebration of the festival and then, apparently satisfied with the Sibylline response, they voted that the games should be held. Here again we do not see an attempt to expiate a prodigy or to appease the wrath of the gods, but simply an attempt to ascertain whether a given ritual is appropriate, which would again normally be the terrain of the pontiffs. This situation is more inexplicable than the prior example, for there was little that could truly be considered a prodigy in the immediate past. Perhaps in these two instances the Senate desired a more explicit divine opinion than the pontiffs could provide, due to the exceptional nature of the situation, i.e. the Gallic sack and the Second Punic War. These are the only known exceptions to the rule that the Sibylline Books be consulted only following prodigies.

One of the most common motives for consulting the Sibylline Books was in order to control a pestilence which was devastating the city.[35] Such pestilences seem to have been regarded as prodigies unto themselves; sickness among the people was held to be a sign of sickness in the Romans' relations with the gods. On six separate occasions the pestilence by itself was enough to warrant asking the Sibyl for help, and on five other occasions the pestilence in combination with other

---

[34] Livy 25.12.
[35] Refer to Appendix Two for a complete list of Sibylline consultations.

prodigies led to this recourse. The severity of the plague, however, appears *not* to have been a factor in consulting the Sibylline Books. On some occasions the Books were consulted only after other attempts at expiation had failed, but at other times Sibylline consultation was the first response to the crisis.[36] Conversely, several plagues which resisted initial attempts at expiation were eventually controlled by other means, without recourse to the Sibylline scrolls.[37] Numerous other plagues which did not last into a second year were also expiated without Sibylline aid. The decision on which pestilences warranted Sibylline intervention belonged to the Senate.[38]

Many other types of prodigies also resulted in Sibylline consultation. Showers of stones provided the pretext for a number of inquiries, often in conjunction with other prodigies. Natural phenomena, such as earthquakes, lightning, or various solar or lunar events, frequently resulted in a retreat to the Books. More exotic prodigies, such as sweat pouring from statues or blood trickling from a hearth, had the same effect. The birth of a hermaphrodite in 207 led to a consultation of the Sibylline Books and an elaborate ritual for expiating this horrific prodigy; the ceremony was repeated on subsequent hermaphrodite births, although we are not always informed that the Books were consulted.[39] Human actions which the Romans recognized as a prodigy, such as the unchastity of Vestal Virgins, might also be expiated according to Sibylline advice.[40] The common denominator

---

[36] Consultations after several years of plague: 433 (Livy 4.25.3), 293 (Livy 10.47), 180 (Livy 40.37). Consultation as the first response to a plague: 346 (Livy 7.27). See the discussion in Chapter One, pp. 21–24.

[37] E.g. in 363 (Livy 7.1–3) and in 331 (Livy 8.18). The pestilence of 365–63 is particularly interesting, because in 364 a *lectisternium*, complete with the first *ludi scenici*, was held to expiate the pestilence, but to no avail. Most scholars have assumed that the celebration of a *lectisternium* implies a Sibylline consultation, so that here the Sibylline Books were consulted and failed to stem the pestilence. However, Livy does not mention any consultation of the Sibylline Books at this time.

[38] While we can not place too much faith in Livy's account of any given incident, the fact that he describes several different outcomes shows that he recognized that there was no "automatic" response to a plague, but that the Senate could respond in a variety of ways.

[39] On these hermaphrodite prodigies, see MacBain (1982), 65–71 and 127–135.

[40] Obs. 37; Val. Max. 8.15.2. Cornell (1981) has argued that such *incestum* was not considered a prodigy, but rather was a religious offence which threatened the *pax deum*. It seems true that *incestum* on the part of the Vestals was not *always* considered a *prodigium*, but could be viewed that way in light of other extenuating circumstances. See the explicit testimony of Livy in regard to the Vestal scandal of 216 that "in the midst of so many other disasters, this impiety, as so often happens,

that all of these signs were considered clear indications that some-
ing was amiss in the Roman relations with the divine, which needed
o be set right before even more drastic calamities befell the state.

Of course, not all prodigies were expiated following a consultation
of the Sibylline Books: the Senate remained the final arbiter on
whether or not to consult the Books. First the Senate had to recognize that a *prodigia* had occurred; in Roman religion a prodigy was
not a prodigy unless the Senate recognized it as such. Then the Senate
had to decide that a given prodigy or group of prodigies warranted
seeking assistance from the Sibyl. This gave the Senate a great deal
of latitude in determining when to consult the Books, and in several
cases it is difficult for us to see why the Senate ordered the *decemviri*
to proceed with a consultation, because similar situations in the past
had not resulted in an appeal to the Books. For instance, a *novemdiale
sacrum* was the standard expiation for a shower of stones. This practice is given a legendary aitiology by Livy, and was normally declared
without the help of the Sibylline Books.[41] However, on some occasions the Senate ordered a *novemdiale* only after consulting the Books.[42]
In one instance, the *decemviri* actually ordered an expiation that had
previously been performed on the orders of the pontiffs. In 207 after
the first hermaphrodite prodigy in Rome, the pontiffs ordered that
twenty-seven maidens should sing a hymn as they marched through
the city; in 200 the *decemviri* ordered the same ceremony following a
similar prodigy.[43] Conversely, situations which in the past had led to
a consultation did not automatically cause the *decemviri* to scurry for
the Books.[44] Thus, prodigies can be seen as a necessary precondition
for consulting the Books, but they were not sufficient. While religious concerns provided the initial motivation, the Senate reserved
discretionary power over exactly when to consult the Books.

We are thus faced with the question of why the Senate felt that

---

was turned into a prodigy" (22.57.4: *Hoc nefas cum inter tot, ut fit, clades in prodigium
versum esset*). Cf. Eckstein (1982), 71–75; Rosenstein (1990), 69–70.

[41] Livy 1.31. For other occurrences, see e.g. Livy 21.62; 34.45.8; 44.18.6.

[42] For Sibyl-ordered examples of a *novemdiale*, see Livy 35.9; 36.37.4.

[43] Livy 27.37, 31.12. According to Livy's account, the *decemviri* became involved
in the events of 207 only after the temple of Juno Regina was struck by lightning
while the maidens were practicing the hymn in the temple of Jupiter Stator, and
even then only after the *haruspices* indicated the prodigy pertained to the matrons. In
200, it is the *decemviri* themselves who give the initial advice to have the maidens
sing the hymn.

[44] See for example the discussion of pestilences above, pp. 21–24 and p. 88. For
another example, cf. Livy 27.37.4 where a series of *prodigia*, similar to those in 216

the participation of the Books was necessary to correct the flaw in the *pax deum* in some instances but not in others. The ancient sources do suggest one possibility. After describing the acts prescribed by the Books in 218 following the battle of Trebia, Livy remarks: "The making of these vows and expiations, as prescribed by the Sibylline Books, lightened men's minds concerning their relations with the gods."[45] One role for the Sibylline Books may thus have been to function as an outlet for fear and a means of boosting morale in times of stress. This does not imply that the Sibylline Books were used by the aristocracy in Rome solely as a means of pacifying and controlling a restive populace.[46] Rather, when confronted with large numbers of prodigies in conjunction with grave national emergencies, many senators may have become equally disheartened and pessimistic about the future. Since the Sibylline Books were viewed as a repository of knowledge for how to appease the anger of the gods, consultation would allow the Senate, along with everyone else, to have confidence that the steps being taken were the correct ones to handle the religious crisis.[47] This would be a more effective means of calming people's fears because the actual written word of the gods could be consulted rather than having to interpret their will through entrails or other signs. Such an attitude seems particularly in evidence during the dark years of the Hannibalic war, as noted by Livy in the citation above and as indicated by the frequent consultations at the outset of the war.[48] The Sibylline Books provided a controlled

---

(Livy 22.36), are expiated not by the Books but according the orders of the pontiffs and the *haruspices*. See also Livy 32.1.14 and 39.22.4.

Cf. Morgan (1990). These examples seem to outweigh his arguments. Of course the severity of the disease which struck Rome might affect the decision on whether to consult the Books, and the pontifical notation in the *Annales* might not reflect this fact; the entry would still read *pestilentium*. But plagues that lasted for two or three years must have been fairly severe. Furthermore, other prodigies were expiated by the advice of the Books on some occasions, but not on others.

[45] Livy 21.62.11: *Haec procurata votaque ex libris Sibyllinis magna ex parte levaverant religione animos.*

[46] Such was the view of Polybius, 6.56.6–15, and glimpses of the same attitude can also be found in Cicero, *De Div.* 2.13.33, and Varro, in Augustine *CD* 4.31, 6.4–5. This notion of Roman religion as a mere "opiate for the masses" had a powerful influence on early studies of Roman religion, but has been rightly discredited in recent years, especially by North (1976), and Liebeschuetz (1979).

[47] Of course once the religious crisis had been resolved satisfactorily and the *pax deum* restored, the Romans believed that the situation on the ground would soon resolve itself in a similar satisfactory manner.

[48] Among other features, this was the first attested time the Books were consulted

outlet for such panic as might occur and restored at least a temporary sense of equilibrium to all members of Roman society.

As for dire circumstances which did not lead to Sibylline intervention, the Senate may have decided that other means of calming the
populace would be more effective in those circumstances. For instance
the pestilences of 363 and 331 were finally expiated by the ancient
Italian ritual of driving a nail into the side of a temple.[49] In this case
recourse was had to a ritual sanctioned more by antiquity than by a
divine source. This ritual was also indigenous, while recourse to the
Sibylline Books, whether one considers them Greek or Etruscan,
involved foreign elements; this factor may have affected the Senate's
decision. One might also note that consulting the Sibylline Books
could be a double-edged sword. While these oracles might be considered the best method for appeasing the wrath of the gods, the
willingness to consult on the part of the Senate might confirm that
the situation was really as grim as the populace believed. Not consulting the Books might have had the effect in some circumstances of
proclaiming to the people that the situation was not serious enough
to warrant a Sibylline consultation. One might compare the effect of
refusing to recognize a prodigy in the first place. The Senate again
had to decide whether more good than harm would come from any
particular recourse to the Sibyl.

Another possible explanation for the Senate's decision to have the
decemviri consult the Books might be to obtain divine sanction for a
particular course of action. If the Sibylline Books endorsed a line of
action, such action was more likely to be approved and accepted by
all concerned parties. Opponents were less likely to materialize, since
they would have a hard time trying to oppose the word of the goddess. We know of only one instance, the Aqua Marcia discussed above,
in which the Senate rejected the Sibyl's advice.[50] Divine sanction
might have been particularly important in those instances where the
religious response had direct political overtones. The introduction of
several temples, and particularly the Magna Mater, fits into this scenario, as we shall see below. Other examples can be adduced however. The oracle which came out against the construction of the Aqua

---

twice in the same year, in 217, both after Trebia (Livy 22.1) and Trasimene (Livy
22.9.8).

[49] Livy 7.3, 8.18.
[50] See pp. 83–84 above.

Marcia is an obvious example; although the oracle failed to prevent the construction of the aqueduct, its purpose was clearly political and opponents of the aqueduct undoubtedly hoped that the divine endorsement would strengthen their efforts. The embassy to propitiate Ceres following the death of Tiberius Gracchus provides another example.[51] B. Spaeth has shown how this embassy fits into the Senatorial propaganda campaign against Gracchus, by claiming that he had violated the *sacrosanctitas* of Octavius, and hence had offended Ceres.[52] The decision to propitiate Ceres at Enna further served the purpose of diminishing the stature of the Ceres in Rome, which was a plebeian stronghold, by proclaiming Enna as more ancient.[53] The backing of a divine source such as the Sibylline Books made the statements behind these actions more authoritative.

The preceding discussion indicates some of the ways in which a Sibylline response might serve political purposes, but we must not view the consultation of the Sibylline Books simply as an attempt at manipulation. Such a view deprives the Books of their religious significance, and in fact most of the responses given by the Sibylline Books did not have political overtones. The primary function of the Sibylline Books, as we have seen, was to restore the *pax deum*, and the overwhelming majority of Sibylline responses consisted of the prescription of rituals for that purpose. These expiations took one of two forms, either an immediate, one-time rite or the creation of a lasting institution. The former category, which is by far more numerous, included such ceremonies as sacrifices, the *lectisternium*, the *supplicatio* and the *lustratio*, while the latter consisted of the foundation of temples or annual games. It is remarkable that, in contrast to Greek oracles such as Delphi, Sibylline responses generally did not contain specific prophecies concerning the future, though on occasion they could.[54]

---

[51] Cicero, *Verr.* 2.4.108.
[52] Spaeth, (1990).
[53] The decision to go to Enna, rather than appease Ceres in Rome, can be seen as part of the Senatorial interpretation that Ceres was to be propitiated, but it can hardly be coincidence that the advice of the Sibyl was so well suited for the Senatorial propaganda campaign. A third possible purpose served by the embassy to Enna may have been to proclaim the pacification of Sicily following the slave revolt of the preceding years.
[54] The only prophecy recorded from the Sibylline Books is so out of character that it may not be genuine. While debating whether to grant Cn. Manlius a triumph in 187, the opponents of Manlius claimed that his legates had barely restrained him from crossing the Taurus by urging that he should not wish to experience the disaster predicted in the verses of the Sibyl for anyone who crossed those fateful boundaries

This feature is characteristic of the fundamental conservatism of the Roman government; the Senate did not want any potential kings or revolutionaries, coming either from inside or outside its ranks, to attempt to justify their actions or drum up support by claiming that their success had been foretold.[55] Rather, the responses found in the Sibylline Books were supposed to help the Senate restore the status quo. First the relations with the gods would be set right, and by easing the crisis which had led to the Sibylline Books, the Senate would calm the fears of the people and reestablish control over the affairs of Rome. Even when they promoted change, fundamentally the Books were a conservative device.[56]

Many scholars have tried to see the Sibylline Books primarily as the source for innovation in Roman religion, particularly with the introduction of Greek elements.[57] As evidence, supporters of this view point to institutions such as the *lectisternium*, when the gods were displayed on ritual couches in front of their temples, and the *supplicatio*, a day of public prayer during which the people thronged the temples; both of these are considered to be *Graecus ritus* introduced by the Books and hence foreign to the original nature of Roman religion. Further evidence is adduced from the foreign deities who were imported under the auspices of the Sibyl, i.e. Ceres, who is considered the Roman version of Demeter, Aesculapius, Venus Erycina, and the Magna Mater. The issues surrounding deities introduced by the Books will be postponed for discussion until Section II of this

---

(Livy 38.45.3). The consultation that produced these verses is not recorded elsewhere. That Manlius and his supporters apparently did not claim the oracle was a fraud provides a powerful argument that there was a genuine Sibylline oracle for Manlius' enemies to use, despite its unusual prophetic nature.

[55] The danger against which the Senate was protecting itself materialized in 63 B.C.E. as part of the Catilinarian conspiracy. According to both Cicero (*Cat.* 3.9–11) and Sallust (47.2), P. Lentulus Sura had tried to sway the Allobrogian ambassadors by referring to a Sibylline prophecy that three Cornelii were to rule the city: Sulla and Cinna had been the first two, and Lentulus was the third. Whether this prophecy was genuine and if so where Lentulus got it remain a mystery, but it was undoubtedly to guard against this potential problem that Augustus eventually ordered all prophetic books to be surrendered to the urban praetor (Suet., *Aug.* 31; Tac., *Ann.* 6.12). The significance of Tarquin, a member of a family no longer existing at Rome, as purchaser of the Books is particularly acute here: no Roman had an inside connection to the Sibyl.

[56] On the odd relationship between conservatism and change in Roman religion, see the article by J. A. North (1976).

[57] E.g. Wissowa, *RKR* 358; Latte, *RRG* 243–5; Fowler, *RERP* 256–65; Bailey (1932), 127; Dumézil, *ARR* 568–9.

chapter. The concern here is with the rites introduced by the Sibylline
Books and we will see that the evidence does not support the theory
that the Sibylline Books were used primarily for Greek innovations
to Roman religion. While it is true that many Greek elements came
to Roman religion by means of the Sibylline Books, to argue that such
activity is the basic function of the Books is a gross overstatement.

To begin with, the injunction to celebrate a *lectisternium* or to build
a temple for a Greek god is far from the only type of order given by
the Sibylline Books. On many occasions, the Books required such
typically "Roman" actions as a sacrifice or a *novemdiale sacrum*, a nine-
day observance, which do not have a Hellenic origin.[58] In one instance the appointment of a dictator *feriarum constituendarum causa*, a
quintessentially Roman institution, followed the consultation of the
Books; the dictator then set a day for *supplicationes*.[59] On at least four
occasions the Books called for a *lustratio*, the ritual cleansing of the
city, which was another Roman rite used especially to mark the end
of the census, and on five other occasions *ludi* were instituted on
account of the Sibyl's response. Even at the height of the panic caused
by Hannibal, the Sibyl recommended that the Romans hold a *ver
sacrum*, an ancient Italic custom in which all animals born during
that spring belonged to the gods.[60] Most of the consultations of the
Sibylline Books did not result in the addition of Greek religious rites
to the Roman religious system.

Even such acts as the *lectisternium* or the *supplicatio* were not as foreign
as they first appear to be. The Roman custom of the *daps* or the
epulum Iovis was long established before 399. While there seems to
have been a significant difference between that ritual and the *lectisternium*, which was more similar to the Greek *theoxenia*, the custom of
providing a meal for the gods was at least known to the Romans.[61]
This implies that the Romans had already begun to anthropomorphise
their gods, contrary to those who wish to place most of the blame

---

[58] E.g. Livy 35.9, 36. 37, 40.45, 42.2.3; Obs. 35.

[59] Livy 7.28.6–8.

[60] The *ver sacrum* is part of long list of expiations which is often taken as evidence
of the Greek intrusions into Roman religion, because it also included temples to
Venus Erycina and Mens, a *lectisternium* and a *supplicatio* (Livy 22.9.8). However, it
also included *ludi magni* for Jupiter in addition to the *ver sacrum*, so the best one can
say about this list is that it involved a mix of imported Greek and native Roman
elements.

[61] On the *epulum Iovis* and the *lectisternium*, see Wissowa, *RKR* 356–57; Altheim,
HRR 238; Fowler, *RERP* 263; Latte, *RRG* 243.

for this feature on the Greeks.[62] Other innovations connected with the *lectisternium* might have no relation to the Sibylline Books. For instance, *ludi scenici* first appeared in 364 following a *lectisternium*, but Livy ascribes this to the superstitious fears of the people after the *lectisternium* had failed to ease the plague.[63] There is no doubt that the *lectisternium* in its full form was a foreign rite, but the degree of innovation has been overstated by those who want to paint a sharp contrast between primitive and pure Roman tradition and degraded Greek practices.

The institution of the *supplicatio* seems even less foreign than the *lectisternium* and owes even less to the Sibylline Books.[64] The first recorded *supplicatio* occurred in 463, ordered by the Senate, without a consultation of the Sibylline Books, because of a raging pestilence.[65] A second such ceremony in 449 was also decreed by the Senate, this time to celebrate a victory over the Sabines.[66] These two examples illustrate the two different purposes of the *supplicatio*: either to beseech the gods for future aid or to thank the gods for their help in the past. Six *supplicationes* had already been held by the time of the first recorded *supplicatio* held at the behest of the Sibylline Books in 218; the only innovation here was that the ceremony was directed to a single deity, Iuventas, in the aftermath of the battle of Trebia.[67] Thereafter, the number of *supplicationes* in Livy decreed by the Senate on its own authority is equal to the number held at the suggestion of the *decemviri*, and in Cicero's time the ceremony was usually decreed by the Senate on its own.[68] Overall, of sixty *supplicationes* recorded by Livy, only seventeen were held at the instigation of the Sibylline Books, while twenty-two were decreed by the Senate or

---

[62] Cf. Bailey (1932), 109–43; Fowler, *RERP passim*.

[63] Livy 7.2.3: *Et cum vis morbi nec humanis consiliis nec ope divina levaretur, victis superstitione animis ludi scenici, nova res bellicoso populo—nam circi modo spectaculum fuerat—inter alia caelestis irae placaminia instituti dicuntur.*

[64] This point was argued as early as 1911 by J. Toutain in his article on *supplicatio* in Daremberg-Saglio, and subsequently reasserted by Hoffmann (1934), 135–38; Lake (1937); and Halkin (1953), 13. Unfortunately the force of Wissowa's opinion has largely obscured this position. Hoffmann was willing to grant that Greek elements did exist in the ritual, but believed that they entered at some point during the third century, while the original ceremony was purely Roman.

[65] Livy 3.7.7.

[66] Livy 3.63.5.

[67] Livy 21.62.

[68] Lake (1937), 248. Cf. the table of all *supplicationes* reported by Livy given by Lake on pp. 250–51.

suggested by the pontiffs.[69] These numbers should definitively refute Wissowa's theory that the *supplicatio* had to be Greek because it generally followed a consultation of the Sibylline Books.[70]

The difference between *supplicationes* decreed by the Senate on their own authority and those recommended by the Sibylline Books reflects the two different purposes for which this ceremony was held. Beginning in 217, the *supplicationes* ordered by the Senate were usually held either as thanksgivings or at the outset of a new war, or at least a new phase of a war. For instance, the Senate ordered a three-day *supplicatio* after the battle of the Metaurus and a five-day celebration when Hannibal left Italy in 203, and also ordered a three-day ceremony at the outset of the war with Philip.[71] *Supplicationes* to expiate prodigies became mainly the province of the *decemviri*, as after 217 only three were held for this purpose without their assistance. In two of those instances, the pontiffs ordered the celebration, while in the other the Senate obtained the help of the *haruspices* rather than the *decemviri* in declaring a *supplicatio*.[72] We can not say for certain why the Senate chose one board rather than another to help expiate the prodigy; the prodigies in these instances do not seem qualitatively different from those which involved the Books.[73] But if one looks at the *supplicatio* as a ritual, including its use as both a thanksgiving and an expiation, it is clear that one can not properly categorize it as a *Graecus ritus*, nor connect it too closely with the Sibylline Books.[74]

---

[69] Livy does not specify what authority ordered the *supplicatio* in the remaining twenty-one instances.

[70] The custom of celebrating the *supplicatio* wreathed with garlands, which occurred for the first time in 193 (Livy 34.55), does seem to derive from Greek sources, but it does not appear to have become a regular feature of the ceremony. Cf. Lake (1937), 248–9; Wissowa, *RKR* 424.

[71] Livy 27.51.8; 30.21.10; 33.24.4.

[72] Pontiffs: 27.37.4; 39.22.4. *Haruspices*: 32.1.14.

[73] As a point of mere speculation, I offer two possibilities. 1) The Senate may have wanted to curb its reliance on the Sibylline Books or the growing power of the *decemviri*. I find this less likely because the evidence for a growing reliance on the Books is dubious, as I have already indicated. 2) In the two instances involving the pontiffs, they acted on their own, i.e. the Senate did not ask for their advice as they did for the *haruspices*. There may well have been a rivalry between the various religious boards in Rome, so that the pontiffs were here trying to expand their power. The episode in 186 (39.22.4) is particularly revealing, for the prodigy was that the temple of Ops had been struck by lightning, and lightning was an area of expertise for the *haruspices*. On rivalry between the various priestly groups, see Bloch (1963) and Gagé (1955), who support the notion, and MacBain (1982), 56–59, who denies it.

[74] Hoffmann, (1933) 68–83 and 135–38, argued that the *supplicatio* was not closely

Before examining the new cults introduced by the Sibylline Books, let us summarize our findings to this point. The Senate kept a tight control on the Sibylline Books and was intimately involved in any action stemming from the Books. The Senate had to order the original consultation, following whatever prodigy they deemed to require it, and then after *decemviri*, who were often senators themselves, had examined the scrolls, the Senate had to take the response and decide on a course of action to implement its advice. The Sibyl's responses were generally limited to recommending a particular ritual in order to appease the wrath of the gods, which if successful would help to ease the crisis and pacify the populace. Many of the Greek rituals which found their way to Rome did arrive through the mediation of the Sibylline Books, but most responses involved rites which were well-known to the Romans and had Italic origins. Bearing these features in mind, we can turn our attention to the new temples which were built in Rome on the advice of the Sibylline Books.

II. *The Sibylline Books and the Construction of New Temples*

II.1 *The Cults and Their Origins*

The Sibylline Books motivated the construction of eight temples in Rome: Ceres, Liber and Libera, dedicated in 493; Aesculapius, in 291; Hercules Custos, probably in the third century; Flora, in 241 or 238; Mens and Venus Erycina in 215; Magna Mater (Cybele), begun in 204 but not dedicated until 191; and Venus Verticordia, begun in 114.[75] Some scholars have sought to add the temples of Mercury, dedicated in 495, and Apollo, dedicated in 431, to this list, mostly because they are Greek gods. However, the reasoning quickly becomes circular: Mercury and Apollo must have been introduced by the Sibylline Books because they were Greek gods, which proves the theory

---

linked with the *lectisternium*, a point with which I entirely agree. It does seem that the *lectisternium* was generally held following a consultation of the Books, and I believe it was the supposed connection between the *lectisternium* and the *supplicatio* which has led to the mistaken belief that the latter was a *Graecus ritus* connected with the Books.

[75] Ceres, Liber & Libera: Dion. Hal. 6.17; Aesculapius: Livy 10.47; Hercules Custos: Ovid, *Fasti* 6.209; Flora: Velleius 1.14.8 (241), Pliny *NH* 18.286 (238); Mens and Venus Erycina: Livy 22.9; Magna Mater: Livy 29.10; Venus Verticordia: Ovid, *Fasti* 4.157.

that Greek gods were introduced by the Sibylline Books. Wissowa
assumed Sibylline involvement in the foundation of the temple of
Mercury, based on that god's participation in the *lectisternium* of 399.[76]
However, we have no evidence at all for the introduction of Mercury into Rome, and, as we have seen, the Greek nature of the god
is not sufficient to prove the involvement of the Sibylline Books.[77]

Apollo's connection to the Books is more problematic. Some scholars
have felt that Apollo's nature as the god of prophecy means that he
came to Rome along with the Sibylline Books.[78] Yet Apollo had no
apparent connection to the Roman oracles until Augustus moved the
Sibylline Books into the new temple of Apollo on the Palatine in 28
B.C.E.; previously they had been stored in the temple of Capitoline
Jupiter, although a temple to Apollo existed from 431. Livy's account of the founding of that temple has often been misconstrued,
leading to further confusion. He states that during a plague, a temple
was vowed to Apollo for the people's health; in the following sentence he reports that the *duumviri* did many things from the Books
for placating the anger of the gods and averting the plague from the
people.[79] The separation of the temple and the Sibylline Books into
separate clauses seems to indicate that the vow of a temple to Apollo
was not one of the things accomplished by order of the Books.[80]
Worship of Apollo in Rome prior to this temple is known by a reference in Livy to a meeting of the Senate in an *Apollinar* in 449, but
we have no evidence for how this cult originated.[81] In the absence of
positive evidence linking the introduction of Apollo or Mercury to
the Sibylline Books, it is best to exclude them from this study and
concentrate on the eight temples which were certainly erected through
Sibylline intervention.

As we examine the cults introduced to Rome by the Sibylline Books,
let us keep in mind the theory of Greek innovations, i.e. that the
prime function of the Sibylline Books was to bring Greek deities to
Rome. As we noted above, supporters of this view point to Ceres,

---

[76] Wissowa, *RKR* 248.
[77] Cf. Latte, *RRG* 162–63; Parke (1988), 212, n. 5; and the argument throughout
this chapter.
[78] Wissowa, *RKR* 239–40; de Sanctis, *SdR* 2.503–504; Bailey (1932), 122–23. Latte,
RRG 221–22, opposed this notion.
[79] Livy 4.25.3: *Aedes Apollini pro valetudine populi vota est. Multa duumviri ex libris placandae
deum irae avertendaeque a populo pestis causa fecere; magna tamen clades . . .*
[80] Only Dumézil, *ARR* 442, to my knowledge has appreciated this point.
[81] Livy 3.63.7.

Aesculapius, Venus Erycina and Magna Mater as the primary evidence. The latter three at first glance certainly seem to support this argument. For instance, in 293 the Sibylline Books were consulted because a serious plague was afflicting Rome and had resisted other attempts at expiation. The Books directed that Aesculapius should be brought from Epidauros to Rome, which was accomplished by an embassy the following year under the leadership of Q. Ogulnius.[82] The cult was brought directly to Rome from Epidauros in the form of a sacred snake; there could be no question that this was the Greek cult of the healing god.

When speaking of Venus Erycina and Magna Mater, one must bear in mind that these were not Greek cults, but rather one Punic and one Phrygian. The argument can only proceed if we expand the theory to include all foreign overseas cults brought to Rome through the mediation of the Sibylline Books. A temple to Venus Erycina was included as part of the list of expiations prescribed by the Books following the battle at Lake Trasimene in 217.[83] This was the Venus from Mount Eryx, a hilltop on the western, Punic-dominated, side of Sicily, with whom the Romans had become acquainted during the First Punic War, when she had proven to be of great assistance.[84] Following the Roman disasters at Trebia and Trasimene in the opening stages of the Second Punic War, the Sibylline Books recommended that a temple be erected to this goddess who had been so helpful in the first struggle against the Punic foe.

At the other end of the war, the Magna Mater was introduced after the fighting in Italy was essentially over. In 205, two years after the battle of the Metaurus had isolated Hannibal in Italy, a Sibylline oracle recommended that "when a foreign enemy should bring war to Italian soil, he may be driven from Italy and defeated if the Idaean mother should be brought from Pessinus to Rome."[85] The Romans accordingly fetched the black stone from Phrygia which was considered to represent the goddess, and installed her in the temple of Victoria on the Palatine hill until her own temple was completed in

---

[82] For the details of Aesculapius' introduction, see Val. Max. 1.8.2; Livy 10.47 and ep. 11; Ovid, *Fasti* 1.291–2 and *Met.* 15.622–744; and *De Vir. Ill.* 22.

[83] Livy 22.9.8.

[84] Cf. Polybius' account of the fighting around Eryx, 1.55–58. The goddess may predate the Carthaginian occupation of this part of Sicily, but in 217 the Romans certainly considered the goddess Punic.

[85] Livy, 29.10.4–5: *quandoque hostis alienigena terrae Italiae bellum intulisset, eum pelli Italia vincique posse, si mater Idaea a Pessinunte Romam advecta foret.*

191.[86] Aesculapius, Venus Erycina, and the Magna Mater are all non-Italian deities whose introduction to Rome was explicitly ordered by the Sibylline Books, and so they could support the "foreign elements" hypothesis.

The case of Ceres, however, does not provide the same solid support for this hypothesis. It has been noted that the Books did not explicitly order the Romans to build a temple to this goddess.[87] According to Dionysius of Halicarnassus, the Sibylline Books commanded that Ceres, Liber and Libera should be propitiated (ἐξιλάσασθαι); Postumius, hearing this, vowed to build a temple and create an annual sacrifice if abundance returned to the land.[88] When the crops did return, Postumius had a vote passed in the Senate to build the temple. The Books only called for propitiation, without specifying the need for a temple; it was the dictator, supported by the Senate, who interpreted the oracle and decided that building a temple was the appropriate action. The role of the Senate and its magistrate were more decisive than the Sibyl in erecting a temple in Rome for Ceres and her cult partners Liber and Libera.

Furthermore, the evidence for Ceres as a Greek deity in 493 is highly questionable. Although Dionysius, our primary source for these events, names the triad as Demeter, Dionysius, and Kore, the identification of Ceres, Liber, and Libera with these Greek deities seems to be a late development, one appropriate in Dionyius's time but not in the early fifth century.[89] The Greek cult was always focused on the twosome Demeter and Kore; when a male divinity was added, he was a subordinate, not a full partner as in the Roman cult.[90] Rather, the cult introduced in 493 seems to be an original Roman creation, produced by combining two Italic dyads, Ceres/Liber and Liber/

---

[86] For the events described here, see Livy 29.10.4–29.11.8; 29.14.5–9; 29.37.2; 36.36.3–5. Cf. also Ovid, *Fasti* 4.249–272; *De Vir. Ill.* 46.1–3; Val. Max. 1.8.11. For modern studies see Graillot (1912); Vermaseren (1977); Thomas, (1984); Gruen, (1990) 5–33; and most recently Burton (1996).

[87] Radke, *RE* col. 1122.

[88] Dion. Hal. 6.17.

[89] Thus the reference in Cicero, *Balb.* 55, to the *sacra Cereris* which were brought over from Greece and supervised by Greek priestesses from Naples or Velia refers to a later development of the cult of Ceres. Both Le Bonniec (1958), 381–395, and Spaeth (1996), 11–12, view this as a new cult introduced in Rome in the second half of the third century.

[90] Cf. the discussion of Demeter and Kore in Burkert (1985), 159–161, where Dionysius is not even mentioned in connection with the Two Goddesses.

Libera.[91] Furthermore, according to Vitruvius the architecture of the temple reflected Tuscan, not Greek, design, and may have had a triple cella such as the temple of Capitoline Jupiter.[92] While there may have been some Greek influence in this cult, as reflected in the tradition that the temple was decorated by the Greek artists Damophilos and Gorgasos,[93] the desire for such Greek artistic influences would hardly justify the use of the Sibylline Books. Since this cult is essentially Italic, the theory of Greek innovation fails to account for its connection to the Sibyl.

Several other deities who can not be considered Greek or foreign also received temples in Rome on the advice of the Sibylline books. It appears that in either 241, according to Velleius Paterculus, or 238, according to Pliny the Elder, a temple to Flora was dedicated following a Sibylline oracle as the result of a prolonged drought.[94] The circumstances were similar to those surrounding the introduction of Ceres and Aesculapius: nature was wreaking havoc on the Roman people. However, Flora was not a Greek deity, but an old established Italian one.[95] Roman legend held that Titus Tatius had erected an altar to her, and she had her own priest, the *flamen Floralis*, a particular feature of some of the oldest cults at Rome.[96] Furthermore, she received, along with such ancient Roman cults as Janus, Jupiter, Juno, and Vesta, sacrifice from the Arval Brethren in their sacred grove.[97] Flora evidently had an established cult in Rome long before the Sibylline Books ordered the erection of a temple to her, so we can not consider that she was introduced to Rome by the Sibyl. Neither novelty nor Greekness can account for the involvement of the Sibylline Books with her temple.

---

[91] Le Bonniec (1958), 292–305, Spaeth (1996), 6–11.

[92] Vitruvius 3.3.5.

[93] Pliny, *HN* 35.154.

[94] Velleius 1.14.8; Pliny *NH* 18.286. These authors, however, mention only the institution of annual games to Flora, with Pliny noting the role of the Sibylline oracle. The temple is known from Ovid, *Fasti* 5.275–330, who mentions the construction of a temple and the celebration of games by the aediles L. and M. Publicius. Tacitus (*Ann.* 2.49) also mentions the Publicii as the founders of the temple, while Varro (*LL* 5.158) and Festus (276 L) mention the Publicii in connection with the construction of the *clivus Publicius*. I follow most modern scholars in accepting that the temple was built at this time; cf. Platner & Ashby (1929); Broughton, *MRR* 1.219–220 and n. 3; Degrassi (1963), 450–452.

[95] For the Italian nature of Flora see Steuding, *Myth. Lex.*, s.v. Flora; Fowler *RERP*, 91–95; Scullard (1981), 110.

[96] Titus Tatius: Varro *LL* 5.74; *Flamen*: Varro *LL* 7.45.

[97] Henzen, *Acta Frat. Arv.* 146.

Still in the third century, the Sibylline Books recommended the construction of a temple to Mens, the personification of Forethought or the Mind. This advice followed the disastrous defeat inflicted on the Romans by Hannibal at Lake Trasimene and was only one of a number of suggestions, including a temple to Venus Erycina as well.[98] Mens is a typical example of a goddess created from an abstract concept, a very Roman practice, following such examples as Concordia (304), Victoria (294), and the two temples to Spes and Fides (First Punic War), among others. Indeed both Cicero and Pliny include Mens when listing good examples of Roman values which warranted deification.[99] There is no justification for viewing Mens as a Greek deity *a priori* because of the connection with the Sibylline Books and Venus Erycina.[100] The temples of Venus Erycina and Mens do have certain connections; not only were they vowed at the same time, but they were dedicated in the same year and their temples on the Capitol were separated by a single water channel.[101] Yet their *dies natales* were on separate days, and they had different functions. The martial aspect of Venus Erycina was very important to the Romans, while Mens served as a reminder to plan the campaign and to choose carefully when to engage in a pitched battle; martial valor was to be reserved for those picked circumstances.[102] The goddesses were clearly complementary, but separate; Mens can not be considered Greek by association. Mens, like Flora, was given a temple by the Sibylline Books even though she followed in a Roman tradition.

The last temple to be built on the order of the Sibylline Books was that of Venus Verticordia in 114, following a consultation pro-

---

[98] Livy 22.9. See above, n. 60.

[99] Cicero, *ND* 3.88 and *Leg.* 2.19 and 2.28, lists Mens with Virtus, Fides, and Pietas. Pliny, *NH* 2.14, gives Mens with Pudicitia, Concordia, Spes, Honos, and Fides. On these "abstract" deities, see Axtell (1907); Fears (1981).

[100] Wissowa (*RKR* 259) wanted to see Mens as part of the Greek circle of gods because of the connection with Venus Erycina and because the consultation of the Sibylline Books served as *a priori* evidence of a Greek deity. The only evidence of Mens as a Greek goddess is the existence of a cult of Bona Mens in the Greek colony of Paestum, as demonstrated by a coin depicting a goddess sitting on a throne with a legend identifying her as Bona Mens (*BMC Italy* 280, 56). However, the coin can not be securely dated, and even so it would be unrealistic to assume that Greek colonies in Italy can only have worshipped Greek deities. The involvement of the Sibyl, as we have shown several times, can not be considered sufficient to establish a Greek heritage. See also Mello (1968).

[101] Livy 23.31.9: *utraque in Capitolio est, canali uno discretae.*

[102] For the martial aspect of Venus Erycina, see Schilling (1954), 243–44; Galinsky (1969), 186.

voked by incest on the part of three Vestal Virgins.[103] By this time
Venus had long been established in Rome and even Venus Verticordia
was already known; the Sibylline Books had previously recommended
that the most chaste of the matrons dedicate a statue to her.[104]
Verticordia was the goddess who changes hearts from lust towards
chastity, and so this temple was dedicated to a different aspect of
Venus, but not to an entirely new deity. In this sense, the temple to
Venus Verticordia parallels the temple to Hercules Custos, which
will be discussed shortly; both were ordered by the Sibylline Books
to a different aspect of deity who had long been worshipped in Rome.
The erection of this temple at this time seems to represent an attempt to turn this goddess back towards a more suitable concept, at
least from the standpoint of the male Roman aristocracy. By the end
of the second century the identification of Venus with Aphrodite had
long been made, and the temple of Venus Erycina *extra portam Collinam*
apparently reproduced some of the more lascivious aspects of its Punic
mother cult.[105] Thus the Sibylline Books in this case were promoting
a distinctly. Roman twist on a goddess whose nature had been al-
tered recently by foreign elements, and for the worse in the eyes of
the Roman ruling elite. This case militates strongly against explaining the use of the Sibylline oracles by reference to the introduction
of Greek elements.

Several Greek deities which came to Rome completely without
the assistance of the Sibylline oracles strike another blow against this
theory. For instance, worship of Hercules goes back as far as Romulus,
according to Livy, and the historian explicitly states that Romulus
used the Greek rite which had been instituted by the Arcadian
Evander.[106] Livy's account of such early worship and the connection

---

[103] Ovid, *Fasti* 4.157–160; Obs. 37.

[104] Val. Max 8.15.12. Sulpicia, wife of Q. Fulvius Flaccus and daughter of Servius
Paterculus, was chosen to dedicate the statue. The episode is therefore usually placed
in the late third century.

[105] Cf. Schilling (1954), 260–262, who analyzes the evidence in detail and describes an "erotic climate" around the temple. His conclusion is based on several
passages in Ovid's *Fasti* (4.133–134, 4.865–868) which indicate the she was particularly favored by prostitutes. An epigraphical note on the calendar even indicates
that the *dies natalis* of this temple was known as the *dies meretricum* (*CIL* I² 316). These
do not seem to be actual "temple prostitutes" such as the Punic cult had, but that
element of the Punic cult may have encouraged the prostitutes of Rome to use this
temple as their base.

[106] Livy 1.7.3: *Sacra dis aliis Albano ritu, Graeco Herculi, ut ab Evandro instituta erant,
facit.*

with Evander may be apocryphal, but it indicates two essential facts:
1) that he considered Hercules to be one of the oldest cults worshipped in Rome, and 2) that he recognized Hercules as a Greek
hero. Other sources confirm that Hercules continued to be worshipped
graeco ritu in Rome.[107] The origins of Hercules worship in Rome went
back beyond the point at which any Roman antiquarian could trace
them, and we may have confidence that it antedated the acquisition
of the Sibylline Books, whenever we wish to place that acquisition. A
temple to Hercules Custos was indeed built on the order of the
Sibylline Books at a later date, probably in the third century.[108] Since
this is not the first known cult of Hercules in Rome, however, it can
hardly be adduced to support the theory that the Sibylline Books
introduced Greek gods and practices to Rome; Hercules was already
known in Rome.

Hercules was not the only Greek god brought to Rome without
the use of the Sibylline Books, so it can not be claimed that Hercules is an exception only because there were no Sibylline Books
when he came to Rome. Examples of Greek deities brought to Rome
without the intervention of the Sibylline Books can be found from
the post-Sibyl period. A temple to the Dioscuri, Castor and Pollux,
was vowed in 499 and dedicated in 484; the construction of this
temple overlapped the construction of the earliest known temple
erected following a consultation of the Sibylline Books, the temple of
Ceres. Castor and Pollux may have come to Rome via Tusculum,
which was a center for their worship in Latium.[109] Such an origin
suits the legend of their participation in the battle at Lake Regillus,
which lay in the territory of Tusculum. However, they may also
have come from Lavinium, where an archaic inscription was found
which reads *Castorei Podlouqueique qurois*.[110] The last word, an obvious

---

[107] Macrobius, 3.16.17, following Varro. See also Plutarch, *QR* 60, which describes the exclusion of women, a feature found in many Greek cults of Hercules.
On the origins of Hercules in Rome, see Bayet (1926). Almost all modern scholars
have accepted Hercules as a Greek hero. In addition to Bayet, see de Sanctis, *SdR*
2.501–502; Latte, *RRG* 214.

[108] Ovid, *Fasti* 6.209. Ovid reports that the inscription names Sulla, which probably points to a Sullan restoration. The third century date is preferred by many
scholars, who place the *supplicatio* at the temple of Hercules in 218 (Livy 21.62.9) at
this temple. Cf. Scullard (1981), 146.

[109] Cf. Wissowa, *RKR* 217–18, among others. Evidence comes from mention of a
temple of Castor and Pollux in Tusculum by Cicero (*De Div.* 1.98) and numerous
inscriptions (*CIL* 14.2620, 2629, 2637, 2639, 2918 and 6.2202).

[110] See Weinstock, (1960), following the initial publication of Castagnoli in *Studi e*

transliteration of κούροις, proves better than anything that this was a Greek cult, however it reached Rome. No Roman tradition connects the Sibylline Books with the introduction of their cult in any way. To argue that Greek deities can only be introduced by the Books necessitates arguing away this very visible exception. The standard interpretation that the Sibylline Books introduced Greek deities or rites to Rome has so many holes that it is best to abandon it altogether.

II.2 *Motivations for the New Temples*

Attempting to explain the construction of temples to these eight extremely varied deities on the basis of supposed common features among them is destined to be fruitless. Rather than looking just at the cults themselves, it will be profitable to take a broader view, to examine these cults in the context of Roman temple building and in their historical contexts. We have seen that the Sibylline Books were consulted several times on account of pestilences, yet only one of these resulted in the introduction of a new god; why that one time and no others? Similarly, showers of stones were normally followed by a *novemdiale sacrum*; why in 205 did the Romans respond by introducing the Magna Mater? The standard explanations, based on the need to expiate the prodigy and reassure the populace, will not suffice.

The most salient feature about these cult introductions is that using the Sibylline Books was the only means by which the Roman Senate initiated the process of erecting a new temple in the city. As we saw in the previous chapters, most new temples arose as a result of a vow made by an individual. That the Senate itself initiated this process only eight times in the history of Rome indicates that generally they were content with the temples being constructed by individuals. But when they wanted to make a particular statement, by introducing a particular cult at a particular time, the Sibylline Books provided the mechanism to do so. Use of this procedure provided the Senate with several advantages. If the decision had been controversial on religious, cultural or political grounds, as we may imagine

---

Materiali 30 (1959), 109ff. This inscription obviously figures in much of the subsequent discussion concerning the Dioscuri. See e.g. Bloch (1960), 144–45; Schilling, (1979), 338–39 and n. 1; Scullard (1981), 65–66. On the temple of Castor and Pollux in Rome, see also Degrassi (1963), 403–404.

that some were, the Books would have the effect of muting the opposition and obscuring its existence; the divine authority would seem to
have made the decision. The combined weight of the gods and the
Senate would appear behind the action, putting that much more
emphasis into the statement. This mechanism also provided the Senate with some coverage; while Senatorial action was necessary to
implement the advice given by the Sibyl, the Books allowed the Senate,
if it so desired, to escape direct responsibility and place the onus on
the divine source. The combination of divine and human authority
gave the Senate a great deal of flexibility in expressing itself through
religious means, as a fresh examination of the new temples indicates.

In the case of the three clearly foreign cults, their introduction is
tied to the diplomatic maneuverings of the Roman Senate, involving
both political and cultural statements. In each case, both the timing
of the adoption of a new cult and the choice of cult itself are highly
significant. The directive to fetch Aesculapius from Epidauros came
only in 293, while a consultation of the Books in 295 for the same
pestilence had apparently produced no mention of Aesculapius.[111] The
key difference between these two dates is that by 293 the outcome of
the Third Samnite War was no longer in doubt. The surrender of
several Etruscan cities the previous year following the decisive battle
at Sentinum had effectively ended any chances for eventual Samnite
victory.[112] Although the Samnites continued to be a thorn in the
Roman side for another thirty years, Roman attention now began
turning toward the world known as Magna Graecia, that part of
southern Italy which was littered with Greek colonies. The Roman
campaigns against the Samnites had brought them in contact, and
indeed into conflict, with the prosperous town of Tarentum in the
southernmost part of Italy. An attempt at rapprochement during the
Second Samnite War had come to nothing. In this context, the introduction of Aesculapius, the first Greek god brought to Rome since
the fifth century, can hardly be coincidence. Only after the course of

---

[111] Livy 10.31. The remedies prescribed by the Books in 295 are not reported by
Livy.
[112] Because of the annalistic nature of Livy's sources, it is unclear whether the
consultation of 295 occurred before or after the battle of Sentinum. However, Livy
explicitly states that "even with these things having turned out thus, there was not
yet peace either with the Samnites or in Etruria" (10.31.1: *his ita rebus gestis nec in
Samnitibus adhuc nec in Etruria pax erat*). Peace with Volsinii, Perusia, and Arretium
was, as Livy says (10.37.4–5) "more important than the fighting had been."

the Samnite war was clear and Roman attention turned to the Greek states of southern Italy did the Romans invite the new god to Rome. The adoption of Aesculapius by the Romans would have been a signal that the Romans sought to enter the world of Greek culture rather than to impose their own Italic customs on southern Italy. As J. Scheid has remarked, "the cult of Aesculapius was able to play the role of federator and integrator for the cities of Magna Graecia."[113]

But there was still another way in which the welcoming of Aesculapius to Rome might serve Roman aims. At this same time, in 291, Rome established a particularly large colony at Venusia.[114] This site was extremely advantageous for the Romans, for it could serve the dual purpose of encircling the defeated Samnites as well as dominating both Lucania and Apulia.[115] The Romans clearly recognized the possibility of trouble coming from the South; an attempt at rapprochement with Tarentum had come to nothing, recent relations with that city had been strained, and the founding of the colony at Venusia could only cause further friction.[116] The extent of the wars with Pyrrhus were probably not envisioned at this time, but conflict may well have seemed likely. In this situation, Roman diplomatic overtures to the Greek colonies of southern Italy take on an added significance. The introduction of the cult of Aesculapius to Rome was not meant merely as a general token of Roman attitudes, but could also have served as a specific bid for support in preparation for a possible conflict in which the support of the Greek towns

---

[113] Scheid (1985), 97–98. See *contra* Musial (1990), 234–5. So far, archaeological evidence of an Asclepium has been discovered only in Latium at Fregellae, but the earliest phase is dated to the beginning of the second century, after the introduction of Aesculapius in Rome, and it appears that this cult reached Fregellae without coming through Rome; see Degrassi (1986). This lack of evidence for worship of Aesculapius in Italy may be due simply to the vagaries of archaeological discoveries. The colonies of Magna Graecia, through their overseas trade with mainland Greece, were surely aware of the cult, especially as the third century saw a tremendous boom in the popularity of Aesclepius in Greece and Ionia.

[114] For the foundation of Venusia see Vell. Pat. 1.14.6; Diodorus 17/18.5.

[115] The importance of the site is noted by Salmon (1967), 275 n. 4.

[116] Appian (*Samn.* 7) reports a treaty "of long standing" between Rome and Tarentum in the context of the outbreak of hostilities in 282. This treaty has been dated anywhere from 348 to 303, but whatever the date it can not be used as evidence of amicable relations in the early third century. Diodorus (20.104.1) reports hostilities between the two sides c. 303, and Roman successes in the Third Samnite War can hardly have eased tensions. Cf. Salmon (1967), 281 and n. 2, who believes that "Tarentine hostility to Rome had long been smouldering" at the outbreak of the war with Rome.

might be decisive.[117] The Sibylline Books allowed the Roman Senate
to put the full weight of divine sanction and their own corporate
approval behind this diplomatic maneuvering.

The action of introducing Venus Erycina to Rome also appears to
be part of a diplomatic initiative, this time in the context of a crisis
at the beginning of a war rather than in anticipation of possible
future conflict. To the best of our knowledge the Roman government had not capitalized on the legend of Rome's Trojan ancestors
prior to the Second Punic War.[118] Rather, it had appeared in some
writers and been used against the Romans by Pyrrhus in 281 B.C.E.
seeking to rouse animosity towards Rome on the basis of the old
enmity towards Troy.[119] It had also been used by states seeking alliance with Rome on the basis on consanguinity, such as when Segesta
defected to the Roman side during the First Punic War on the basis
of a claimed common ancestor, Aeneas.[120] Eryx had played a major
role in the fighting in the latter stages of the First Punic War, and
the Romans had responded by paying honors to the tutelary goddess
of the mountain stronghold. Thirty years ago D. Kienast showed
how the legends of Trojan descent for both Rome and Eryx facili-
tated the Romans' taking control of the sanctuary following that war.[121]
And yet the timing of the goddess' actual entry into Rome was not
accidental; the situation in 217 demanded further action. Sicily had
been the major theater of war in the First Punic War, and in particular the western part of Sicily, including the area around Mt. Eryx,
had been a Carthaginian possession for a significant period of time
prior to the First Punic War. Even the cult of Venus on Mt. Eryx
was essentially Punic.[122] The Romans had good reason to be appre-
hensive about their position in Sicily; there was no guarantee that
the states there would not defect back to Carthage when given the
chance. Furthermore, given the damage which Hannibal was wreak-

---

[117] The importance of Venusia in conjunction with the introduction of Aesculapius
was also noted by Altheim, *HRR* 283.

[118] On the Trojan legend in Rome, see in general Perret (1942); Galinsky (1969);
Gruen (1992), 6–51.

[119] Pausanias 1.12.1.

[120] Zon. 8.9.12. See also Diodorus 23.5. Segesta also minted coins depicting Aeneas
carrying Anchises on his back: *BMC Sicily*, 59ff.

[121] Kienast (1965).

[122] Cf. Schilling (1954), 233–242, and Kienast (1965), 480. This conclusion is based
on evidence for the worship of Astarte, along with the presence of rituals such as
temple prostitution and the annual release of a dove from the sanctuary. Cf. *ILS*
5505; Val. Max. 2.6.15; Aelian, *Var. Hist.* 1.15.

ing in northern Italy, secure possession of Sicily and her grain supply was doubly important to the Romans. Bringing the goddess to
Rome and adopting her as part of the Roman state religion made a
significant statement to the inhabitants of northwest Sicily. By welcoming the Venus of Mt. Eryx into their own home and installing
her in a place of honor on the Capitoline hill, the Romans publicly
affirmed the kinship between the two peoples, a kinship which had
only recently been "discovered". By this act the Romans hoped to
bind those states more tightly to them and solidify their allegiance
for the coming struggle.

Similar characteristics can be seen in the introduction of the Magna
Mater at the other end of the Second Punic War. E. Gruen has
recently argued that the desire to bring Cybele to Rome arose not
from a feeling of despair and weakness during a dark moment of the
Hannibalic war, but represents an attempt to foster relationships with
the states of the Greek East.[123] Although the war with Hannibal was
not over when this temple was vowed in 205, the battle of Metaurus
had cut off Hannibal from supplies and relief forces and it was clear
to the Romans that the danger had passed.[124] The only remaining
issue was how best to bring the war to its conclusion, and in this
context a Sibylline oracle referring to driving a foreign enemy from
Italian soil must be regarded with suspicion. Even more suspicion is
raised by the fact that the consultation was occasioned by repeated
showers of stones, a relatively frequent prodigy that was normally
expiated by a *novemdiale sacrum* without consulting the Books.[125] There

---

[123] Gruen (1990) , 5–33. The notion that Rome reached out for the Magna Mater
in a time of crisis was championed by H. Graillot (1909) and recently defended
against Gruen's view by P. Burton (1996). The danger in assuming that the Romans only adopted foreign cults when they felt their own gods to be insufficient has
already been pointed out; cf. Chapter One, pp. 12–14.

[124] Gruen (1990), 6–7. Cf. Polybius 11.3.6, and Livy 27.51.10, 28.11.8–11, for
recognition by the Romans of the significance of the battle at the Metaurus. Burton
(1996), 38–41, tries to downplay this evidence by pointing to 1) the lapse of time
between the battle and consultation of the Books in 205 and 2) other problems
faced by Rome in 205, including a potential new threat from Mago. In regard to 1),
Livy reports (28.9.6–7) that the whole populace streamed out to the temple of Bellona
to greet the victorious generals; the subsequent joint triumph in late 207 and the
sending of a golden wreath to Delphi precisely in 205 (Livy 28.45.12) would have
continued to highlight the importance of the battle. In regard to 2), the Senate can
not have been panicked by this threat if they sent an army of ex-slaves to guard the
Gallic frontier while allowing Scipio to continue his preparations in Sicily for an
invasion of Africa.

[125] E.g. Livy 1.31, 23.31.15, 35.9.3–5. Cf. MacBain (1982), 82–106, for a index

was neither a military crisis nor a religious crisis which demanded
that the Romans import a new cult in order to handle this situation, which strongly implies that ulterior motives are involved here.[126]
Both the timing and the deity chosen for acceptance in Rome need
explanation.

The Roman shortcomings in the First Macedonian War provide
the clue.[127] Regardless of the degree of Rome's committment to this
war, the Peace of Phoenice concluded in 205 had left Rome with a
bad reputation in the East.[128] The Roman adoption of the Magna
Mater was undoubtedly intended to make a declaration to all parties
concerned about Rome's continuing interest in the region and may
have helped the cause of Roman diplomacy in three ways. First, it
reaffirmed Rome's alliance with Attalus, whose help was actively sought
in bringing the Magna Mater to Rome.[129] Secondly, it warned Philip
that the Romans had not permanently departed from Asia Minor,
but were merely taking a temporary hiatus to conclude their business with Hannibal. Finally, just as it served to warn Philip, so it
reassured the Greek states of the area that the Romans continued to
have a strong interest in this region, by emphasizing their cultural
links and perhaps even their common ancestry. Gruen has argued
that the Magna Mater was actually summoned from Mt. Ida in the
Troad and thus represented an attempt, as with Venus Erycina, to
capitalize on the legend of Trojan origins.[130] Yet the specific home

---

of prodigies which includes many other instances of a *novemdiale sacrum*. This prodigy
is hardly "alarming" enough to account for the "gloomy picture" which Burton, 42
and n. 29, wants to describe.

[126] Burton, 61, shies away from suggestions of "tampering" with either the Sibylline Books or the Delphic oracle in 205. Yet instances of tampering with the Books
have been discussed already, and tampering with Delphi was possible also; cf. the
Alcmaeonid bribery of the oracle in their attempts to remove the Peisistratids from
Athens (Hdt. 5.62). Such tampering in no way negated or reduced the religious
efficacy of the action.

[127] For a fuller treatment of this point, see Gruen (1990), 27–33.

[128] Cf. Polybius 9.37.5–8, 9.39.1–3, 11.5.4–8, 31.31.19, 32.21.17; Livy 29.12.1,
31.29, 32.22.10.

[129] For the role of Attalus, see Livy 29.11.2–7; Varro *LL* 6.15. Even Burton, 62,
acknowledges that "the Magna Mater episode comprised a reassertion of friendship
between the two states."

[130] Gruen (1990), 15–20, who bases his conclusions on the account of Ovid (*Fasti*
4.247–348) and on repeated references to the *mater Idaea* (Livy 29.10.5, 29.14.5;
Cicero *De Sen.* 45). In fact, the *Fasti Praenestini* (admittedly of Augustan date) indicate
that the goddess was officially known in Rome as the *mater deum magna Idaea* (*Inscr.
Ital.* 13.2, 127). Burton (1996), 43–58, however has reaffirmed the standard view
that the Magna Mater came from Pessinus, based on Livy, 29.10.5 and Cicero *HR*

of the goddess may be less important than the overall statement made by the importation of a goddess hailing from Asia Minor whom the Romans *claimed* as an ancestor; the Romans thus made it clear that they had no intentions of exiting the Greek world for good.[131] The Sibylline Books provided the perfect medium for bringing the Magna Mater to Rome, putting the divine stamp of approval onto the statement being made to Attalus, Philip and the Greeks.[132]

In the case of Ceres, the relevant feature for her introduction was not her place of origin, but rather her links with the plebs of Rome. The battle of Lake Regillus had seen the dictator A. Postumius vow a temple to Castor and Pollux, the patron of cavalry and hence of the wealthier segment of the Roman population. According to the tradition on the Struggle of the Orders, plebeian agitation grew in the ensuing years, culminating in the first Secession of the Plebs. Furthermore, the dearth reported by Dionysius as the immediate motivation for the temple would have affected the plebs disproportionately.[133] The construction of a temple to Ceres, in addition to addressing the problem of famine, may have been intended to ease tension with the plebs. Ceres had numerous ties to the plebs, at least

---

27–28. However, Cicero's evidence is of little value; his representation that Italy was "worn out by the Punic War" is a rhetorical flourish, and the orator refers to Pessinus only as "the seat and dwelling place of the mother of the gods." As Gruen points out (19), while Pessinus may have been the most ancient sanctuary of the goddess, that consideration need not have affected the events of 205/4. Given the evidence of nomenclature, of the apparent lack of contact between Rome and Pessinus prior to 189, and of numerous other Roman attempts to capitalize on the Trojan link at this time, Gruen's suggestion is persuasive.

[131] Even while denying the Idaean origins of the Magna Mater, Burton (1996), 58, acknowledges that there were "overtones of Trojan ancestry" in the events of 205/4 which "reflect *Roman* predilections" (emphasis original). This is precisely the point: whether or not the goddess was viewed this way in Asia Minor, the Roman willingness to adopt this interpretation and make a public statement of consanguinity sent a powerful message.

[132] It is worth noting that there were actually *two* stamps of divine approval in this case, for the Romans also checked with the Delphic oracle as to whether their action was correct. The Delphic oracle may have been a more respectable and reliable divine authority than the Sibylline Books for the members of the Greek world. This again indicates that Rome saw herself as fully a member of that world, despite her current preoccupation with Hannibal.

[133] Livy 2.23–30. Dion. Hal. 6.17. Livy (2.27.5) may record a trace of the famine when he notes that the Senate referred to the people for a decision on who was to dedicate the temple of Mercury, for he indicates that this person was also to have charge of the grain supply. The people gave this task to neither consul, but to a senior centurion, M. Laetorius, whom they obviously trusted more than the consuls. This story may be apocryphal, highlighting the divisions between the Orders, but the mention of the grain supply may be a genuine detail.

one of which is attested at an early date; persons violating the sac-
rosanctity of the *tribuni plebis* were to have their goods consecrated to
Ceres.[134] Roman tradition dated the First Secession of the Plebs and
the creation of the tribunate to the same year as the foundation of
the temple to Ceres; while this dating may be ahistorical, the linkage
reflects the linkage which existed between the temple and the plebs
in Roman minds.[135] A further confirmation of this connection is the
location of the temple itself on the Aventine hill, site of the plebeian
secessions. The temple of Ceres eventually seems to have served as
the headquarters for the plebeian aediles, including the archive of
the plebs and a treasury.[136] The temple of Ceres may have been intended to balance out the temple of Castor: one predominantly plebeian, one predominantly patrician, both initiated by A. Postumius.
The involvement of the Sibylline Books allowed the Senate to walk
a fine line in making a peace gesture, taking some responsibility for
interpreting the Books but not appearing to capitulate completely to
the plebs.

    Similar internally directed messages can be easily read in two more
deities introduced on the authority of the Sibylline Books. The temple
to Mens was ordered at a particularly fortuitous time, as this quality
was essential for Fabius and his new tactics.[137] The Sibylline Books
would have seemed to be endorsing Fabius' strategy, a result Fabius
no doubt intended when he pushed for consultation in the first place
and whose result he, as an augur, might have been able to arrange
through friends on the decemviral board.[138] Similarly, the temple to
Venus Verticordia had unmistakable moral overtones in the light of
the recent discovery of the unchastity of three Vestal Virgins. The
Senate no doubt wanted to impress, not just on the Vestal Virgins
but on all Roman women, its views on sexual restraint. In both these
cases the Sibylline Books provided the means by which the Senate
could introduce cults on its own, but also provided a more authoritative divine backing for the statement made by the new cult.

---

[134] Dion. Hal. 6.89; 10.42. Livy 3.55 says that the person guilty of violating a
tribune was *sacer Iovi*, but that the goods were to be sold at the temple of Ceres. On
this and other links between Ceres and the plebs, see Spaeth (1996), 81–102.

[135] Creation of the tribunes: Livy 2.33.1–3.

[136] The archive is dated to 449 by Livy (3.55.13), but this is part of his confused
account of the Valerio-Horatian laws. Cf. Spaeth (1996), 83–85.

[137] Cf. Dumézil *ARR*, 474, who makes a similar point.

[138] Certainly Fabius was closely involved in religious affairs; in addition to the
augurate, he was chosen to fill a vacancy in the pontifical college in 216.

II.3   *The Sibylline Books as an Authority*

Perhaps the most perplexing feature surrounding the Sibylline Books
is the willingness of the Romans to use clearly foreign oracles written
in Greek hexameters as the authority for making innovations, many
of them involving Greek elements, in Roman religion. J. North has
suggested that "the Sibylline oracles combine in a most economical
package the four most obvious sources of religious legitimation available at Rome—a portent, ancient tradition, foreign wisdom and
priestly authority."[139] The initial prodigy provides the sign from the
gods, then the use of the Books offers "a guarantee based on alien
wisdom and experience" and a "missing link with antiquity." As the
foregoing discussion has indicated, these points are all well-taken. Yet
it is still a curious feature that the Romans should have placed foreign wisdom on an equal level with their own ancient traditions. We
need to dig a little further, in an effort to uncover why "alien wisdom
and experience" should have mattered to the Roman ruling class.

I believe the answer lies in how the Romans wanted to present
themselves to the world around them and to themselves. Almost every
study of Roman religion has noted that the Romans were particularly tolerant of and receptive to foreign religions.[140] This is true, but
only up to a point; the Romans did not blithely accept any new cult
which they encountered as they expanded their territorial possessions. Individual Roman generals rarely made vows to foreign deities. Rather, the introduction of foreign cults and foreign rites was
left in the Senate's hands, and the Senate chose to exercise this
prerogative on only a handful of occasions, when it found something
that could be used to further Roman interests. The Sibylline Oracles,
the very mechanism by which many of these changes were introduced, exhibit this same characteristic attitude: the Roman state was
open to innovation, but that innovation had to be carefully controlled, by the Senate itself naturally, and had to be acceptable within
a Roman context. The subjection of the Sibylline Books to Roman
secular authority solved a number of problems. First and foremost, it
controlled a potential threat to the state, in the form of a religious
authority which an individual might use to seize power. The elimi-
nation of this subversive potential was the primary prerequisite for

---

[139] North, (1976), 9.
[140] See Wissowa, *RKR* 42–46 and 239–271; Fowler, *RERP* 223–269; Latte, *RRG*
148–94, 213–63; Dumézil, *AAR* 2.407–31, 446–56.

the admittance of foreign rituals. With the safeguard of the Senate's supervision, the Books themselves were made palatable to the Senate's tastes, just as foreign cults were made palatable by restricting or removing objectionable features before they were permitted entry in Rome.[141] Even with restrictions, the important statement was that the Romans were willing to adopt foreign elements, and doing so by using the Sibylline Books, themselves a foreign element, made this statement simply and eloquently. From the first use of the Sibylline Books in 496, the Roman Senate presented itself as looking outward, willing to accept religious elements of value it found in foreign traditions.[142] The legend of Tarquinius Superbus is relevant here; the story indicates that Tarquinius was reluctant at first to accept a foreign innovation, yet his eventual recognition that the Books were valuable and subsequent purchase indicate a willingness to change his ways and learn from other traditions. The story provided a superb metaphor for the Romans.

Yet there is a more significant point to be made concerning the acceptance of foreign wisdom and its subjection to the Senate's authority. The Senate not only permitted the existence of the Sibylline Books, but adopted this institution to its own use, making political statements via the embassy to Sicily in 133 or the introduction of cults such as Aesculapius and Venus Erycina. This implies not only willingness to allow foreign influences into the state, but demonstrates mastery over them; the Senate made a point of controlling the Sibylline Books, rather than letting the Books control them. Gruen has recently pointed out how the Roman reaction to things Greek functioned not only to show that Rome partook of Greek culture, but used it to further Roman ends and demonstrate Rome's own cultural ascendancy.[143] The Sibylline Books provide another *exemplum* of this tendency, demonstrating Roman competence and indeed mas-

---

[141] For instance, the sacred prostitutes were stripped from the Punic cult of Venus Erycina before it arrived in Rome, and numerous restrictions were placed on the cult of the Magna Mater, including limiting the membership and public appearances of the *galli*. Note that these restrictions were intended to make these cults more palatable to *senatorial* tastes. The populace was often happy with these "objectionable" features, as the popularity of the temple of Venus Erycina *extra portam Collinam* attests.

[142] In this context it may be useful to note the Senate's use of Etruscan *haruspices* as another means of expiating prodigies. Two of the three groups—the third being the pontiffs—most involved in expiating prodigies thus depended on foreign wisdom. On the *haruspices* in Rome, see now MacBain (1982), 43–59.

[143] Gruen (1990), *passim*, and (1992), especially ch. 6. This is also the period which

tery of a foreign religious institution. It would be stretching the evidence to say that the presence of the Sibylline Books in Rome from the fifth century indicates that this notion was fully conceptualized at such an early date, but the seeds of this attitude were clearly in place at this time.

This attitude helps explain why the Senate never commissioned a Latin translation of the Sibylline Books. In the Early Republic, such a translation might have compromised the Senate's claim to exclusive control through the *decemviri*. Verses written in Greek hexameters clearly required men with special training and a knowledge of Greek, and such men were to be found in the Early Republic primarily amongst the upper classes who constituted Rome's ruling elite. The admission of plebeians to the decemviral board in 367 would not have affected this consideration, for by then those plebeians would have shared the interests of the ruling class. More importantly, a translation at this time or later would have compromised the Romans' claims to be fluent in Greek language and culture. The continued use of Greek oracles for Roman purposes demonstrated the Roman command of Greek culture.

The introduction of new cults by the Sibylline Books fits right into this matrix of cultural statements. The message is made more powerful by the introduction of both Greek and Roman cults, rather than just one or the other. The introduction of only Roman cults might indicate that the Romans were wary of allowing Greek cults into the city, expressing a fear that perhaps Roman religion was not strong enough to withstand such influences. The introduction of only Greek cults conversely might indicate that the Senate was able to use the Books only in the context of foreign cultures, but did not have the capacity to expand beyond that frontier. The use of the Sibylline Books to introduce both Greek and Roman cults indicates that the Romans had truly mastered the Books. The introduction of new cults via the mechanism of the Sibylline Books conveyed messages on several different levels at the same time.

---

saw the majority of our attested Sibylline consultations, although as indicated above (p. 85) this fact may simply be a reflection of our sources.

CHAPTER FOUR

THE CONSTRUCTION

The construction of a new temple in fulfillment of a vow, the next stage in the process, presents as many difficulties as the making of the vow itself. The key issue here is determining how the construction of these temples was financed, by private means or with public funds. Temples ordered by the Senate following a consultation of the Sibylline Books were certainly built with public funds, but temples built following a general's vow are more problematic. Many modern scholars have endorsed a theory of manubial building, wherein generals used the proceeds from their victorious campaigns—*manubiae*—to erect the temples they had vowed on their campaigns. On this view, these temples were lavish monuments which were intended as a lasting testimony to the *gloria* of the victorious commander; by the second century, temple building had become simply another field in which politicians strove to outdo one another. This theory implies that the Senate played no role in the construction process, and assumes that a general could vow and build a new temple in Rome without any oversight on the part of the Senate. Yet we shall see that there is little direct evidence to support the theory of manubial building; it is based on assumptions about what generals did with their *manubiae* when they returned to Rome. The previous chapters have already called into question some of these assumptions, particularly that an individual could enact permanent changes in the Roman religious system without the supervision of the Senate. This chapter will reexamine the evidence for the financing of new temples in Rome, the key element in the manubial building theory. First we will investigate the definition of *manubiae* and the uses which the ancient sources describe for this money, and this analysis will show that in fact *manubiae* were seldom used for the construction of state temples. The study then turns to consider other ways in which temples might be built, an investigation which will reveal that the Senate played a much more active role in this process than has been commonly thought. This conclusion in turn points towards a new interpretation of the significance of temple building in Rome.

I. *Manubiae*

I.1 Manubiae, Praeda, *and Victorious Generals*

The term *manubiae* and its relationship to the term *praeda*, both of which in some fashion refer to the spoils of war, present a legion of problems. The only fact which seems certain is that the victorious general possessed the initiative in arranging the distribution of these spoils. The precise definition of these terms is a vexed question unto itself, and has resisted several attempts to arrive at a definitive solution. This lack of definition of course makes any further analysis a hazardous endeavor, but there are many other questions to be answered. For instance, we do not know how the spoils were divided into the categories of *manubiae* and *praeda*, or how much booty fell into each category. The victorious commander's role is murky; did he make the division? Did he keep a portion for himself? Was he restricted either in the quantities set aside for various uses or in the actual uses of the money? Many analyses have tried to answer these questions in a legalistic manner, attempting to find legal categories for the booty and to determine the legal authority of the general vis-à-vis the booty. Yet in Chapter Two we saw that the Romans did not operate in a constitutional system with well-defined legal positions, and the same may be true of *manubiae* and *praeda*. Such restraints as were imposed on victorious generals are not likely to have come from legal pronouncements, but from the *mos maiorum* and from *ad hoc* decisions of the Senate. Thus we should not look for legal definitions and rules regarding *manubiae* and *praeda*, but for customary practices and the factors which may have shaped those practices. This approach suits our purposes particularly well, because we want to know if Roman generals actually spent their *manubiae* on temples, not whether they were entitled to do so, or conversely required to do so.

The major problem in defining *manubiae* and *praeda* stems from the fact that none of the three definitions for these terms found in the ancient sources is earlier than the second century c.e., and none of these definitions is convincing or consistent with ancient usage. One of the three can be discarded without much effort. As reported by Gellius, common second century c.e. wisdom held that *manubiae* and *praeda* were the same thing.[1] This view is already rejected by Favorinus,

---

[1] Gellius, 13.25.3–4: *manubiae enim dicuntur praeda, quae manu capta est.*

one of the protagonists of this dialogue of Gellius, and has not found
a single modern supporter. While the terms are occasionally used as
synonyms by ancient sources, usually this is for purposes of *variatio*;
for the most part the sources do make a distinction between the
terms, often using them alongside one another.[2] "Favorinus" then
offers his own definition: *praeda* means the actual items which are
captured, but *manubiae* refers to the money collected by the quaestor
from the sale of the *praeda*.[3] This view, implying that *manubiae* were
a subset of *praeda*, was endorsed by Mommsen, and has subsequently
been accepted by the majority of scholars.[4] The third definition is
offered by a scholiast on Cicero's Verrine orations, known as Pseudo-
Asconius: *manubiae* are the general's share of the *praeda* captured from
the enemy, again implying that *manubiae* were a subset of *praeda*, but
of a different sort.[5] The more recent studies of Bona and Shatzman
both favor the latter definition.[6]

The difficulty in accepting either of the latter two definitions is
that some ancient writers used the terms in a manner consistent with
the former, that *manubiae* is the cash raised from the *praeda*, while
others used them as if following the latter, that the *manubiae* belonged
to the general. For instance, the first extant use of the term, in a
fragment from Cato the Elder, perfectly suits the definition offered
by "Favorinus". Cato is quoted as follows: "*numquam ego praedam neque
quod de hostibus captum esset neque manubias inter pauculos amicos meos divisit,
ut illis eriperem qui cepissent.*"[7] The apposition implies that *praeda* is made
up of "what was captured from the enemy" as well as "*manubiae*",
which could well mean the money derived from the sale of booty.
The *manubiae* are clearly a subset of *praeda* in Cato's view, just as
"Favorinus" would have us believe. Although this passage is capable

---

[2] Cf. *TLL*, s.v. *manubiae*, and Shatzman (1972), 179.

[3] Gellius, 13.25.25–26: *Nam praeda dicitur corpora ipsa rerum quae capta sunt, manubiae
vero appellatae sunt pecunia a quaestore ex venditione praedae redacta.*

[4] Mommsen, *RS* 1.241–42. Bona (1960), 106–113, and Shatzman (1972), 177–79,
both provide capsule sketches of the previous literature on the topic.

[5] Two scholia, on *Verr.* 2.1.154 and 2.1.157 [Stangl 224–25], offer largely the
same definition. *Verr.* 2.1.154: *Manubiae sunt praeda imperatoris pro portione de hostibus
capta.* *Verr.* 2.1.157: *spolia quaesita de vivo hoste nobili per deditionem manubias veteres dicebant;
et erat imperatorum haec praeda, ex qua quod vellent facerent.*

[6] F. Bona, *SDHI* (1960), 105–175; Shatzman, *Historia* (1972), 177–205. Bona's
article remains the most exhaustive and complete treatment of the ancient sources.
Shatzman offers more analysis of the supposed instances of *peculatus* trials, and provides some useful correctives to Bona's views.

[7] *ORF*[2], fr 203.

of other translations,[8] this is certainly the most natural rendering. Cato apparently understood *manubiae* and *praeda* in the same way that "Favorinus" did.

Ciceronian usage, on the other hand, seems to prefer the definition proposed by pseudo-Asconius. In the two speeches on the agrarian bill proposed by Rullus, Cicero twice uses *manubiae* and *praeda* in a way which is incompatible with a definition based on monetary and non-monetary items, the "Favorinus" definition. In the first passage, cited by Gellius but missing in the texts of Cicero, the orator complains that "the decemviri will sell (*vendent*) the *praeda*, the *manubiae*, the *sectio*, and finally the camps of Pompey while the imperator sits by."[9] That Cicero could have actually used the phrase *vendent manubias* is proved by its occurrence in a passage that we do have: "will he sell the general's spoils (*vendet manubias*) in his own province?"[10] As Shatzman points out, unless Cicero is speaking nonsense, *manubiae* can not simply be equated to money, for it makes no sense to speak of selling money.[11] In the second passage, an actual citation from the agrarian bill quoted by Cicero, we read: "the gold, the silver, from the *praeda*, from the *manubiae*, from the *aurum coronarium*" shall be returned to the *decemviri*.[12] Again, Shatzman points out that this passage is not compatible with the definition proposed by "Favorinus", for the bill conceives that gold and silver could come from both the *praeda* and the *manubiae*.[13] Shatzman also indicates several other passages where Cicero does not use *praeda* and *manubiae* to refer to non-monetary and monetary items respectively.[14] One should also note that Cicero uses *manubiae* and *praeda* as parallels, and not as if one were a subset of the other. Ciceronian usage, combined with the definition of pseudo-Asconius, would lead one to conclude that *manubiae* was the general's share of the booty, while *praeda* was another part of the booty, perhaps that destined for the state treasury.

Livian usage is perhaps the least helpful of all, for he seems to use the terms in both senses. In one passage he uses *manubiae* and *praeda*

---

[8] See in particular Shatzman (1972), 184.

[9] Gellius 13.25.6: *praedam, manubias, sectionem, castra denique Cn. Pompei, sedente imperatore, decemviri vendent.*

[10] Cicero, *Leg. Agr.* 2.53.

[11] Shatzman (1972), 179–80.

[12] Cicero, *Leg. Agr.* 2.59: *aurum, argentum, ex praeda, ex manubiis, ex coronario . . .*

[13] Shatzman (1972), 181.

[14] Cf. Cicero *Ad Att.* 5.20.5; *De Prov. Cons.* 28; *De Off.* 2.76; *De Or.* 3.10.

in a way compatible only with the "Favorinus" definition. Describing the activities of C. Lucretius Gallus in 170, Livy notes that he built an aqueduct to carry water from the river Loracina to Antium *ex manubiis*, for which he let the contract at 130,000 *asses*, and at the same time he decorated the shrine of Aesculapius with paintings *ex praeda*.[15] Decoration of a temple would most naturally be accomplished through the dedication of artworks taken from a defeated enemy, as examples from several sources indicate.[16] In the passage concerning Gallus, therefore, Livy apparently views *manubiae* as equivalent to money and *praeda* as equivalent to material objects, just as Cato and "Favorinus" did. Yet whenever Livy describes a distribution made to the soldiers at the conclusion of a campaign, he notes that such donatives came *ex praeda*, a usage which is hardly consistent with "Favorinus" and a non-monetary definition of *praeda*.[17] This usage hardly conforms to the pseudo-Asconian definition either, for the victorious commander took the money for this distribution out of money which nominally did not belong to him. This difficulty might be overcome by arguing that *praeda* referred to the money which the general was to turn in to the state treasury, but over which he maintained control until that time, which would be after his triumph and subsequent distributions. This line of reasoning also explains the usage concerning Gallus in the 170's in a manner which is consistent with the Pseudo-Asconian definition as well as "Favorinus".

One other text relating to *manubiae* needs to be brought into the discussion, an inscription on a statue base of Hercules recorded by Pliny the Elder. Pliny reports the inscriptions as follows: "*L. Luculli imperatoris de manubiis; aliter, pupillum Luculli ex S.C. dedicasse; tertius, T. Septimium Sabinum aed. cur. ex privato in publicum restituisse.*"[18] The first clause indicates that the statue was part of the *manubiae*, and allows us to firmly dismiss the definition offered by "Favorinus": *manubiae* did not simply consist of money, but could include statues. Furthermore, the next clause indicates that Lucullus owned the statue until his death, since it was only afterwards dedicated by his minor son in

---

[15] Livy 43.4.6–7.

[16] Cf. the temple of Honos and Virtus, decorated with spoils from Syracuse (Livy 25.40.1, 26.32.4); the temple of Hercules Musarum, filled with statues of the Muses (Pliny, *NH* 35.66); temple of Felicitas, decorated with art from Mummius' campaigns in Greece (Strabo 8.6.23; Pliny, *NH* 34.69).

[17] E.g. Livy 10.46, 30.45.3, 31.20.7, 34.46.3, 39.5.17, 40.43.7.

[18] Pliny, *NH* 34.93. Cf. Shatzman (1972), 188.

accord with a *senatus consultum*. That Lucullus himself did not dedicate the statue is significant, for it indicates that he considered the
statue to be his own property; he did not need to make a public
dedication. From this one may conclude that Lucullus considered at
least this piece of the *manubiae* to be his share of the booty and part
of his personal property. The passage of an *s.c.* prior to the dedication of the statue is noteworthy; perhaps the Senate's involvement
was occasioned by the age of the boy, or perhaps because of the
location of the statue on public property near the rostra. Nevertheless it is a clear attestation of the Senate's continued involvement
with the *manubiae* of a triumphant general. It is also curious that
somehow this statue had fallen into private hands following its dedication, so that a state magistrate had to take action in order to return
the statue to public display. By itself, this inscription is sufficient to
confound our notions of public and private property in Rome, and
to frustrate any attempt to declare *manubiae* the exclusive property of
either the individual or the state.

This survey of the most important texts relating to *manubiae* and
praeda should have indicated the hopelessness of arriving at a conclusive definition. Moreover, insisting on legalistic hair-splitting to reach
a defensible position would be to miss the point being raised in this
study. Such categories as *manubiae* and *praeda* clearly existed, as is
evident from the ancient sources, but the significance of this distinction has been overemphasized in modern studies. The distinction
simply may not have been as important to the Romans as it seems
to us, for Roman authors made no attempt to use these terms in a
consistent fashion nor did they define these terms until after the
distinction was moot. The one fact which seems certain is that the
victorious commander had a measure of control over the disposition
of both *manubiae* and *praeda*. The line between these two categories
may never have been clearly drawn, precisely because they both
derived from the spoils of war and their distribution was controlled,
at least initially, by the triumphant general. Once again, as we saw
in the matter of general's vows, the distinction between public and
private could be extremely blurry in Rome.

Modern scholars have also tried to look for restrictions on the
general's use of these funds, particularly legal restrictions. Most have
held that the general had wide freedom of action, but with the restriction that the spoils be spent on a work of public utility. Mommsen
argued that a general who did not use his *manubiae* in this way was

subject to a charge of *peculatus* and Bona, while differing with
Mommsen over the definition of *manubiae*, agreed with him on this
point.[19] Vogel, following closely the second part of the definition of
manubiae given by Pseudo-Asconius, argued that the general had
absolute authority over his *manubiae* and could spend it as he wished;
there was no legal basis for a charge of *peculatus* as regards the
manubiae.[20] Shatzman is one of the few scholars who has supported
this view, with particular reference to the known *peculatus* trials during the Republic.[21] Here again certainty is near impossible, and again
misses the larger point. The Romans had no written constitution
laying out the rights and obligations of magistrates, so we should not
expect an actual law or *senatus consultum* defining what a magistrate
could or could not do with the booty brought back from a successful
campaign. Rather, certain customs had evolved over time concerning the appropriate uses of booty, and social or political pressures,
based on the *mos maiorum*, played a more significant role in limiting
expenditures to those appropriate uses than legal threats. As long as
an individual was willing to ignore these pressures, he could use the
manubiae in almost any manner he wished, as Lucullus' possession of
the statue of Hercules has already indicated.[22] The question should
rather focus on determining the norms of behavior, the ways in which
a Roman general might be expected to utilize the spoils of his campaign. This issue has direct bearing on our study of new temples, for
it has often been postulated that one of these expected uses of *manubiae*
was to build a temple which had been vowed during the campaign.

I.2   *Generals' Use of Booty*

The behavior of the consuls of 293 provides one of the best illus-
trations of the right of the general to dispose of the spoils of war
according to his own wishes and also allows us to glimpse what was

---

[19] Mommsen, *RStFr*, 765, n. 5 and 7; Bona (1960), 160–67.
[20] K. Vogel (1948), 394–423.
[21] Shatzman (1972), 188–203.
[22] To the extent that one can answer the purely legal question of the general's
authority over his *manubiae*, it seems to me that Shatzman is correct in arguing,
based on an analysis of the *peculatus* cases, that there were no legal restrictions on
the general's use of this money. It is likely that there were some laws pertaining to
peculatus under which these cases were tried, but the content of those laws has been
lost, and there are no grounds for asserting that one or more of these laws defined
the position of the general in regard to the *praeda* and *manubiae*.

considered appropriate behavior. Both consuls, L. Papirius Cursor and Sp. Carvilius Maximus, fought successful campaigns and celebrated triumphs over the Samnites, but they used the booty in diametrically opposed ways.[23] Papirius gave all the bronze and silver to the treasury and gave nothing of the *praeda* to the soldiers. This aroused great ill-feeling among the plebs, all the more so because they had been taxed in order to pay the troops, which otherwise could have been paid from the booty. Nonetheless, no legal action was taken. Papirius also dedicated the temple of Quirinus and decorated it with the *spolia* taken from the enemy. Livy emphasizes that the father had vowed the temple, so the *manubiae* can not have been used for the construction, but only for the decoration. Carvilius, on the other hand, gave the treasury 380,000 pounds of bronze, and with the remaining money let the contract for a temple to Fors Fortuna *de manubiis* and gave 102 *asses* to each soldier and twice that amount to each centurion and horseman *ex praeda*.[24] Carvilius was correspondingly more popular with the plebs than Papirius because of his donative. There is no indication that the Senate either approved or disapproved of the actions of either general; no attempt was made to force Carvilius to deposit more of the booty into the treasury, although one might think that would be a Senatorial interest. The implication from Livy is that both generals acted within accepted norms of behavior, although Papirius had to face the wrath of the plebs.

Several other Roman generals endured the same experience with the plebs as Papirius; those who did not give suitable donatives to their soldiers incurred the hostility of the plebs.[25] The plebs clearly considered such withholding of booty to be inappropriate behavior, and the consuls of 455 were even condemned and fined, according to the tradition preserved by both Livy and Dionysius.[26] Giving the soldiers a donative was a very common use of booty, although where the source is specified such gifts always came from the *praeda*. The

[23] Livy 10.46.

[24] The implication in this passage is that *manubiae* and *praeda* are distinct from one another, and that both are distinct from the money paid into the state treasury. Both come out of the *reliquo aere* after the 380,000 pounds of bronze had been deposited in the treasury.

[25] Cf. Livy 2.41, 3.31, 4.53, 5.5; Dion. Hal. 10.48–49. Some of these incidents may be apocryphal, especially as they date from before the Gallic sack, but if invented they show what an ancient author would have expected in such a situation. Cf. the treatment of these cases by Shatzman (1972), 188–198.

[26] Livy 3.31; Dion. Hal. 10.48–49.

amount of the donative varied from general to general, apparently
at the general's discretion, and was usually doubled or tripled for
centurions and *equites*. The general would no doubt be influenced by
the total amount of booty brought back from his campaign and might
be led to give proportionally more if he wished to curry particular
favor with the plebs. Factors such as these, and not any legal curbs,
determined the amount the triumphant commander gave his troops.

Somewhat surprisingly, we do not know of many controversies
caused by the opposite tendency, giving too much to the plebs and
too little to the state treasury. One is reported for 495, when the
consul Ap. Claudius Sabinus opposed his colleague's triumph on these
grounds, and another only in 89, when Pompeius Strabo gave nothing from Asculum to the treasury.[27] The reason for this silence is
most likely that few generals chose to favor the plebs excessively at
the expense of the state treasury; one would expect to find a chorus
of Senatorial complaints at this practice. The conclusion to be drawn
is that the division of spoils between the soldiers and the state treasury was left entirely to the discretion of the general, subject to his
feelings on offending either the army or the Senate. The few recorded instances of controversy indicates that in most cases the donatives given were apparently enough to satisfy the army without
transgressing what the Senate deemed to be a suitable amount.

The actions of Carvilius in 293 reveal another accepted use for
the booty brought back from a successful campaign: the construction
of a public building. We know of several public works which were
undertaken from *manubiae*, and many modern authorities have believed that most of the new temples in Rome were financed in this
way, that is the so-called "manubial building".[28] To quote just one
of these scholars: "Temples vowed in battle, built by means of spoils,
and dedicated in connection with a triumph are most common in
the annals of the Republic and early Empire" and again "temples
vowed in battle were usually paid for, during the Republic, by the
victorious general out of the spoils of victory."[29] This hypothesis is
attractive because many temples were vowed by generals on campaign, and it is plausible that the money they brought back to Rome

---

[27] 495: Dion. Hal. 6.30.2. 89: Oros. 5.18.26.
[28] Cf. H. Bardon, (1955); F. Bona, (1960); D. E. Strong, (1968); M. G. Morgan,
(1973a); I. Shatzman, (1975), 90–91; J. E. Stambaugh, (1978); L. Pietilä-Castrén,
(1987); and most recently A. Ziolkowski, (1992).
[29] Stambaugh (1978), 557, 564.

as a result of their triumph would be used in part to fulfill that vow. Under this hypothesis, the temple served not only as a thank-offering to the god who had aided the consul during the campaign, but also as a means of self-aggrandizement and a continual reminder to his fellow Romans of his success in battle. To use money actually won in that war to build the temple seems likely enough in this scenario.

A passage from Cicero's speech on the Rullan land bill seems to provide a *prima facie* case that it was customary for generals to use their *manubiae* to build public monuments, and temples in particular. One section of this bill ordered generals to render an account to the *decemviri* of any money from *praeda, manubiae,* or *aurum coronarium* that was not deposited in the treasury or spent on a public monument.[30] An exception was to be made for Pompey, to which Cicero objects: "For if it is just that generals should not devote *praeda* and their own *manubiae* on monuments of the immortal gods nor on adornment of the city, but should have to carry them to the *decemviri* as if to masters, then Pompey seeks nothing in particular for himself, nothing."[31] While defending Pompey from charges of special treatment, Cicero of course believes the opposite, that it was perfectly acceptable for generals to spend their booty in this way.[32] As uses for this money, he mentions "adornment of the city" which could refer to any type of building, and also specifies "monuments of the immortal gods." The provisions in the Rullan bill and Cicero's comments on it have

---

[30] Cicero, *De Lege Agr.* 2.59: *"Aurum, argentum ex praeda, ex manubiis, ex coronario ad quoscumque pervenit neque relatum est in publicum neque in monumento consumptum" id profiteri apud decemviros et ad eos referre iubet.* Since Bona believed that such money already had to be spent on public monuments, he viewed the institution of the decemvirate as the primary innovation in this bill (167–170). Shatzman argues correctly that the entire restriction on the use of *manubiae* is an innovation, further evidence that there was no previous imperative for generals to spend their *manubiae* on public monuments (199–201). For our purposes, however, we need to know not merely whether it was required for generals to spend their *manubiae* in this way, but also whether it was customary to spend it, and specifically to spend it on temples.

[31] Cicero, *De Lege Agr.* 2.61: *Nam si aequum praedam et manubias suas imperatores non in monumenta deorum immortalium neque in urbis ornamenta conferre, sed ad decemviros tamquam ad dominos reportare, nihil sibi appetit praecipue Pompeius, nihil.* Cicero's language here supports the definition of *manubiae* as specifically pertaining to the general; he uses *suas* to modify *manubias,* indicating that the *manubiae* in some sense belongs to the general, while *praedam* is left without a modifier.

[32] Cicero's argument is actually slightly off-target here, for the Rullan bill in fact made an exception for generals to employ such money in building monuments; the point was to restrict other uses of this money. Cf. the language in 2.59, quoted in n. 30 above.

thus been used to indicate the existence of a tradition of building temples in Rome from booty.

These passages, however, are not sufficient grounds on which to draw this inference. In the first place, the agrarian bill itself does not mention temples, or "monuments of the immortal gods", but merely public monuments. For the purposes of Roman religion, there is a significant distinction between temples built from *manubiae* and other public buildings built from *manubiae*. The former implies an ongoing religious commitment by the state to the worship of a deity, often a new deity. The latter is simply a building for the use of the populace, such as a portico or a library; it requires no such commitment on the part of the state. We shall see that a number of generals did build public monuments in Rome from their *manubiae*, but only a handful of these were temples. Rullus' bill recognizes the erection of such monuments as a legitimate use of booty, but does not insist that the monument be a temple, because that was not a necessary part of the tradition.

Cicero himself is the one who brings up the connection between generals, *manubiae*, and "monuments of the immortal gods." Note that Cicero does not even mention temples; monuments of the immortal gods could include statues or other dedications in addition to temples. Even the link to such monuments is only circumstantial. Cicero says that both *praeda* and *manubiae* have been used to build both *monumenta* and *ornamenta* of the city, not merely that *manubiae* are used for *monumenta*.[33] The inclusion of the immortal gods here may be intended for rhetorical effect, in order to drum up emotional and religious opposition to Rullus: are generals to be deprived of the opportunity to pay honor to those deities who have helped them and the state in a time of need? Certainly the addition of monuments combined with the omission of the *aurum coronarium* provides Cicero with a nice symmetry to his sentence: two sources of income, *praeda* and *manubiae*, and two areas of expenditure, *ornamenta* and *monumenta*. There is some basis for the inclusion of temples by Cicero, for we will see that some generals did build temples with their *manubiae*. Yet we should not assume from Cicero's rhetoric that this was an established cus-

---

[33] In fact, the positioning of the terms may argue against this. *Praeda* appears first as do the monuments of the gods, while *manubiae* appears second and is paralleled by *ornamenta*. Without laying too much stress on this point, it may indicate that subconsciously Cicero recognized that temples were not frequently linked to *manubiae*, and thus when he wrote the speech he linked *ornamenta* to *manubiae*.

tom. We need to examine carefully the history of monumental building during the Republic to determine if temples were in fact erected
as a result of manubial building.

I.3 *Manubial Building of Temples, Reconsidered*

Some confirmation of the hypothesis is often sought in the early part
of the second century, since the most dramatic period of growth in
the number of temples in Rome occurred in the aftermath of the
Second Punic War. A total of fourteen temples were dedicated in
the fifteen years between 194 and 179, only three of which were
holdovers that had been vowed during the Hannibalic war.[34] In
addition to the indemnity flowing in from Carthage, the Romans
also conducted successful campaigns on several fronts during this
period. There was thus ample opportunity for military campaigns
and for booty, so that manubial building appears to be an attractive
explanation for the sudden boom in the construction of new temples.
Unfortunately, explanations seldom prove that simple.

One problem with the theory of manubial building arises from a
close examination of the first explosion in the number of new temples
in Rome. From 304 to 291, nine temples were built, a pace which is
only slightly slower than that of the early second century, but which
far outpaces any other period during the Republic.[35] For this period,
our sources are actually relatively explicit in reporting the source of
funds used to construct these temples. Of these nine temples, only
one, the temple of Fortuna, is specifically stated to have been built
from spoils, while three others, those of Concordia, Venus and Victoria,
were built with money raised by fines imposed by aediles. This hardly
conforms to a picture of manubial temple building, especially as the
great victory at Sentinum in 295 and the subsequent victories in 294

---

[34] The temples are: Juno Sospita, Faunus, Vediovis (on the Tiber island), and
Fortuna Primigenia (vowed during the Second Punic War) in 194; Vediovis (on the
Capitoline) in 192; Iuventas and Magna Mater (both vowed during the Second
Punic War) in 191; Venus Erycina (outside the Porta Collina) and Pietas in 181;
Fortuna Equestris in 180; and Lares Permarini, Diana, Juno Regina, and probably
Hercules Musarum in 179.

[35] The temples are: Concordia in 304; Salus in 302; Venus, started in 295, although perhaps not finished until after the Third Samnite War; Victoria and Jupiter
Stator in 294, although again Jupiter Stator may not have been finished for a few
years; Bellona, Quirinus, and Fors Fortuna in 293; and Aesculapius in 291. Even
seven temples in thirteen years (leaving out Venus and Jupiter Stator) is a pace
unmatched during the Republic except for the early second century.

had brought great amounts of spoils into Rome. Nor can one argue that the lack of manubial temples stems from the pressing military needs Rome continued to face until the end of the war; no temples are known to have been built in the aftermath of the final Samnite surrender. Besides, *manubiae* constituted the general's share of the spoils, and so would not have been available to the state treasury for the prosecution of the war anyway. The construction pattern of the 290's strikes a damaging blow to the notion of manubial building of temples.

Even the rash of building following the Second Punic War does not follow the pattern demanded by a hypothesis of manubial building. None of these temples is specifically attested to have been built with booty. In fact the only temple of this group for which we have an attested source of financing was again built with the fines collected by the aediles.[36] Indeed, it is reasonable to suppose that the state treasury financed this particular construction boom. The primary source of income at this time derived from indemnity payments, including two hundred talents, roughly 1.2 million *denarii*, from Carthage annually and one thousand talents, six million *denarii*, annually from Antiochus after 187.[37] Some generals at this time brought great sums of money to Rome, but there is no correlation between those who brought back more booty and those who vowed and built temples. For instance, the campaigns against Antiochus were quite profitable, but only two temples were vowed by generals fighting Antiochus. Both L. Aemilius Regillus and M'. Acilius Glabrio built temples, although the former displayed only 500,000 *denarii* in his triumph and the latter 1.5 million *denarii*; Flamininus and Scipio

---

[36] The temple of Faunus: Livy 33.42.10, 34.53.3.

[37] Cf. Livy 30.37.5 and Polybius 15.18 for the Carthaginian indemnity. Cf. Livy 37.45.14 for the settlement imposed on Antiochus. The figure for the latter does not include the three thousand talents collected in 187 itself. See T. Frank, *ESAR* 1.125–141, for a summary of the sources of income, particularly booty, acquired by the Romans from 200–157. In the discussion that follows, I have generally converted the sums of money brought to the treasury into *denarii* for ease of reference. Obviously we must recognize that strict accuracy is not possible here, but the figures provide a good method for comparing the relative amounts of booty brought in by various campaigns.

On pp. 138–141, Frank presents a summary of his estimates on the sources of income for the period 200–157. Far and away the largest source of monetary income for Rome derived not from booty, but from the indemnity payments of defeated enemies. These included not only Carthage, but also Philip, Antiochus, and Nabis among others. Frank's estimated total of 150,000,000 *denarii* from indemnity payments is more than double the amount of booty brought from the East and quadruple that brought from Spain. Gaul and Histria contributed a mere 2,000,000.

Asiaticus, who each triumphed with over 5 million *denarii*, did not build temples.[38] The Spanish campaigns, and the proceeds of the mines in Spain, also brought large sums of money back to Rome, yet again the more profitable campaigns did not result in temples; Q. Fulvius Flaccus, who brought only 330,000 *denarii* back, did vow a temple, while L. Stertinius (four million *denarii*) and Q. Minucius Thermus (three million) did not.[39] On the other hand, the Roman campaigns against the Gauls and the Ligurians in the 190's and 180's, which resulted in the vowing of six temples, did not provide large amounts of booty to victorious generals or to the treasury.[40] For instance, in 200 L. Furius Purpurio brought the equivalent of only 125,000 *denarii* into the treasury, while C. Cornelius Cethegus displayed less than 100,000 *denarii* in his triumph of 197, yet both these men vowed temples.[41] Realistic estimates of building costs are hard to derive, but such sums hardly seem sufficient for an impressive manubial monument, especially if Cethegus paid the donative to his soldiers out of that 100,000 *denarii*.[42] That those who had large sums of money available did not erect temples while those who did erect them had much smaller sums should cast doubt on the view of the early second century as a period of intense manubial building of temples.[43]

Supporters of the theory of manubial building also point to a list of monuments built with *manubiae* which at first sight appears extremely impressive.[44] On closer examination, however, these references

---

[38] Regillus: Livy 37.58.4. Glabrio: 37.46.3–4. Flamininus: 34.52.4–11. Asiaticus: 37.59.3–6.

[39] Flaccus: 42.34.9. Stertinius: Livy 33.37.3–4. Thermus: 34.10.5–7.

[40] Cf. Frank's estimate, mentioned above in n. 37, that Gaul and Histria brought only two million *denarii* into the state treasury over this forty year period.

[41] Livy 31.49.1–3, 33.23.7.

[42] Cethegus gave each soldier almost four *denarii*, each centurion eight, and each *eques* twelve. Given that Cethegus had two legions assigned to him (32.27.9), roughly forty thousand *denarii* must have been distributed, even assuming a legionary strength of only 3000–4000. That would leave only 60,000 *denarii* available for building a temple, let alone depositing anything into the treasury.

[43] It is curious that when Frank, *ESAR* 1.145, devises a balance sheet of income and expenses for the Romans in the period 200–157, he is left with a surplus of 30,000,000 *denarii* unaccounted for. Of course he also assumes that the temples built during this period were constructed using *manubiae*. Obviously these numbers are highly speculative, but I suggest the possibility that some of this supposed surplus in the state treasury may actually have been spent on the construction of temples which have heretofore been considered manubial.

[44] E.g. Shatzman (1975), 90–91, n. 37.

do little to advance the hypothesis of temples built from *manubiae*. A number of these references involve building projects other than temples, such as *fornices*,[45] porticoes,[46] aqueducts,[47] or walls.[48] Many others refer to monuments built after the fall of the Republic,[49] which can hardly prove the thesis sketched earlier, that during the Republic generals built monuments from *manubiae* as a means of propaganda and thus provided themselves with an advantage in the aristocratic competition. Julius Caesar may have been motivated by a desire to glorify his achievements, but it can not be seriously maintained that the building of public monuments was necessary for him to support his position. Similarly while the works undertaken by Augustus played an important role in the creation of a new ideology which allowed the Principate to take root, the meaning of these monuments was completely different than in the Republic; political competition no longer existed in Rome, and the Augustan regime did not depend on such monuments for its survival. Monuments undertaken by others during this time, for instance Asinius Pollio or L. Munatius Plancus, similarly did not hold the political meaning which they are supposed to have held under the Republic.

Evidence for the manubial construction of temples is lacking for all but a limited number of temples. Livy tells us that the contract for the temple of Fors Fortuna in 293 was let from the *manubiae* of the consul Sp. Carvilius Maximus.[50] Later in the third century, Cn. Papirius Maso dedicated a shrine to Fons *ex Corsica*, probably in

---

[45] Livy 33.27.3. The use of *manubiae* for the construction of the *fornix* of Stertinius confirms the interpretation offered in Chapter Two, pp. 71-72, that this monument focused attention primarily on the individual. On the significance of the uses of *manubiae*, see below, pp. 135-37 and 160-61.

[46] Pliny, *NH* 34.13, Vell. Pat. 1.11.3.

[47] Livy 43.4.6–7.

[48] *ILS* 22.

[49] E.g. Caesar built his forum from *manubiae* (Suet. *Jul.* 26.2); see further pp. 197–98. Other building projects at this time undertaken *de manubiis* include: the rebuilding of the temple of Saturn by L. Munatius Plancus (*ILS* 41 and 886); the library of Asinius Pollio (Isidor. *Etymol.* 6.5.2); an unknown building by Domitius Calvus (*ILS* 42); and various works either of Augustus himself (Suet. *Aug.* 30.1–2, *RGDA* 21.1) or encouraged by him (Suet. *Aug.* 29.4–5). Although Augustus encouraged generals to use their *manubiae*, as Plancus did, his pleas fell on somewhat deaf ears, and this can not be taken as firm evidence of a long-standing Republican tradition.

It should also be noted that Florus (1.7.7) claims that King Tarquin built the temple of Jupiter Capitolinus *de manubiis*. However, no other author mentions this fact and even if it were true, manubial building by the kings, like manubial building after Caesar, hardly supports the theory.

[50] Livy 10.46.14.

gratitude because the sudden appearance of a spring had saved his army while in Corsica.[51] In the middle of the second century, L. Licinius Lucullus built a temple for Felicitas out of the money from his Iberian war.[52] D. Iunius Brutus, consul in 138, apparently built a temple to Mars from his manubiae, and an Augustan elogium attests that the temple built by Marius to Honos and Virtus was constructed de manubiis Cimbris et Teuton.[53] These are the only Republican temples for which we have ancient testimony that manubiae were utilized for the construction.

A number of other temples have been added to the list by modern scholars, but without sufficient grounds. For example, some have argued that both the temple of Victoria Virgo, dedicated in 193, and the temple of Lares Permarini, dedicated in 179, were built with manubiae.[54] Yet Livy says nothing about the use of manubiae for these temples, nor does any other source.[55] The conclusions seem based more on assumptions about what Roman generals did with their manubiae than on any evidence, e.g. "it is evident that Regillus used his manubiae for constructing the temple."[56] Without a pattern of manubial temple building, such an assumption for these temples is unjustified. A few other temples are included in the manubial list for other reasons, however, and we need to take a closer look at those cases.

Plutarch claims that the temple of Honos and Virtus was built by M. Claudius Marcellus out of the spoils of his Sicilian campaign.[57] Plutarch, writing in Greek, naturally did not use the term manubiae, but the context strongly implies that he was referring to Marcellus' own share of the spoils. However, the many Roman sources who

---

[51] Cicero, ND 3.52. I think that the phrase dedicavit ex Corsica has been correctly interpreted by Pietilä-Castrén (1987), 53, who understands by this phrase "that he had made the vow evidently after having found the spring during his campaign and that he built the temple from his share of the booty and, thirdly, that he dedicated it himself."

[52] Dio, Book 22, frag. 76.2. As Dio wrote in Greek, we obviously can not be sure that Lucullus used manubiae. However Dio's phrasing, ἐκ τοῦ Ἰβηρικοῦ πολέμου, almost exactly parallels Cicero's ex Corsica and surely refers to the spoils of war. Pietilä-Castrén (1987), 126, n. 15, who accepted that ex Corsica referred to spoils, instead took this phrase temporally, that Lucullus built the temple "after the Iberian war", which would remove this temple from the list of those built with manubiae.

[53] Iunius: Val. Max. 8.14.2. Marius: ILS 59.

[54] Shatzman (1975), 257, 244; Pietilä-Castrén (1987), 83, 93; A. Astin (1967), 53.

[55] Cf. Livy 35.9.6; 40.52.4.

[56] Pietilä-Castrén (1987), 93.

[57] Plut. Marc. 28.1: ἐκ τῶν σικελικῶν λαφύρων.

speak of this temple do not mention that it was built from *manubiae*. Rather, they remark on the number and quality of the artworks taken from Sicily which were placed in the temple as dedications.[58] The temple was the natural place for the display of objects captured in war; a long-standing feature of Roman temples was that they served for the display of works of art or for the display of important public documents, and these uses date back to the earliest days of the Republic.[59] Pliny's *Natural History* makes it clear that the typical place for the display of statues and paintings was in temples; indeed it seems that sometimes the Romans treated temples almost as if they were museums.[60] The pieces in the temple of Honos and Virtus undoubtedly came from Marcellus' *manubiae*, and this may have led Plutarch to conclude erroneously that the temple was built from *manubiae*. This distinction between dedications to a deity from the *manubiae* and construction of a temple from the *manubiae* is significant. The former implies no ongoing commitment, while the latter, as we have seen, has lasting repercussions for the state.

This confusion between dedications to a deity and the construction of a new temple has led several scholars to posit that the temple of Hercules Musarum was built from *manubiae*.[61] The main support for this view comes from a remark of Cicero: *[M. Fulvius Nobilior] non dubitavit Martis manubias Musis consecrare.*[62] Cicero does not say that Fulvius built the temple to the Muses from his *manubiae*, but rather that he consecrated his *manubiae to* the Muses. Again, as with Marcellus, we have ample testimony that Fulvius took a great deal of artwork as part of his *manubiae*.[63] Thus it is most natural to take Cicero as referring to the artwork dedicated by Fulvius in the temple of the Muses, certainly an appropriate place for the display of artwork.

---

[58] Cf. Livy 25.40, 26.32, 27.25; Cicero, *Verr.* 2.4.121; *Rep.* 1.21.

[59] The temple of Ceres was reported to have been decorated by the Greek artists Damophilos and Gorgasos and also to have contained many other works of art, while the temple of Salus contained paintings by C. Fabius Pictor. The temple of Jupiter Optimus Maximus was a noted repository of public documents, and even lesser structures could be used in the same way; the temple of Tellus is reported to have contained a map of Italy within its precinct, while Cn. Flavius placed a legal calendar in his shrine to Concordia.

[60] Pliny, *NH passim*. The temples of Ceres, Liber and Libera, Apollo, Salus, Honos and Virtus, and Felicitas, among others, are known to have contained notable artworks. This subject is worthy of a study in its own right.

[61] Shatzman (1972), 252; Pietilä-Castrén (1987), 101.

[62] Cicero, *Arch.* 27.

[63] Livy 38.9.13; 39.5.15; Pliny, *NH* 35.66.

Beyond this evidence, there is no reason to assume that *manubiae* were involved in the construction of the temple. A late source even states explicitly that Fulvius built the temple *ex pecunia censoria*.[64] This evidence is mostly discounted, firstly as a facile connection by a late source to the censorial building tradition and secondly because the temple is generally considered to have been dedicated in 179, the year of Fulvius' censorship.[65] However, the date of dedication is not known for certain, and we may not want to discard the only explicit evidence for the funding of this temple. Certainly one should not press the claim that the temple of Hercules Musarum was definitely built with the *manubiae* of M. Fulvius Nobilior.

The same problem of dedication as opposed to construction appears to have confused Pliny the Elder as well. Pliny claims that Pompey dedicated a shrine to Minerva *ex manubiis*, and he quotes an inscription as evidence; the inscription, however, indicates merely that Pompey made a dedication to Minerva.[66] We have seen that such dedications were often made in the temple as ornamentation rather than the temple itself, and a parallel report of an inscription set up by Pompey seems to confirm this interpretation. This latter inscription, a record of Pompey's achievements in Asia, is preserved by Diodorus, and toward the end it reads: "[Pompey], having taken the statues and the other images of the gods and the other valuables of the enemy, has dedicated to the goddess twelve thousand sixty gold pieces and three hundred seven talents of gold."[67] Again, the inscription describes the dedication of money to the goddess, not the construction of a temple out of that money. Furthermore, while Pompey built several temples in Rome, we do not know that any of them were built with *manubiae*, and we have no knowledge of a temple to Minerva in Rome dedicated in the first century.[68] As Pliny does not

---

[64] Eumen. *Pro rest. Schol.* 7.8.

[65] L. Richardson Jr. (1977), 355; M. Martina (1981), 49.

[66] Pliny, *NH* 7.97. Pliny's words run as follows: *in delubro Minervae quod ex manubiis dicabat.* The inscription has no main verb, and after listing the accomplishments of Pompey in the east, ends with the following three words: *votum merito Minervae.*

[67] Diodorus 40.4: τούς τε ἀνδριάντας καὶ τὰ λοιπὰ ἀφιδρύματα τῶν θεῶν καὶ τὸν λοιπὸν κόσμον τῶν πολεμίων ἀφελόμενος ἀνέθηκε τῇ θεῷ χρυσοῦς μυρίους καὶ δισχιλίους εξήκοντα, αργυρίου τάλαντα τριακόσια ἑπτά.

[68] See *contra* Palmer (1990b), 1–13. Although acknowledging that "no temple with a known site can be attributed to Pompey", Palmer suggests that the temple was built at the foot of the Pincian hill. However, this conclusion is based on several inferences drawn from evidence of the Imperial period, which do not create a convincing link between Pompey and a temple to Minerva.

actually state that the temple was in Rome, it is quite possible that
the temple, if in fact there was a temple, was built in the East, especially considering that Pliny was describing Pompey's eastern exploits.
Thus this dedication of Pompey to Minerva can not be used to prove
the relevance of manubial temple building in Rome.

One other example remains to be considered. Cicero, in his attack
on C. Verres, complained that Verres during his urban praetorship
had made *manubiae* for himself out of the *manubiae* of Metellus, and
that Verres spent more on refurbishing four columns than Metellus
did for the whole temple.[69] The reference is to the temple of Castor
which Metellus had renovated in 117, and it has therefore been
suggested that the renovation was carried out with the *manubiae* of
Metellus.[70] Yet it is not clear that the building activity here was
financed by *manubiae*, for Cicero's use of *manubiae* in relation to Verres
is clearly metaphorical, i.e. that Verres has appropriated for himself
some of the *manubiae* of Metellus. The use of the term in relation to
Metellus must refer to some of the dedications inside the temple, as
Verres could hardly appropriate the entire building for himself. In
addition, the other surviving reference to Metellus' work on this temple
remarks on the paintings and statues that Metellus placed in the
temple.[71] Once again the evidence points to *manubiae* used to make
dedications in the temple and not for the actual (re)construction of
the temple. It would be reaching to insist that these construction
projects were financed by war-booty.[72]

This survey of the use of *manubiae* reveals that only five temples
are clearly attested as having been built from *manubiae* during the
Republic. This is a remarkably low number to begin with, considering that over eighty temples were dedicated in Rome in this period;
it hardly provides a strong argument for the prevalent practice of
manubial temple building at Rome. Six temples were also built by
the aediles out of the money they collected from levying fines, yet no
one would argue for the importance of aedilician temple building in

---

[69] Cicero, *Verr.* 2.1.154.

[70] For the rebuilding of the temple by Metellus, see Cicero, *Scaur.* 26, with Asconius
(Stangl 28). The use of *manubiae* was suggested by Morgan (1973b), 36.

[71] Plut., *Pomp.* 2.4.

[72] Even if the renovation was carried out with *manubiae*, this does not go far toward establishing a theory of manubial temple building. Renovating an already existing
temple differs from erecting a brand new temple, for the former does not imply any
new religious commitments, while the latter brings with it the establishment of another
series of cultic obligations.

Rome, nor is that the intention here.[73] Furthermore, some of these temples built from *manubiae* do not appear in any copies of the *fasti*, which implies that they were not part of the official state religion, with annual celebrations at public expense. The celebration of a Fontinalia does appear on the calendars, but this celebration seems older than 231, when Maso built his shrine.[74] Similarly, no *dies natalis* is recorded for the temple of Felicitas built by Lucullus. Under July 1, the *fasti* do record a temple of *Felicitas in Capitolio*, but we know that the temple of Lucullus was situated on the Velabrum, so this can not be the temple indicated on the calendar.[75] The Venusine *fasti* indicate a celebration for Mars Invictus was held on May 14, but most scholars doubt that this festival was the *dies natalis* for the temple built by Iunius Brutus.[76] The temple of Fors Fortuna, which we considered at the very beginning of this discussion, is the only temple for which we have solid evidence that it was both built from *manubiae* and a part of the public cult, and it thus appears to be the exception rather than the rule.[77] The available evidence does not support the idea that state temples were erected from *manubiae*.

In fact where *manubiae* are mentioned in connection with a temple, the usage is often as dedications inside the temple rather than as the source of money for the actual construction of the building. The tradition of dedicating a portion of the *manubiae* as decoration inside a new temple reaches back to the early Republic. As we noted above, in 293 L. Papirius Cursor decorated the temple of Quirinus with spoils taken from the enemy; this was the same year in which the other consul Sp. Carvilius let the contract for his temple to Fors

---

[73] Temples built by aediles included: the temple of Concordia in 304 (Pliny *NH* 33.19); the temple of Venus in 295 (Livy 10. 31.9); the temple of Victoria in 294 (Livy 10.33.9); the temple of Flora in 241 or 238 (Pliny *NH* 18.286); the temple of Libertas, probably in the 230's (Livy 24.16.19); and the temple of Faunus in 194 (Livy 33.42.10).

[74] Degrassi (1963), 520. Cicero calls Maso's construction a *delubrum* instead of an *aedes*, the standard word for temple; this may also imply that the shrine of Fons was not a public temple.

[75] Suet., *Iul.* 37.2; Dio 43.21.1.

[76] See Degrassi (1963), 457.

[77] See above, pp. 123–25. Even this temple is problematical because of the many temples to Fortuna ascribed to king Servius Tullius. Cf. Plutarch, *De Fort. Rom.* 10 and *QR* 74. As the temple of Carvilius was supposed to be located near one of Servius (Livy 10.46.14), the notice in the *fasti* could refer either to a temple of Servius or the temple of Carvilius. On the problems posed by these multiple temples of Fortuna, see Degrassi (1963), 461 and 473, and more fully Champeaux (1982), 199–207.

Fortuna from his *manubiae*.[78] Furthermore, Livy was at some pains to emphasize that the temple of Quirinus was *not* erected with proceeds from the sale of the spoils, for he knew of "no ancient author [who stated] that it had been vowed in that very battle, nor by Hercules could it have been completed in such a short period of time."[79] Livy was thus aware of a tradition in which the victorious general placed a portion of the booty to the gods in a newly dedicated temple. Yet modern scholars have not paid sufficient attention to this tradition, a tradition which dates back as far as the first temple built from *manubiae*.

In later periods, this custom of making dedications from the *manubiae* inside the temple is actually better attested than the construction of temple. In the late third century this practice received a notable boost from M. Claudius Marcellus; as noted above Marcellus placed numerous statues and paintings which he had taken following the capture of Syracuse in 212 into his temples of Honos and Virtus built following the campaign.[80] These two temples were true show-pieces, for Livy reports that "the temples dedicated by M. Marcellus by the Porta Capena used to be visited by foreigners on account of their remarkable decoration of that sort."[81] This notice in Livy's account highlights one of the significant differences between making dedications in a temple and erecting the temple itself. By placing captured artwork in a newly constructed temple, a general might focus attention on his achievements; when Roman citizens and others viewed the contents of the temple, they would be reminded of the campaign and the individual who had brought those objects to Rome. Nor was this practice only limited to the commander in chief; even staff officers might make such dedications following a successful campaign.[82]

Several recent studies have underlined the point that the public

---

[78] Livy 10.46.7: *exornavit hostium spoliis.* The spoils in this case may refer to arms or armor taken from the defeated Samnites. On the display of such spoils, see Wiseman (1987); Rawson (1990).

[79] Livy 10.46.7: *quam in ipsa dimicatione votam apud neminem veterem auctorem invenio neque hercule tam exiguo tempore perficere potuisset.*

[80] Livy 25.40.1–3. Cf. 26.30–32, where Marcellus had to overcome a complaint lodged in the Senate against him about his looting of artworks by the defeated Sicilians. Cf. above, pp. 131–32.

[81] Livy 25.40.3: *Visebantur enim ab externis ad portam Capenam dedicata a M. Marcellus templa propter excellentia eius generis ornamenta.*

[82] Cf. *ILLRP* 100 and 221 for separate dedications *de praidad* to Mars and to Fortuna by the military tribune M. Furius.

display of spoils was more significant than the construction of a building. For instance, T. P. Wiseman has compared the house of a Roman senator to a temple decorated with *manubiae*:

> his *vestibulum* and *atrium* could advertise his glory to the Roman people as effectively as a temple with his name on the architrave. Perhaps even more effectively, to judge by Sallust's phraseology: "they decorated the temples of the gods with honor, and their own houses with glory." In fact, there are some striking parallels between house and temple: the *spolia* around the door, the honorific statues in *vestibulum* or *pronaos*, and in all probability also paintings of glorious *res gestae* within.[83]

Similarly, before her untimely death E. Rawson drew our attention to the display of *spolia* at the home of the *triumphator*; according to Pliny the Elder, even subsequent owners were not allowed to take down these objects, so that "the houses' triumphs continued even when their owners changed."[84] The key element needed to create a *monumentum* is not the erection of a structure, but the decoration of that structure with items commemorating the glorious exploits of the individual, a point which Wiseman hints at in another article on *monumenta*.[85] In particular, self-portrait statues and pictorial representations would be effective means of advertisement, items which might be, and often were, dedicated in a newly-built temple. *Manubiae* would thus be more effective in advertising the virtues of the victorious general when used for the decoration of a temple rather than for the construction.[86]

The early second century provides several examples of this phenomenon; other generals followed Marcellus' lead with the obvious intention of furthering their political ambitions, as the case of M. Fulvius Nobilior and the temple of Hercules Musarum demonstrates. As discussed above, Cicero notes that Nobilior dedicated the spoils of his campaign in the temple, and other sources indicate that the temple was indeed filled with statues of the Muses and with other artworks taken from Greece.[87] In fact, Nobilior's plundering of

---

[83] Wiseman, (1987) 395 = (1994) 99–100. The citation from Sallust is *Cat.* 12.4 Wiseman provides several examples each of temples decorated with *spolia*, statues, and paintings.

[84] Rawson (1990), 159–166. Pliny, *NH* 35.2.7: *triumphabantque etiam dominis mutatis aeternae domus.*

[85] Wiseman (1986), pp. 87–89 = (1994) 37–39.

[86] Cf. Kyrieleis (1990), who sees in some of these projects the origins of the later Imperial fora.

[87] Cicero, *Arch.* 27.

artworks—over one thousand bronze and marble statues were displayed in his triumph—became the subject of heated debate within
the Senate due to the machinations of his *inimicus* Aemilius Lepidus.[88]
The presence of these statues in the temple would have helped to
associate Nobilior' successes more closely with the structure. Furthermore, as discussed in Chapter Two, Nobilior's emphasis on the Muses
and the innovation this decision represented would have caused this
temple to stand out even further from the normal temple built following a campaign.[89] These actions seem intended to fuel Nobilior's
personal ambition and were directed toward helping Nobilior win
election to the censorship, an office which he sought unsuccessfully
in 184 before attaining it in 179. In this regard it is noteworthy that
Nobilior vowed *ludi* as well as a temple during his campaign.[90] Vowing two separate items is hard to understand on purely religious
grounds, but would have provided Nobilior with another prime opportunity to impress himself in the minds of the Roman populace.
In this case, Nobilior seems not to have worried that vowing a new
temple would unduly emphasize the role of the gods and the importance of the state, because the nature of his temple, its decoration
and the conjunction of this vow with the celebration of *ludi* kept
attention firmly focused on himself.

Many of these same features are visible in the actions of Q. Fulvius
Flaccus, a contemporary of Nobilior in the early second century. In
179, Flaccus told the Senate that he had vowed games to Jupiter
Optimus Maximus as well as a temple to Fortuna Equestris.[91] Livy's
account implies that Flaccus made both his vows at the same moment, although either games or a temple individually should have
been enough to insure the favor of the gods. This double vow again
provides an indication that such battlefield vows were not motivated
solely by religious needs, but also by political or personal consider-

---

[88] Livy 38.43–44; 39.4. In the end, it does not appear that Nobilior was forced
to return the art, although he did have to submit to the jurisdiction of the pontiffs.
That the sculpture ended up in the temple, rather than in Nobilior's house or elsewhere, may thus have been partly determined by the pontiffs, but still would have
redounded to Nobilior's credit. Nobilior's ability to prevail in this debate was undoubtedly aided by the fact that his supporters pointed to the precedent set by
Marcellus thirty years earlier. Cf. *CIL* 6.1307, an inscription on a statue base indicating that the statue had been captured by Nobilior from the Ambraciots.

[89] Cf. above, pp. 65–66.

[90] Livy 39.5.7.

[91] Livy 40.44.9. For the vow itself, cf. 40.40.10.

ations. Like Nobilior, Flaccus had grandiose ambitions and desired every opportunity to promote his name in Rome. Because he had fought his campaign against the Celtiberians, he did not have the same opportunity to dedicate captured artworks in his temple. Instead, during his censorship he attempted to take the marble tiles from the roof of the temple of Hera Lacinia at Croton and use them on his own temple.[92] This would have been the first temple in Rome with a marble roof, and thus would have caused it to stand out from the other temples built in this period. Unfortunately for Flaccus, when the Senate got wind of the plundering of roof tiles, a great outcry arose and Flaccus was forced to return the tiles to Croton.[93] Nonetheless Flaccus' attempt to distinguish his temple by its decoration provides another example of how a Roman general might counter the normal implications of building a temple and provide himself with an additional opportunity to impress the Romans with his own personal accomplishments. These examples make it clear that the importance of *manubiae* in connection with temples lies in the decoration of the structure, and not in the construction itself.

II. *The Construction of New Temples*

Since *manubiae* were not often used to finance the construction of new temples, we must ask ourselves how in fact these temples were built. The first item in attempting to answer this question is to discover who let the contracts for new temples, since the *locatio* was the first step in the construction of any public building in Rome.[94] Hand

---

[92] Cf. Livy 42.3 for this incident. Cf. the discussion of this temple by Champeaux (1987), 132–154, especially 136–139 where she discusses the ambitious character of Fulvius.

[93] In 172 Fulvius committed suicide by hanging himself, and Livy reports (42.28.10–13) that many people believed that the wrath of Juno Lacinia had unbalanced his mind.

[94] The idea of Ziolkowski (1992), 203–208, that *locatio* refers to the selection of a site for the temple and not to the contracting has no merit to it. Even if one grants that the word *locare* in the fourth century B.C.E. meant "to place", which is a dubious proposition in the first place, Livy certainly used the term in the standard first-century sense of "to hire out". This meaning would hold whether he referred to an action that took place in the fourth century or the first century; it is absurd to believe that Livy would have changed his usage according to the usage of the period he was describing. Despite the efforts of Ziolkowski, 214–219 and Mommsen, *RS* 2.618–623, among others, we know absolutely nothing about the process by which the site was chosen for a new temple. The topographical spread of temples

in hand with the notion that temples were commonly built from *manubiae* is the largely unspoken notion that the magistrate who vowed the temple often let the contract immediately on his return from the campaign. Yet we can point to a great many instances where this is simply not the case; the letting of the contract could languish for several years before any action was taken.[95] This fact provides yet another reason to regard the theory of manubial building with great skepticism. It will be worthwhile to review the evidence for the letting of contracts for new buildings in Rome, beginning with public structures other than temples. The comparison of temple building with the erection of other public buildings in Rome will help to isolate the potential means by which new temples were constructed in Rome. The differences between erecting temples and other public structures will also be useful in understanding the religious feelings of the Romans.

II.1 *Contracts for Public Buildings*

Most construction in Rome was undertaken by the censors, elected every five years and serving for eighteen months.[96] The Senate allotted a sum of money to these magistrates, but allowed the censors to choose the projects they would undertake. The censors were responsible for contracting to have the actual work done, and for maintaining general supervision of the project. There was no coordinated building program from censorship to censorship, but the censors were generally cognizant of Rome's needs and chose their projects accordingly. Thus, censorial contracts resulted in the construction of walls, aqueducts, basilicas and other structures essential to urban life in Rome. In the absence of censors, i.e. during the three and a half years between censorships, consuls are known to have let contracts, and praetors also let contracts in the absence of a consul.[97] In all

---

seems to indicate that conscious thought went into choosing a site, but no ancient source gives any testimony as to whether the Senate, the people, or the magistrate involved made the final decision.

[95] See below, p. 154 and n. 153.

[96] Mommsen, *RS* 1.449–455; de Ruggiero (1925), 47–49, 172–77; Strong (1968), 97–98; Robinson (1992), 48–50. See also Polybius 6.13.3. Examples of censorial contracts are too numerous to mention, but for a selection see Livy 29.37.2, 34.6.17, 41.27, 42.3.8.

[97] Mommsen, *RS* 1.236–243, 2.108–9, 2.232–8; de Ruggiero (1925), 49–51, 55;

these cases, when the magistrate was acting as the agent of the state in making a contract, the state treasury paid for the fulfillment of the contract.

Other building projects in Rome were carried out by the aediles as part of their *cura urbis*.[98] Such projects might involve mere ornamentation, such as the erection of a statue or a statue group, as when the Ogulnii set up a representation of the twins being suckled by the wolf at the *ficus Ruminalis* in 295.[99] Other aediles actually erected public buildings, as when two Aemilii constructed two porticoes and a wharf on the Tiber in 193, while another portico was added by the aediles of the following year.[100] The aediles did not draw on the state treasury for their building projects, but rather used money which they had collected from the fines they imposed on lawbreakers during their term of office. Thus public building projects always involved public officials and money which did not come out of the magistrate's pocket. The question before us now is to decide to what extent the procedure for erecting a basilica or an aqueduct was similar or dissimilar to building a new temple. Of particular concern is to determine who let these contracts, because that fact will help to illuminate the source of funding for new temples.

II.2   *Contracts for Temples*

The records of who let contracts for the construction of new temples are extremely sparse, as Livy's reports for the *votum* or the *dedicatio* of temples far outweigh his statements on *locatio*. Nevertheless, we have a certain amount of information which will be very useful if analyzed thoroughly. We will find that, just as with other building contracts in Rome, a number of different officials let contracts to build new temples. However, the Romans also created on occasion a separate office whose sole function was to oversee the construction of a particular temple, the *duumviri aedi locandae*. This is but one indication that contracts for the building of temples were placed in a separate

---

Strong (1968), 99; Robinson (1992), 48. For some examples, see Cicero, *Verr.* 2.1.130; *Ad Att.* 4.1.7; *Phil.* 14.38.

[98] Mommsen *RS* 2.496, 505–512; de Ruggiero (1925), 57–61; Strong (1968), 99; Robinson (1992), 48. Cf. also Varro, *LL* 5.81 and Cicero, *Leg.* 3.3.7, for the general *cura urbis* of the aediles.

[99] Livy 10.23.11–13.

[100] Livy 35.10.12, 35.41.10.

category from other public buildings. The fact that these buildings
possessed religious significance undoubtedly contributed to the fact
that they received special treatment.

The most startling difference between the construction of new
temples and other public buildings was noticed long ago: censors did
not ordinarily let contracts for the construction of new temples.[101]
We know of only two situations in which censors let temple contracts:
1) when they themselves had vowed that particular temple during a
previous year in office, and 2) when the temple was built on the
orders of the Sibylline Books. In the first instance, the personal connection to the temple seems to have provided the primary justification for letting the contract. C. Iunius Bubulcus, censor in 307, let
the contract for the temple of Salus, which he had vowed while serving
as consul in the Samnite War.[102] Similarly, M. Livius Salinator vowed
a temple to Iuventas at the battle of Metaurus in 207, and then let
the contract for the temple while serving as censor three years later.[103]
A third example may be provided by the temple of Fortuna Primigenia, although there are major problems with Livy's text here. Livy
refers to P. Sempronius Tuditanus as the person who vowed the
temple in 204, but when the temple was dedicated in 191, Livy
remarks that P. Sempronius Sophus had vowed the temple and let
the contract as censor.[104] Tuditanus must be right, for no Sophus is
known to have been active at this time; Livy's confusion was probably caused by the fact that Tuditanus held the censorship before
the consulship. This order of office-holding would have seemed highly
irregular to Livy, and may account for his attempt to have Tuditanus
let the contract before the consulship in which he actually vowed the

---

[101] Cf. Mommsen, *RS* 2.456–57; Marquardt (1888), 108–110; De Ruggiero (1925),
49; Strong (1968), 99; Stambaugh (1978), 565. This applies only to the construction
of new temples, and not for upkeep or repair to existing temples, which apparently
was the responsibility of the censors.

[102] Livy 10.1.9.

[103] Livy 36.36.5. In these instances where a censor let the contract for a temple
which he had vowed on an earlier campaign, it is unclear what money he used to
pay for the contract. Pietilä-Castrén (1987), 62, argues that the fact that M. Livius
Salinator was censor when he let the contract "certainly does not mean that he
used the *pecunia censoria* for this purpose." While this is true, the timing is suggestive,
and we may question whether after a lapse of several years an individual would still
have a separate tabulation of his *manubiae* to show that this was the source of funds
for the new temple. The question must remain open, but I seriously doubt whether
a temple whose contract was let several years after its vowing could be called manubial.

[104] Livy 34.53, 36.36.5. Cf. Briscoe (1981), 132–33. For the Sempronii and their
careers, cf. Broughton, *MRR*.

temple.[105] Nevertheless he does believe that the man who vowed the temple also let the contract while he was censor.

The second scenario, the letting of the contracts for a Sibylline-sponsored temple by the censors, is attested by only a single example, and thus may not represent a general practice. This was the temple of the Magna Mater, and that this case was somewhat exceptional should need little argument. The impetus for the temple had come from the Sibylline Books, which of course means that no individual was particularly associated with the cult's introduction. Even though an individual magistrate may have made the vow on behalf of the state, letting the contract for a Sibyl-motivated temple could not be considered his responsibility.[106] Under such circumstances, we might surmise that the responsibility for letting the contract would automatically pass to the censors, if there were any currently in office; the censors of 204, however, obtained a special decree of the Senate before they let the contract for the temple of the Magna Mater.[107] The censors apparently could not, or did not want to, simply exercise the prerogative of their office to let the contract, but rather they sought a *senatus consultum*. Temples built on the order of the Sibylline Books clearly depended on Senatorial authority, and as such an *s.c.* was obtained in order to let the contract. This example only confirms that censors did not regularly let temple contracts unless they themselves had vowed the temple in question.[108]

The aediles provided the other major source for building projects in Rome, and aediles did in fact build several temples using the money collected from fines. Aediles are known to have built six temples in Rome, including one built on order of the Sibylline Books.[109] Only

---

[105] Livy's attempt to have Tuditanus let the contract as censor may be significant. It would have been easy for Livy to have Tuditanus let the contract as consul on his return from the campaign. That Livy did not do so indicates that he did not believe this to be a regular practice, another factor arguing against the manubial building theory and consuls letting contracts immediately on their return to Rome. See further pp. 145–47.

[106] Cf. the temples of Venus Erycina and Mens in 217, which were vowed by the dictator Fabius Maximus and the praetor Titus Otacilius respectively.

[107] Livy 36.36.4. In 217 there were no censors in office, and we have no evidence to indicate how the contracts for the temples of Venus Erycina and Mens might have been let.

[108] The further example of the temple to Fortuna Equestris, which will be considered in more detail below pp. 155–57, provides an even stronger confirmation of this point.

[109] The temples are: a shrine to Concordia (Livy 9.46.6), temples to Venus (10.31.9), Victoria (10.33.9), Flora (Pliny, *NH* 18.286), Libertas (Livy 24.16.19), and Faunus

in one instance does Livy specify that the aediles actually let the
contract for a temple, but that instance shows that it is legitimate to
infer that fact from his statement that aediles built the temple. Under
the year 196, Livy reports that the plebeian aediles built a temple of
Faunus *in insula* from the fines which they had collected.[110] Two years
later, when reporting the dedication of the temple, the historian
remarks that the contract had been let by the aediles of 196 out of
the fines.[111] Thus, for the other cases where Livy merely indicates
that the aediles built a temple, we may conclude that this includes
the actual *locatio* of the structure. It is possible that aediles, like the
censors of 204, might have needed special permission from the Senate to let contracts for temples, particularly for the temple of Flora
built on order of the Sibylline Books, but we have no record of any
such *senatus consulta*. Note that Livy never reports that the censors
"built" a temple, again confirming that censors did not normally let
contracts for temples. While aediles occasionally did let such contracts, we have seen that temples initiated by aediles rather than by
generals are the exception in Rome, not the rule.[112]

One dictator is reported to have let the contracts for a temple
after returning from a triumphant campaign, but this temple is again
clearly exceptional. The dictator M. Furius Camillus performed an
evocatio on the Juno of Veii during his campaign of 396.[113] After his
return to the city, he let the contract for the temple to Juno Regina
before he resigned the dictatorship.[114] No one would deny that the
dictator possessed the legal authority to let a contract, but Camillus
is the only dictator known to have done so. The gradual disuse of
the military dictatorship may play some role in explaining this soli-
tary example. Nevertheless, this is also the only firmly attested example
of an *evocatio*, and there may be some link between these two unique
occurrences. We must note that Camillus did not attempt to discharge the vow of a tithe to Apollo before he resigned his commission, even though that vow had been made at the exact same moment

---

(33.42.10). For the temple of Libertas, Livy reports only that it was built with fines
by Ti. Gracchus, but the parallel to the other temples indicates he must have been
aedile when he did so.
[110] Livy 33.42.10.
[111] Livy 34.53.3.
[112] See Chapter One.
[113] Livy 5.21.
[114] Livy 5.23.7.
[115] For the vows, see Livy 5.21.1–3. The order of presentation in Livy 5.23 is as

as the vow to Juno.[115] The *evocatio* may have created a special circumstance where the dictator felt he himself had to let the contract immediately, before he resigned his office. It is impossible to take this incident as the basis for a more general practice for letting temple contracts.[116]

Most analyses of temple building in Rome have assumed, sometimes without stating it directly, that the consuls let the contracts for their temples on their return from the campaign, just as Camillus did as dictator.[117] Yet there is a major obstacle to this theory, in that our sources provide precious little evidence in support. In 293, the consul Sp. Carvilius returned from his triumphant campaign over the Etruscans and let the contract for a temple to Fors Fortuna while he was still in office; Livy describes these events before he describes the elections for the following year.[118] As we saw above, this is one of the few cases in which our source explicitly states that *manubiae* were used to finance the construction. There is thus some justification for connecting temples whose contracts were let by returning consuls with temples built with *manubiae*. Yet only one other temple might conform to this scenario; Livy remarks that the temple of Juno Sospita in the Forum Holitorium was vowed and contracted for by C. Cornelius in the Gallic war.[119] However, Livy provides no further details on the letting of this contract, and there are several reasons to be wary of this passage.[120] Even if the notice is accurate, two

---

follows: Camillus celebrates a triumph (4–6), lets the contract for Juno Regina and dedicates Mater Matuta (7), and resigns the dictatorship (7). Only then is the discussion of the gift to Apollo raised (8ff.).

[116] Again note that we do not know how the contract was let for the temple of Venus Erycina, vowed by the dictator Fabius Maximus.

[117] Mommsen, *RS* 3.1049–51; Bardon (1955), 166–74; Morgan (1975), 500, n. 2; Stambaugh (1978), 557–565; Robinson (1992), 48. De Ruggiero (1925), 51–55, lists thirty-six temples built by consuls.

[118] Livy 10.46.

[119] Livy 34.53.3.

[120] This passage is riddled with errors, textual or factual or both: 1) Livy has apparently confused the temple of Juno Sospita and Mater Matuta, for he calls the goddess "Juno Matuta" in this passage; 2) This notice is included with the notice about the temple of Fortuna Primigenia, where Livy has made mistakes in the magistrate's name and his office (see further pp. 142–43); 3) At the end of this passage Livy's text reads "*Haec eo anno acta*" even though the next chapter continues to deal with the same year. In addition, Livy claims that all four of the temples mentioned in this section had their contracts let by the same man who had first promoted the temple: one (Faunus) by aediles, one (Juno Sospita) by a censor following up his consular vow, one (Vediovis) by a consul following up a praetorian vow, and one (Fortuna Primigenia) where the offices are muddled. The "*locataque*" in reference to

examples do not constitute a recurring pattern, as two other temple contracts let by consuls will indicate.

In 200, L. Furius Purpurio, serving as praetor in Gaul, vowed a temple to Vediovis in the heat of battle.[121] When the temple was dedicated in 194, Livy remarks that the same man had let the contract while serving as consul, an office Purpurio held in 196.[122] Although this contract was let by a consul, the picture is a far cry from the returning general immediately setting about the temple construction. Rather, it seems much closer to the example of censors who let contracts for temples which they had vowed several years earlier as consul. Because Purpurio had only been praetor when he vowed the temple, he was able to let the contract as consul, his next magistracy. This incident confirms that it was the personal connection, not the specific magistracy of the censorship, that lay behind the previous temple contracts for Salus, Iuventas, and Fortuna Primigenia let by Bubulcus, Salinator, and Tuditanus.[123] Commanders who had vowed temples used their next available magistracy, if they obtained one, to let the contracts for their temples.

One other consul is known to have let the contract for a temple on his return from the campaign, but he seems not have done so in his capacity as consul. M'. Acilius Glabrio vowed a temple to Pietas during the battle with Antiochus at Thermopylae in 191. Livy reports that he also let the contract for that temple *ex senatus consulto*.[124] Livy does not state whether he let the contract before or after he celebrated his triumph. It would seem more likely that he did so afterwards, as he would have been occupied before the triumph with ensuring that the Senate in fact voted him a triumph and then the preparations for the celebration. If in fact Glabrio let the contract after his triumph, he would no longer have held proconsular *imperium*. Recognizing these facts, Mommsen believed that the phrase *ex senatus consulto* implied that Glabrio was appointed a *duumvir aedi locandae*, since we have no examples of a private citizen letting a contract for

---

C. Cornelius has a certain suspicious look; the contract was not let while Cornelius was fighting the Gauls, and though Livy mentions the vow earlier during the battle (32.30.10), he makes no separate reference to the contracting.

[121] Livy 31.21.12.

[122] Livy 34.53.7. This is one of the four temples mentioned in n. 120 above. Again we may doubt whether this temple, whose contract was let four years after its vow, could actually be built from *manubiae*. Cf. n. 103 above.

[123] See above, p. 142.

[124] Livy 40.34.5–6.

a public building.[125] Even if Glabrio still had the legal authority to let the contract, the fact that he obtained a *senatus consultum* to do so indicates that he felt the letting of contracts for temples depended on Senatorial authority. Although Glabrio himself had vowed the temple, he acted just as the censors of 204 did in regard to the temples built according to the Sibylline Books. Whether such permission was actually necessary in the legal sense is unclear, but less important; Glabrio at least felt that such permission was desirable in achieving his aims. This example counterbalances that of Sp. Carvilius and Fors Fortuna, and perhaps outweighs it, for the Senate's role as regards Carvilius is unspecified; they might have been involved in 293 as well. Returning consuls or proconsuls seem not to have used the bare authority of their office, if they still had it, in order to let the contract for temples which they had vowed.

To this point we have examined all of the regular offices we might expect to have let contracts for the construction of temples, but the standard procedure for such contracts remains elusive. None of the standard magistracies assumed this role; censors, consuls, dictators, and aediles all let contracts for temples, but none can be considered to have regularly performed this task. This point highlights the fact that the Romans treated religious affairs with special care, to ensure the *pax deum* and the safety of the Roman state. Only one rule can be discerned with relative security: if an individual who had vowed a temple later attained another magistracy before the contract had been let, he could use that office to perform this task. This principle applied whether he obtained the censorship or the consulship, for both offices possessed the authority to let contracts. Otherwise, no patterns can be discerned. Thus, we have exhausted the regular magistracies of the Roman republic, and now must consider the role of the special magistracy created solely for the purpose of letting temple contracts, the *duumviri aedi locandae*.

II.3 *The Creation and Employment of* Duumviri Aedi Locandae

The institution of *duumviri* played a significant role in the foundation of new temples, both in construction and dedication. *Duumviri aedi locandae* let contracts for at least three temples, those of Juno Moneta,

---

[125] Mommsen, *RS* 2.623, n. 1, followed by Pietilä-Castrén (1987), 88.

Concordia, and Fortuna Equestris.[126] Their counterparts, *duumviri aedi dedicandae*, are reported to have dedicated a total of ten temples built during the Republic, beginning with the temple of Castor and Pollux in 484 and continuing through the temples of Pietas and Venus Erycina in 181.[127] The institution may even have survived into imperial times, as it has been suspected that Augustus bestowed this position on his nephews Gaius and Lucius for all buildings erected in Rome.[128] Yet remarkably little is known about these men, in terms of the circumstances under which they were appointed and who appointed them. Livy's reports on their actions are laconic at best, and modern authorities have not focused much attention on the *duumviri*.[129] In this section we will be primarily concerned with the *duumviri aedi locandae*; the *duumviri aedi dedicandae* will be discussed in the next chapter, although they will be brought in to this analysis whenever it will help clarify the position of *duumviri* in general.[130] It will rapidly become apparent that the use of *duumviri* in the construction of a new temple implies a high degree of Senatorial involvement in that process, including funding from the state treasury.

The evidence for the process by which the *duumviri* were chosen is decidedly ambiguous. For this point, we will consider both *duumviri aedi locandae* and *duumviri aedi dedicandae*, since the selection process seems to have been similar for both offices. This will provide a larger data base on which to base conclusions. Of the thirteen known instances of *duumviri*, Livy provides no hint for how six of those pairs were chosen. In the seven instances where Livy does include some detail on how the *duumviri* obtained office, he always uses a passive form of the verb *creo*, usually the participle *creatus*. This form of the verb in reference to magistrates usually, but not always, denotes that the office was attained by popular election.[131] For instance, the military tribunes of 388, or the praetors and consuls of 191, were *creati* by the *comitia*.[132] However, the word is also used for the selection of

---

[126] Livy 7.28, 22.33.7, 40.44.9–10.

[127] Livy 2.42.5, 40.34. Cf. Appendix Four for a list of the known *duumviri*.

[128] Dio 55.10. Cf. Mommsen, *RS* 2.621, n. 1, and 2.624.

[129] For modern treatments, cf. Mommsen, *RS* 2.618–624; Pauly-Wissowa *RE* vol. 5, cols. 1801–1802; Daremberg-Saglio, 416 Wissowa, *RKR* 338–39; de Ruggiero (1925), 174–76. Only Mommsen devoted more than a paragraph or two to these men, and his interests were primarily legal and constitutional and not on the significance of their existence in Roman religion.

[130] The *duumviri aedi dedicandae* will be discussed in full in Chapter Five.

[131] Cf. Packard (1968).

[132] Livy 6.4.7, 36.45.9. These are only a few examples of many. The word *facti*

augurs, who were coopted until the *lex Domitia* of 104, and for the appointment of a *flamen Martialis* by the *pontifex maximus*.[133] The word *creatus* by itself is therefore not sufficient to indicate whether *duumviri* were elected by the populace or appointed by the Senate or a senior magistrate.

Fortunately, we do have two instances in which Livy provides more than just a simple participle to describe how *duumviri aedi locandae* or *duumviri aedi dedicandae* obtained office. In 217, the dictator Q. Fabius Maximus vowed a temple to Venus Erycina on the order of the Sibylline Books, while at the same time the praetor T. Otacilius vowed a temple to Mens for the same reason.[134] Two years later, when the temples were ready for dedication,

> Q. Fabius Maximus asked the Senate for permission to dedicate the temple of Venus Erycina which he had vowed as dictator. The Senate decreed that Ti. Sempronius the consul-designate, when he first entered office, should propose to the people that they order that Q. Fabius be *duumvir* for the sake of dedicating the temple.[135]

Accordingly, in the following year, "Q. Fabius Maximus and T. Otacilius Crassus were made *duumviri* for dedicating temples, Otacilius for Mens and Fabius for Venus Erycina."[136] Despite the use of the words *creati sunt* in the second passage, we should not envision a full-scale election with multiple candidates. Note that Ti. Sempronius brought a proposal to the people, and his proposal was not that the people should hold an election for *duumviri*, but that the people should order that Fabius be *duumvir*. It is significant that the proposal does not include the term *creatus*, but rather uses the word *iuberent* in regard to the people's action regarding Fabius.[137] The people were simply asked for their approval of the men chosen by the Senate and officially

---

could also be used of magistrates elected by the *comitia*, as with the consuls in 193 (Livy 35.10.10) and the praetors in 190 (Livy 37.47.8).

[133] Augur *creatus*: Livy 27.36.5. *Flamen Martialis creatus*: Livy 29.38.7. See Beard and North (1990), 19–25 for the methods by which Republican priests were chosen, especially 23, n. 5 for *flamines* and 24, n. 1 for augurs. For the *lex Domitia* see Cicero, *Leg. Agr.* 2.18.

[134] Livy 22.9–10.

[135] Livy 23.30.13–14: *Q. Fabius Maximus a senatu postulavit ut aedem Veneris Erycinae, quam dictator vovisset, dedicare liceret. Senatus decrevit ut Ti. Sempronius consul designatus, cum primum magistratum inisset, ad populum ferret ut Q. Fabium duumvirum esse iuberent aedis dedicandae causa.*

[136] Livy 23.31.9: *duumviri creati sunt Q. Fabius Maximus et T. Otacilius Crassus aedibus dedicandis, Menti Otacilius, Fabius Veneri Erycinae.*

[137] Cf. the language in the proposal put to the *populus* concerning the *ver sacrum* in 217 (Livy 22.10.2): *Velitis iubeatisne haec sic fieri?*

proposed to them by the consul, not to choose *duumviri* themselves. *Creati* in this context indicates approval by the *comitia*, but not election by it. Such comitial approval may not have been necessary in all cases, but even if it was, the essential decision on the identity of the *duumviri* had already been made by the Senate.

The other detailed example of the selection process involves *duumviri aedi locandae* rather than *duumviri aedi dedicandae*. In 217 *duumviri* were appointed to build the temple of Concordia, which was vowed by the praetor L. Manlius during a mutiny in Gaul: "C. Pupius and K. Quinctius Flamininus, created *duumviri* for this purpose by M. Aemilius the urban praetor, let the contract for building the temple on the *arx*."[138] *Creati* translated as "elected" here would strain the text; it seems more likely that the role of the urban praetor here was to appoint the *duumviri*, rather than to secure their election by the *comitia*. We might compare this passage to the creation of *duumviri navales* in 182, where the consuls are ordered to *creare* the two naval commissioners.[139] Interestingly, in the other instances where praetors are known to have appointed special commissions, they did not do so without higher authorization. Rather, either the Senate or the people ordered them to appoint commissioners for various purposes.[140] Such an order is not recorded for 217, but this is the only such instance where it is not recorded; surely we must imagine that either the people or the Senate directed the praetor to appoint *duumviri*.[141]

This supposition is borne out by two other instances in which Livy

---

[138] Livy 22.33.8: *Itaque duumviri ad eam rem creati a M. Aemilio praetore urbano C. Pupius et K. Quinctius Flamininus aedem in arce faciendam locaverunt.*

[139] Livy 40.18.7: *Duumviros in eam rem consules creare iussi.* The translation of the Loeb edition, that the Senate ordered the consuls "to secure the election of" *duumviri navales* seems farfetched. It is much more natural to translate this passage as "the consuls were ordered to appoint *duumviri* for this purpose," although there may be a sense in which the consuls were ordered to obtain comitial approval for the appointments. See above, pp. 148–49, and Packard (1968) for other examples of *creare* in Livy.

[140] The Senate decreed in 201 that the praetor should appoint *decemviri* for the purpose of surveying and dividing the land in Samnium and Apulia (Livy 31.4.3) and in 190 that the praetor, L. Aurunculeius, should appoint *triumviri* for leading out a colony (Livy 37.46.10). In 296 the tribunes were given the responsibility of conducting a plebiscite which ordered the praetor, P. Sempronius, to appoint *triumviri* again for leading out colonists (Livy 10.21.9).

[141] The phrase *in religionem venit* could refer either to the people or the Senate as the instigator of this action; both had good reason for wanting to see this temple built as soon as possible.

provides a little more context for the selection of *duumviri*: both show the Senate ordering that *duumviri* be created. When Camillus resigned his command after vowing a temple to Juno Moneta, "the Senate ordered that *duumviri* be created in order to build this temple in a style worthy of the grandeur of the Roman people."[142] A similar procedure is reported in 179, when Flaccus brought up the issue of the games and the temple to Fortuna Equestris which he had vowed: "The games were decreed and also that *duumviri* should be created for letting the contract for the temple."[143] These examples make it more likely that the Senate, rather than the people, ordered M. Aemilius to appoint *duumviri* for the temple of Concordia. Such a scenario suits the general picture of Roman religion, as the Senate was usually unwilling to let the people play a significant role in the state religion.[144] Thus, the use of *creo* in the passive does not necessarily imply a role for the *comitia*, although most uses do point to some sort of role. In regard to the creation of *duumviri*, such a role would have been limited to mere approval of the Senate's choices, as with Fabius and Otacilius.

These two parallel procedures raise the question of whether there was a difference, in religious authority or otherwise, between *duumviri* who were approved by the *comitia* and those who were simply appointed. This phenomenon may be related to the gravity which the Romans attached to certain vows. The Romans seem to have valued some vows as being more important than others, as evidenced by the speed with which the temples were built and the scrupulousness with which the construction was performed. The temples to Mens and Venus Erycina were part of the religious response aimed at repulsing Hannibal, an action of the highest importance for the whole state and of equal importance to all the members of the state. The construction of these two temples took only two years, despite the immense resources which had to be committed at the same time to the defense of the city itself. The referral to the *comitia* for approval of the *duumviri* contributed to the emphasis placed on this religious act, involving the whole community in the fulfillment of the vow and not just the upper levels of the government. Having the *comitia*

---

[142] Livy 7.28.5: *Senatus duumviros ad eam aedem pro amplitudine populi Romani faciendam creari iussit.*

[143] Livy 40.44.10: *Ludi decreti et ut duumviri ad aedem locandam crearentur.*

[144] Cf. Mommsen, *RS* 3.1050; Wardman (1982), 38–39; Beard & North (1990), 30–34.

approve the selection of *duumviri* gave an indication of the gravity of
the moment and sent a message to the heavens that the whole Roman
state was beseeching the aid of the gods.[145] In other, less extreme
situations, such complete involvement was not required.

Two basic facts emerge from the evidence on the creation of
duumviri, which as we have seen is by no means uniform. On the one
hand, the Senate did not, to the best of our knowledge, directly appoint
the *duumviri* which it selected. This practice would be in keeping with
the Senate's role as a consultative body which did not usually execute
its own decisions, but delegated that responsibility to others. On the
other hand, regardless of whether comitial action was necessary in
order to approve them, the decision on when to appoint *duumviri*
and whom to appoint as *duumvir* was taken by the Senate. Again this
practice was in keeping with the Senate's practice of keeping affairs
of religion out of the hands of the populace as far as possible.

Because the Senate was responsible for the appointment of *duumviri
aedi locandae*, we might expect that the state treasury would pay for
the temples built by these men, and an examination of the temples
built by these men confirms this supposition. The *duumviri* for the
temple of Concordia could have drawn on no other source than the
state treasury. Manlius had not conducted a very successful campaign and had only vowed the temple during a mutiny, not a battle
with the enemy, so his booty is not a plausible source of financing.
Nor is it possible to conceive of *duumviri* being directed to spend
money from Manlius' personal estate. The treasury is the only logical alternative. Similar reasoning holds for the temple for Juno Moneta,
although Camillus was more successful in his campaign. If he had
brought booty back from his campaign, the *duumviri* would not be
able to spend money that he kept for himself. They would have
access only to that part which had been deposited in the state treasury. For the temple of Fortuna Equestris, we know that Flaccus
collected money from the Spaniards for the fulfillment of his vows.[146]
However, it seems that this money was intended to be spent on the
games which Flaccus had vowed, since the remainder of that chapter in Livy deals with the restrictions which the Senate placed on the

---

[145] Note that the people's approval was also required for approval of the *ver sacrum*
(Livy 22.10). The latter could be explained on economic grounds, that the farmers
were not to be deprived of a part of their livelihood without a chance to vote, as
well as on religious grounds.

[146] Livy 40.44.9.

collection and expenditure of money to be spent exclusively on games.[147] The *duumviri* would therefore not have had access to this money, and again must have relied on the state treasury to pay for the contracts which they had let.[148] The involvement of *duumviri aedi locandae* clearly implies that the state treasury would assume responsibility for the construction of the new temple.

Let us now turn to an examination of the circumstances under which *duumviri aedi locandae* were employed. In all three known instances, we can point to specific, practical reasons for their appointment. In 345, the dictator L. Furius Camillus vowed a temple to Juno Moneta in the heat of battle against the Aurunci, and then resigned his command when he returned to Rome.[149] As a private citizen, Camillus could not let the contract for a public building, and no one else was available to do the job; there were no censors in 345, and censors, as we have seen, were not generally involved with temple construction anyway. Someone else had to be chosen to ensure that the temple was constructed in a timely fashion. Recourse was thus had to the creation of a separate board of men, the *duumviri*, "in order to build a temple worthy of the greatness of the Roman people."[150] The sequence of events is presented as entirely unexceptional. The Senate assumed responsibility for building the temple only after Camillus resigned, but there is no reason to believe that they expected Camillus to remain in office until the contract for the temple had been let. It was not part of his job. Nor can one postulate that the Senate's action was prompted by the location of the temple on the property of a condemned man; the Senate did have to approve the use of public land for a temple, but could have done so without appointing *duumviri*.[151] The *duumviri* were needed precisely because no one else was suited to letting the contract for this temple.

---

[147] Livy 40.44.10–12.

[148] The *duumviri* might have been able to utilize any excess funds collected by Flaccus which the Senate did not let him spend on the games. If Flaccus had agreed to this, the *duumviri* would still have drawn on the state treasury for any money they needed which was not provided by Flaccus. There may in fact have been little money left over after the games, for Livy reports that they were celebrated *magno apparatu* (42.10.5). Cf. Pietilä-Castrén (1987), 113.

[149] Livy 7.28.4.

[150] Livy 7.28.5: *Senatus duumviros ad eam aedem pro amplitudine populi Romani faciendam creari iussit.*

[151] The only other example of a temple built on land of a condemned person is the temple of Tellus, built in the 260's on the land of Spurius Cassius who had been condemned for aiming at the monarchy in 485. Florus reports that P. Sempronius

The temple of Concordia presented a different set of circumstances, but again the appointment of *duumviri* was meant to ensure the timely construction of a new temple. Livy reports the following events in 217:

> There was also a religious concern that the [contract for the] temple of Concordia, which the praetor L. Manlius had vowed during a mutiny two years earlier in Gaul, had not been let up to this time. Therefore, C. Pupius and K. Quinctius Flamininus, having been appointed for this purpose by the urban praetor M. Aemilius, let the contract for building the temple on the *arx*.[152]

The religious concern at this time was prompted no doubt by the Roman failures against Hannibal. Under normal circumstances, a two-year lapse of time between the vow and the letting of the contract would not have seemed threatening, but the situation in 217 was far from normal.[153] The temple of Concordia would have seemed particularly important at this time in order to indicate a renewed *concordia* amongst the Romans as they united to face Hannibal. The previous years had seen a great increase in tension within the state, as Flaminius pushed his reformist agenda in the face of much Senatorial opposition. In the light of Flaminius' election to the consulship earlier in the year, the decision to expedite the construction of the temple to Concordia should be seen as a public attempt at reconciliation on the part of the Senate.[154] It may also have attempted to

---

Sophus vowed this temple when an earthquake struck during a battle against the Picenes, but we know nothing about the other aspects of the construction of this temple.

[152] Livy 22.33.8: *In religionem etaim venit aedem Concordiae, quam per seditionem militarem biennio ante L. Manlius praetor in Gallia vovisset, locatam ad id tempus non esse. Itaque duumviri ad eam rem creati a M. Aemilio praetore urbano C. Pupius et K. Quinctius Flamininus aedem in arce faciendam locaverunt.*

[153] Several temple vows went more than two years without a contract being let and without the Senate or the praetor stepping in to appoint *duumviri*. Cf. the temple of Salus, whose contract was let in 307 although it had been vowed at least four years earlier (Livy 9.43.25); the temple of Honos et Virtus of M. Claudius Marcellus, which was originally vowed in 222, but whose contract had not been let by 211, when the vow was renewed (Livy 27.25.7, Val. Max. 1.1.8); the temple of Iuventas, which was vowed in 207 but the contract was not let until 204 (Livy 36.36.5); and the temple of Vediovis *in insula* whose contract was let in 196 although it had been vowed in 200 (Livy 34.53.7).

[154] Temples to Concordia seem to have functioned as a means of attempting to secure concord amongst the Romans following a period of civil unrest. The first such foundation, which is probably legendary rather than historical, was ascribed to Camillus in 367 following passage of the Licinian-Sextian laws. The first actual shrine to Concordia was the dedication by the aedile Cn. Flavius in 304, following his publication of a legal calendar. The most famous dedication of a shrine to Concordia

ensure a renewed sense of *concordia* with the gods, and therefore ensure success in the upcoming struggle with Hannibal. As Manlius was no longer in office, the expediency of *duumviri* was employed by the Senate to insure the prompt completion of this temple.[155]

The construction of the temple for Fortuna Equestris presented a third different scenario, but again one solved by the appointment of *duumviri*. Q. Fulvius Flaccus had vowed this temple as propraetor in 180, and the following year, after his election to the consulship, he brought the question of this vow before the Senate, which ordered *duumviri* to be chosen to let the contract for the temple.[156] Unlike Purpurio, who had used his subsequent consulship to let the contract for his temple, Flaccus did not take advantage of his subsequent magistracy to do this, perhaps because he was shortly to depart Rome for his campaign in Liguria and thus could not stay in Rome to supervise this stage of the process. Nor was responsibility for the temple given to the censors of this year, and perhaps no other example demonstrates as vividly that censors did not ordinarily let contracts for temples as part of their public works programs. The censors of 179, M. Aemilius Lepidus and M. Fulvius Nobilior, were notable for their building activity, and yet the Senate gave the task of letting the contract for Fortuna Equestris to a separate commission.[157] Contracts for temples were clearly considered a separate category by the Senate and assigned to a separate board of men.

The example of Fulvius Flaccus also proves that employment of *duumviri aedi locandae* did not necessarily terminate the involvement of the vower in the construction of the temple. Fulvius was elected censor in 174 and devoted himself to an ambitious building program, and he did not neglect this temple:

> Q. Fulvius Flaccus the censor was striving with zealous exertion that there would not be any temple in Rome larger or more splendid than

---

was also the least successful; the rededication of a shrine by the consul L. Opimius following his attack on C. Gracchus and his followers was met with great hostility on the part of the plebs. On these foundations, see Momigliano (1942).

[155] We can only speculate on why Manlius himself was not appointed a *duumvir*. Perhaps he had been killed at Trebia or Trasimene, or perhaps he was off on campaign or unavailable for some other reason. It is also possible that he did not have enough friends in the Senate to support him. The sources reveal no particular support for any of these hypotheses. It seems difficult to believe that the Senate held Manlius personally responsible for the religious breach, since he had not yet held an office in which he could have let the contract.

[156] Livy 40.44.9–10.

[157] See Broughton *MRR*, 1.392, for the building activity of these censors.

the temple of Fortuna Equestris, which he had vowed as praetor in Spain during the Celtiberian war. Thinking that it would add much ornamentation to the temple if the roof tiles were made of marble, he set out for Bruttium and stripped the temple of Juno Lacinia of half its tiles, thinking that this would be enough to cover what was being built.[158]

Even though Flaccus had arranged for *duumviri* to begin building the temple, he himself, as censor, took an active role in the temple's completion. This was no doubt due to his position as censor; Flaccus must have used censorial money to transport the tiles to Rome, and it was only his office which kept the citizens of Bruttium from preventing his removal of the tiles. One should also note that this action was more in the line of decoration than construction, and we have already seen how other Romans used *manubiae* to decorate their temples. Flaccus caused a stir precisely because he did *not* use his *manubiae*, but attempted to despoil an Italian sanctuary.[159]

Still, it is noteworthy that Flaccus brought the matter of his vows before the Senate himself. On the one hand, the Senate did not high-handedly intervene and force a particular resolution on him involving his temple and games. On the other hand, Flaccus felt that it was necessary to seek the cooperation and support of the Senate rather than single-handedly pressing ahead with his projects or delegating responsibility on his own authority. This is all the more remarkable considering the ambitions of Flaccus, for he has been held up as an example of those nobles of the early second century "who knew no rule other than their pleasure or their ambition."[160] And yet exactly here, in his erection of a building which was apparently intended to further his own political career, we find Flaccus consulting with the Senate and we find *duumviri* placed in charge of the actual construction. The implications of this action deserve special emphasis. For one, Flaccus may not be quite the "individualist" as he has been characterized or better, the whole opposition which modern scholars have set up between "individualists" and "commu-

---

[158] Livy 42.3.1–2: *Q. Fulvius Flaccus censor aedem Fortunae Equestris, quam in Hispania praetor bello Celtiberico voverat, faciebat enixo studio ne ullum Romae amplius aut magnificentius templum esset. Magnum ornatum ei templo ratus adiecturum, si tegulae marmoreae essent, profectus in Bruttios aedem Iunonis Laciniae ad partem dimidiam detegit, id satis fore ratus ad tegendum quod aedificaretur.* The Senate eventually forced Flaccus to drop this plan, and the tiles were returned to Bruttium, where they remained on the ground because no one could figure out how to reinstall them on the roof.

[159] For a further discussion of the implications of this incident, see above, pp. 138–39.

[160] Champeaux (1987), 136.

nalists", i.e. supporters of the Senate, may be overdrawn. Roman politicians could, and did, work to distinguish themselves amongst the other members of the oligarchy *at the same time* as they enhanced the control of public affairs by that same oligarchy. A politician could not long survive in Rome without caring both for the interests of the state and for the interests of the Senate.[161] If an ambitious man such as Flaccus worked in cooperation with the Senate to build his temple, it argues strongly that this procedure was the best way for Flaccus to look after his own interests. Thus, we should not be surprised if most other generals also brought the question of their temples vows before the Senate, permitting the Senate to play a major role in the construction of these monuments.

Other evidence shows that this may in fact have been the normal procedure for the fulfillment of vows made by generals on campaign. Much of this evidence is drawn from vows made for games, but the parallel is appropriate because both were vowed by generals during campaigns. The example just discussed of Flaccus, who vowed both games and a temple, indicates that the Senate did hold a similar competence for both vows.[162] In an incident discussed earlier, Livy reports the following meeting of the Senate in 205: "There, the question being raised by Publius Scipio [the future Africanus], a decree of the Senate was passed that he should celebrate the games which he had vowed during the mutiny of the soldiers in Spain, drawing upon the money which he himself had brought into the treasury."[163] Some familiar elements are present here: Scipio made a vow and brought the matter before the Senate, which approved the vow and directed that money to pay for the games should come from the state treasury. A similar scenario occurred fifteen years later, except that the Senate refused to pay for the games vowed by Scipio Nasica. This case is clearly exceptional, however, for it is the only place where Livy records the rejection of such a request.[164] It is clear that Nasica fully expected the Senate to pay for his games, and he had good reason for that expectation; in addition to the example of Africanus, other examples illustrate that it was the normal action for

---

[161] Cf. the remarks of Brunt (1990), 49ff.

[162] If anything, one would expect the Senate's competence to be greater in the case of temples, which involved a permanent addition to the Roman pantheon and a continuing financial commitment.

[163] Livy 28.38.14. Cf. the discussion in Chapter Two, pp. 55–60.

[164] Livy 36.36.

the Senate to approve the request.[165] The procedure for both games and temples vowed on campaign is clear: a general makes a vow, brings that vow to the attention of the Senate and requests public approval and funding, and then fulfills the vow in accord with the Senatorial decision.

There is thus no reason to view the appointment of *duumviri aedi locandae* as an extraordinary occurrence. Although we have only three firm examples of these *duumviri*, we have only two examples of consuls on their return to Rome letting contracts for temples vowed in the heat of battle; we also know of two censors and one consul who let a contract for a temple vowed as praetor.[166] M'. Acilius Glabrio has not been included in any category; as discussed above, he seems most likely to have been a *duumvir aedi locandae*. In addition, the Senate ordered the construction of the temple to Jupiter Stator in 294, which had been vowed in battle against the Samnites that year; the means available to the Senate for building this temple would have been the appointment of *duumviri aedi locandae*.[167] There were thus two mechanisms for letting contracts to build new temples: the person who vowed the temple might let the contract, usually during a subsequent magistracy but possibly before laying down his *imperium*, or the Senate might employ *duumviri* for this purpose. No rule existed indicating how long the Senate would wait for the vower to obtain a subsequent magistracy and let the contract; rather this time period might depend on the individual's strength within the Senate as well as the individual's desire to personally let the contract.[168] The evidence as we have it indicates that both procedures were used in roughly equal measures and in fact, because only one in five consuls could attain the censorship, *duumviri* may have let the majority of temple contracts, especially as iteration became increasingly infrequent.[169] Livy or his sources, more concerned with vows and dedications, simply neglected these details about the *locatio*.

---

[165] Cf. Livy 31.49.5, 39.5.7, for other games vowed by generals in battle.

[166] P. Sempronius Tuditanus is omitted here because of the corruption in the passage referring to him. See above, pp. 142–43.

[167] Livy 10.37.16.

[168] Of course, since censorial elections were held only once every five years, only one in five consuls could go on to become censor. The Senate might thus have considered failure to win the next censorial election reason enough to proceed with the construction of the temple, rather than waiting another five years on the slim chance that the politician involved would win that election.

[169] Morgan (1975), 500 n. 2, expresses an opposite view. He considers, but ulti-

III. *Conclusions*

The central focus of this chapter has been to refute the notion that new temples in Rome were commonly erected by a victorious general singlehandedly by the use of his *manubiae*. Rather, the Senate played an active role by appointing special commissioners to let the contract and by providing the funds for construction. Private initiative mingled with public oversight to create a situation in which both sides shared in the rewards; a sharp distinction between private and public is again not possible. Thus Livy can record the involvement of the Postumii, father and son, in the vowing and dedication of the temple of Castor and Pollux, while Dionysius of Halicarnassus writes merely that the city built the temple.[170] We need not exercise our ingenuity to determine which account is more reliable, for there is no contradiction in these reports; the individual did make the vow, but the Senate paid for the construction.

The use of *duumviri aedi locandae* has both religious and political significance. The Romans did not entrust the construction of sacred structures to the same men who were responsible for other public buildings in Rome. Rather than utilizing the ordinary magistracy of the censorship, they appointed men whose only task was the construction of an appropriate temple. For all of the discussion in modern literature concerning the mingling of secular and religious in Rome, temple building is one area where the religious was carefully separated from the secular. The Romans were not willing to place the fulfillment of these vows in the hands of the censors or other regular magistrates. Perhaps they felt that these magistrates would not be able to devote sufficient attention to the important task of building a suitable home for a new deity, or perhaps they were afraid that human rivalries would interfere, if one man's *inimicus* happened to be in office when the contract for his temple needed to be let.

---

mately rejects, the notion that it was customary for a consul to request the appointment of *duumviri*, preferring instead to postulate that the consuls let these contracts themselves. However, he does not face the objections to this view raised above and, while he notes the relative scarcity of *duumviri aedi locandae*, he apparently does not recognize that these examples are more plentiful than those of consuls letting contracts themselves.

[170] Livy 2.20, 2.42; Dion. Hal. 6.13.4. Compare the temple of Tellus; Florus (1.14.2) mentions the vow made during the earthquake by P. Sempronius Sophus, while Valerius Maximus (6.3.1b) claims that the Senate built the temple and Dionysius of Halicarnassus (8.79.3) again says that the city built the temple.

These factors presented potential problems which might put the Romans' relationship with their gods in jeopardy. Such considerations would not be an issue if the vower himself was in office; these men could be trusted to fulfill their own vows properly. These explanations are speculative; the fact is that Roman religious feeling demanded that special care be taken with the construction of new temples.

The conclusions reached in this chapter also square well with the conclusions reached in the previous chapters. As noted earlier, it would be strange indeed if the state had little or no control over the new cults and temples which became part of the state religion. Yet widespread manubial building would entail just that, for the general had almost total control in that scenario; he vowed the temple while on campaign, and then he built the temple with his own money when he returned, leaving little leeway to the Senate. Under the scenario presented here, however, the Senate played a significant role in the construction of new temples in Rome, even those which had been vowed by generals on campaign, which means that the Senate and its magistrates had to cooperate closely. Magistrates, particularly consuls, were still responsible for making vows and initiating the process, but on their return to Rome they sought approval from the Senate. The Senate, in approving these vows, reciprocated by often providing the funds necessary to fulfill the vow.

The use of state funds in the construction of new temples had distinct advantages for the individual. For one, use of state funds would free up a general's *manubiae* for other uses, whether that be personal enjoyment or other attempts at ingratiating himself with the electorate. A strict adherence to the manubial theory would also disadvantage those who fought campaigns against enemies who could not be expected to produce much in the way of spoils. Yet we have seen such generals were not disadvantaged, as four temples were vowed by generals who fought the Ligurians and several others who fought against Gauls.[171] Nor were those who fought in Greece or Asia Minor automatically advantaged, for only a few temples were vowed by generals fighting in those areas.[172] The use of state funds in the erection of temples provided a level playing field for all generals who wished to vow temples while on campaign. This provided a means

---

[171] Against the Ligurians: Honos (233), Venus Erycina (181), Diana (179), and Juno Regina (179). Against Gauls: Juno Sospita (194) and Vediovis (194).

[172] Pietas (181), Lares Permarini (179), and Hercules Victor (142).

of minimizing potential conflict between the consuls-elect over the assignment of campaigns as much as possible. Even the consul-elect who drew the less desirable campaign would be able to vow a temple and reap the benefits of this action.

In an ironic fashion, the findings in this chapter actually support the notion at the heart of the manubial building theory even while militating against the idea that temples were let by consuls on their return to Rome and built with *manubiae*. It remains a fact of Roman political life that there were benefits to the individual who vowed a temple, for temples did serve as a means of increasing a general's *gloria*. In his neglect of the *locatio*, Livy may be reflective of a more general feeling concerning the construction of new temples in Rome. The *locatio* was not as significant a moment as either the vow or the dedication. Making the vow would inextricably link the general's name with that temple; even today we know the names of over half the men who vowed temples, more than for those who let contracts and dedicated temples combined. The dedication was a public ceremony, a festive occasion where the dedicant played the central role; his name would be on everyone's lips. By contrast, the *locatio* occurred in less visible surroundings, out of public view. It was the behind-the-scenes activity without which the temple could not be built, but for which there was little *gloria* to be gained; as such, it provided a less useful vehicle for promoting one's name. Some Roman commanders were clearly content to have the Senate appoint someone else to take care of the actual construction and hope for the opportunity to dedicate the temple, a hope which, as the next chapter will indicate, was often fulfilled. A general did not have to use *manubiae* and oversee the temple from start to finish, since performing the vow and the dedication would provide him with the requisite *gloria*, but he could still use his *manubiae* to decorate the structure and in that way attempt to display his own individual prowess. Building temples should no longer be seen as merely "a means of perpetuating a name and of winning popularity."[173] Rather, it shows another way in which the *gloria* of the individual could be greatly enhanced by the association of his accomplishments with the interests of the state.

---

[173] Morgan (1973a), 223.

CHAPTER FIVE

THE DEDICATION

The final step in the addition of a new temple to the Roman religious system was its dedication. After construction of the temple was completed, a ceremony was held to formally consecrate the structure to the appropriate deity. At first glance it might appear that this ceremony is less significant for our study, because it involves a *fait accompli*. The temple has been built: a vow has been made, land and money set aside, architects engaged, a structure erected. The ceremony simply marks the official birthday of the cult. Nevertheless several aspects of the dedication are full of implications for Roman politics and for Roman religion, particularly the identity of individuals who performed the dedications. As we have already seen, the person who vowed a new temple provided himself with a lasting fame, as his name was likely to be remembered in connection with the temple. But the dedication, which was performed with great pomp and often accompanied by games, offered a more immediate form of *gloria*, more directly applicable to the competition among the aristocrats in Rome. On most occasions, the dedication was performed by the same man who had undertaken the vow (or his son), so that he (or his family) would earn both the immediate and the lasting *gloria*. This tendency for the same man to vow and dedicate the temple offers further confirmation that from a religious viewpoint the temple vows were considered personal vows, *vota privata* in the sense that they were to be fulfilled by the same man who undertook them. Of course, religion and politics were inextricably linked in Rome: we shall see instances both where the normal procedure was abandoned because of political concerns, and where it was abandoned because of religious concerns. The maneuvering which occurred around dedications provides a sure indication that this ceremony was by no means viewed as an insignificant anticlimax.

I. *The Legal Authority to Dedicate a Temple*

As with several of the other aspects of temple building, we should begin with an examination of who possessed the authority to perform this action, and in this case we actually have two texts which directly address this issue. Cicero and Livy both indicate that there were laws which placed restrictions on who could dedicate a temple.[1] There are some differences in their two accounts, however, and modern scholarship has expended much ink in attempting to determine whether they refer to the same law or two different laws.[2] The proper place to begin our inquiry is thus with an analysis of these two texts and an attempt to discover not only whether they refer to one law or two, but more importantly what the content of the law(s) might have been.

Under the year 304, Livy describes the dedication of a shrine to Concordia by the curule aedile Cn. Flavius. In this account, Cornelius Barbatus, the *pontifex maximus*, was reluctant to dictate the formulaic words for a dedication to Flavius, asserting that according to the *mos maiorum* only a consul or a commanding general (*imperator*) could dedicate a temple. Nonetheless Barbatus was forced by the will of the people (*consensu populi*) to dictate the proper formula to Flavius. Following this incident, the Senate passed a resolution, which the people voted into law, that no one should dedicate a sacred precinct or an altar without orders from the Senate or a majority of the tribunes of the plebs.[3]

Many elements in this episode are open to question, especially as the first decade of Livy's work must be treated with great care. Although some scholars have taken the claim of Barbatus to indicate the situation prior to 304, this claim must be regarded with skepticism. The temple of Concord was in fact *not* the first to be dedicated

---

[1] Livy 9.46.6–7; Cicero, *De Domo* 49.127 and *Ad Att.* 4.2.3.

[2] The argument in favor of the identification of the two laws was made most strongly by Willems (1878–1883), 306–309, and opposed by Niccolini (1934), 76, 403–404. The *communis opinio* has now come to rest on Niccolini's position. See Rotondi (1912), 235; Nisbet (1939), 176; Broughton, *MRR* 2.471; Bleicken (1975), 155 and n. 59; Stambaugh (1978), 558; Linderski (1986), 2224; and most recently Tatum (1993), who accepts that the two laws were different while attempting to "shatter this academic concord" on the actual formulation of Cicero's law. Ziolkowski (1992), 224–227, provides a quick summary of the scholarship on this issue. See further pp. 167–68 and n. 16.

[3] Livy 9.46.7: *Itaque ex auctoritate senatus latum ad populum est ne quis templum aramve iniussu senatus aut tribunorum plebei partis maioris dedicaret.*

by a magistrate other than a consul or an *imperator*: according to
Livy, the temple of Mercury had been dedicated in 495 by a senior
centurion, while two other temples had been dedicated by *duumviri*.[4]
Nor can one view the claim of Barbatus as a Livian retrojection of
the situation of his own day; a glance at the records of who dedicated temples reveals no such custom even in Livy's day, for fewer
temples were dedicated by consuls and *imperatores* than by other
magistrates.[5] If in fact Barbatus did object to Flavius' action on the
grounds of the *mos maiorum*, it would seem that he was merely using
this as a pretext in an attempt to prevent Flavius from dedicating
this shrine. Certainly his statement can not be taken as the norma-
tive situation in regard to dedicants prior to 304.

There are further problems with which to contend in Livy's account
of these events. Given that the objections of Barbatus were based on
the rank of the person making the dedication, it is noteworthy that
the subsequent law made no ruling on the issue of who could perform dedications, but concerned itself entirely with the issue of who
could *authorize* such dedications. Furthermore, the stories of the dedications of both the temple to Concordia and the prior temple to
Mercury fit far too smoothly into Livy's scheme of opposition between the patricians and the plebs to provide us with much confidence in the details. This concern is particularly acute when the events
of 304 are juxtaposed with the passage of the *lex Ogulnia* in 300,
opening the augurate and the pontificate to plebeians.[6] These considerations should again make us aware of the danger in placing too
much weight on the specific details of these events as reported by
Livy. Certain elements in the story of Flavius may not be accurate,

---

[4] For Mercury, see Livy 2.27. The temples dedicated by *duumviri* prior to 304
were Castor and Pollux in 484 (Livy 2.42) and Mars in 392 (Livy 6.5).
None of the scholars holding to Barbatus' formulation of the *mos maiorum* offers
an explanation for the temple of Mercury, while the *duumviri* are discounted by
arguing that they were invested with a quasi-consular power which gave them the
ability to perform dedications. On this theory, cf. Mommsen, *RS* 2.622. Two objections may be raised: 1) Barbatus did not speak of magistrates *cum imperio*, but rather
named specific magistrates which in his view had the right to dedicate temples; it is
modern scholars who have brought the issue of *imperium* forward; 2) Mommsen's
theory has no evidence to support it, but relies on this assumption that *imperium*
was necessary to dedicate temples and therefore *duumviri* must have been invested
with a type of *imperium*. In fact, of the six temples with known dedicators prior to
304, three were dedicated by consuls or imperatores, while three were dedicated by
others.
[5] See Appendix One for the known dedicators of temples.
[6] Livy 10.6.3–9.2.

and Livy may have placed the episode in what he felt was an appropriate time period, so we must proceed very cautiously.

It does appear that Livy's account may be trusted on the facts of most importance to our investigation, the dedication of a shrine by Flavius and the subsequent passage of a law. For the former, Pliny the Elder confirms that the aedile Flavius did indeed dedicate a shrine to Concordia.[7] For the latter, we may have some confidence in the passage of the law and its substance as reported by Livy precisely because it does *not* conform to a neat scheme involving increased plebeian rights. A recent study has tried to argue from the relation of the law to the Struggle of the Orders that Livy must have reported the substance of the law incorrectly, for the plebs had just won a victory by forcing the *pontifex maximus* to dictate the dedication formula to Flavius: "Why should the people have given back the victory they had just won and make the Senate, even if on par with the college of tribunes of the plebs, the dispenser of the right to *dedicatio*?"[8] Yet the fact the law of 304 violates the simplistic progression of plebeian rights which Livy wants to portray is a good reason for believing not only in the authenticity of the law but also that Livy recorded its provisions properly. He would not have invented a law which violated his schema, but rather must have found a notice of this law in the annalistic record. Although he may have been mistaken in his attempt to link the law of 304 to the expansion of plebeian rights and the dedication of the temple of Concordia by Flavius, Livy correctly reported its substance.

The context of patrician-plebeian relations in fact seems to be an erroneous way to view the thrust of this law. The law of 304 did not result in a dramatic change in the identity of dedicants, for no aedile or tribune is known to have dedicated a public shrine after Flavius.[9] Rather, the issue confronted and settled in 304 may have been one of secular versus pontifical authority. Despite the presence of numerous priestly specialists (i.e. the pontiffs, augurs, *decemviri*, haruspices, et al.), the direction of Roman religion remained firmly under secular control. Whenever the Senate consulted any of these experts, strictly speaking they did so only for advice; the Senate maintained the final

---

[7] Pliny, *NH* 33.19.

[8] Ziolkowski (1992), 228.

[9] Cf. Appendix One. On Clodius' attempt to dedicate a shrine of Libertas in Cicero's house while tribune, see below, pp. 166–67.

authority to decide whether or not to accept that advice.[10] In 304, the *pontifex maximus* had attempted to interfere by asserting who was or was not qualified to dedicate a temple. The law passed in response declared that henceforth only the Senate or the tribunes were competent to approve, or conversely disapprove, potential dedicants. The provision allowing a majority of tribunes to approve dedications may reflect the increasing influence of the plebs in religious matters; the Senate managed to avoid direct popular involvement, but in order to get the law approved may have been forced to grant this power to the tribunes. The issue confronted in 304 thus may not have involved agitation for increased involvement of the people or of plebeian offices in the dedication of temples, but rather concerned Senatorial vs. priestly control over the approval of dedicants.

Cicero's evidence on the necessity for dedications to be properly authorized is of a slightly different nature. This evidence is preserved in his speech *De Domo Sua* and in the letter to Atticus which informs his friend of the results obtained by the speech (4.2). The sequence of events can be summed up briefly. Cicero, on his return from exile in 57, discovered that Clodius had consecrated a shrine to Libertas in his house on the Palatine. Clodius was attempting to deprive Cicero the use of his house, for consecrated land was considered *res sacra* and could not ever be returned to secular use.[11] Cicero contended that the consecration had not been legally performed, and therefore that he should be able to remove the shrine and take possession of his house again. To determine if in fact the consecration was legal, a hearing was convened before the pontiffs, who had jurisdiction because at issue was whether the consecration had been properly performed. At this hearing Cicero delivered the *De Domo*, in which he referred to "an old tribunician law which forbids any shrine, land or altar to be dedicated without authorization of the plebs."[12] This law, proposed by the otherwise unknown Q. Papirius, is not attested by any other source.[13] In order to provide a precedent for his case,

---

[10] See Beard & North (1990), Chapter One; and above, Chapter Three, pp. 81–85.
[11] Watson (1968), 21.
[12] *De Domo* 49.127: *Video enim esse legem veterem tribuniciam quae vetet iniussu plebis aedes, terram, aram consecrari.*
[13] Because this Q. Papirius is otherwise unknown, the *lex Papiria* is undated. A *terminus ante quem* is provided by Cicero's reference to the failed effort by the censor C. Cassius Longinus to dedicate a statue in 154 (*De Domo* 50.130). Several dates have been proposed for a *terminus post quem*: Niccolini (1934), 403–404, proposed

Cicero cites another instance in which the requirement for popular approval was applied: Licinia, a Vestal Virgin, who had dedicated an altar, a little shrine, and a sacred couch in 123 to the Bona Dea. When the praetor, after consulting the Senate, referred this case to the college of pontiffs, the decision followed that "that which Licinia, daughter of Gaius, dedicated in a public place without the order of the people, was not deemed sacred."[14] The judgment of the pontiffs in Cicero's case was subsequently based on the tribunician law: "if the one who claims that he performed the dedication was not placed in charge of this task by name either by order of the people or by vote of the plebs and if he was not commanded to do it either by order of the people or by vote of the plebs, then it seemed that it was possible for that part of the site to be restored to me without sacrilege."[15]

The principle recorded by Cicero on the dedication of shrines is clearly similar to that recorded by Livy; both deal with the authorization necessary to dedicate a shrine on behalf of the Roman state. Two important questions need to be faced: is the *lex Papiria* the same as the law of 304 recorded by Livy, and if not, why was the *lex Papiria* needed, if there was already a law on the books which covered essentially the same territory? In answer to the first question, the two laws appear to be distinct. Livy's law derived from a *senatus consultum*; procedurally such a law would normally have been proposed to the people by a consul or praetor, but Cicero's law was proffered by a tribune. This objection might be sidestepped by postulating that the Senate might have employed a tribune to bring this bill before the assembly, but there is a more serious objection to the identity of the two laws. The *lex Papiria* of Cicero commanded that

179, when the censor M. Aemilius Lepidus dedicated three temples (Livy 40.52); Broughton, *MRR*, 2.471, followed by Linderski (1986), 2224, offered 174; while Tatum (1993), 325, suggested 167, when Livy's text breaks off. Livy's silence has been taken to imply that the law was not passed in the years 218–180; however, this argument would not apply to the years 292–219. Stambaugh (1978), 558, has therefore argued that the *lex Papiria* should be placed prior to 216, when Gracchus was instructed to bring the nomination of Fabius Maximus as *duumvir* before the plebs (Livy 23.30–31). However, there is no reason to assume that this was an application of the *lex Papiria*. On this episode, see further, Chapter Four, pp. 149–50.

[14] *De Domo* 53.136: *Quod in loco publico Licinia, Caii filia, iniussu populi dedicasset, sacrum non viderier.*

[15] *Ad Att.* 4.2.3: *Si neque populi iussu neque plebis scitu is, qui se dedicasset diceret, nominatim ei rei praefectus esset neque populi iussu aut plebis scitu id facere iussus esset, videri posse sine religione eam partem areae mihi restitui.*

approval be obtained from the people or the plebs, as opposed to the Senate or the tribunes as ordered by the law of 304. Thus, to argue that Cicero's *lex Papiria* is identical to the law of 304 described by Livy necessitates assuming that Livy and/or Cicero made at least one and possibly two significant mistakes: on the procedure by which the law was passed and on the substance of the law itself. This seems most unlikely.[16]

The existence of two separate laws concerning the *ius publicum dedicandi* raises the question of what purpose the *lex Papiria* served. Theoretically, the law of 304 already controlled who could authorize the dedication of public shrines: why was a second law necessary? The lack of a secure date for the *lex Papiria* eliminates the possibility of placing this law in a historical context and reduces any hypothesis to mere guesswork. Perhaps the *lex Papiria* was a strike for increased popular involvement in religious matters. The Senate generally liked to keep the populace far removed from religious decision-making; this bill may have vested the authority solely in the plebs as a counter move.[17] Alternatively, if the *lex Papiria* was passed in the early second century, it may have been meant as a reaffirmation of the earlier law in the face of a sudden renewed burst of temple building. Enforcement of the law of 304 may have fallen into abeyance, and the *lex Papiria* could be seen as part of the Senate's campaign to rein in its magistrates.[18] It seems fruitless to speculate further lacking a more specific context for this law.

Two recent studies have suggested that these laws drew distinctions based on whether the dedicant held *imperium*: A. Ziolkowski has argued that magistrates *cum imperio* were exempt from the provisions

---

[16] Ziolkowski (1992), 228–231, has recently revived the argument that the two laws were actually the same. He argues that the plebs would not have accepted a limitation on their right to authorize dedications at this time, particularly not after having forced the *pontifex maximus* to acquiesce in Flavius' dedication. Therefore, the law of 304 must simply have written into law the precedent established by events of that year—that the people had the ability to authorize dedications—and thus its purport "would have practically been identical with that of the *lex Papiria*." Yet we have already seen (p. 165 above) that the failure of the law of 304 to fit the schema of expanding plebeian rights provides good reason for accepting the wording of the law as preserved by Livy.

[17] Cf. Mommsen, *RS* 3.1050 on the Senate's desire to remove religious matters from the whims of the people. The danger, from the Senate's viewpoint, of allowing the people to have a significant role in religious affairs, is evidenced by the events of 213, when the people neglected Roman rites for "petty priests and prophets" (Livy 25.1.6–12).

[18] On this campaign, see further below, pp. 185–87.

of both laws, while J. Tatum focuses more narrowly on the *lex Papiria* and argues that it applied *only* to magistrates *cum imperio*.[19] Yet there is little evidence to support either contention. Both laws as we have them imply that they applied to all Romans; Livy uses the phrase *ne quis dedicaret* while Cicero's formulations use the passive to deny that temples could be consecrated without approval.[20] In regard to the law of 304, it is unlikely that either the Senate or the plebs would have accepted a law which limited the prerogatives of their leaders but not those of the other; the law must have applied equally to everyone.[21] If this is so, it becomes difficult to argue that the *lex Papiria* applied only to magistrates *cum imperio* wishing to make a dedication, and not to censors, tribunes, or aediles, for it would be highly unusual if the later law applied to fewer people than the earlier one.[22] There is simply no reason to justify discarding the formulation

---

[19] Ziolkowski (1992), 231–34; Tatum, (1993), 322–28, esp. 325. Willems (1878–1883), 306–309, and Wissowa, *RE* 4.2, 2356–57 and *RKR* 402–403, staked out the opposing positions in this debate, the former believing that all dedications required approval and the latter arguing that magistrates *cum imperio* were exempted from seeking special authorization. Tatum is the first to raise the possibility that magistrates *sine imperio* were exempt from these laws.

[20] The decision of the pontiffs as recorded by Cicero in his letter to Atticus seems similarly broad, and Cicero would have little reason to fabricate the terms of the pontifical decree.

[21] Ziolkowski undermines his own analysis of the patrician-plebeian relationship at the time, for he implies that the plebs were willing to accept this limitation on their magistrates, the tribunes and the aediles, even though they had just forced the *pontifex maximus* to accept Flavius as dedicator. Ziolkowski's statement that "the Senate would not have given its support to a law limiting the prerogatives of its leaders" can be easily turned around: the plebs would not have approved a law limiting the prerogatives of their leaders (and no one else's). This argument is completely inconclusive and we have already seen that this entire line of reasoning in regard to the law of 304 may be misguided. Ziolkowski offers no evidence to justify discarding what Livy and Cicero have to say. Tatum (323) admits that the law of 304 applied to "anyone wishing to dedicate a temple or an altar."

[22] Tatum's argument fails to make a strong case for a narrow formulation of the *lex Papiria*. He places too much weight on the phrase *vis huius Papiriae legis* (*De domo* 130), which he takes to indicate Cicero's recognition that the actual wording of the law did not apply to Clodius. This phrase does not seem as central to Cicero's case as Tatum would like. To the extent that Clodius' defense can be discerned from the statements of Cicero, he seems to have argued not that the law did not apply to him, but only that he had received authorization from the plebs: *tuleram, inquit, ut mihi liceret* (*De Domo* 106). Similarly, after the hearing, Clodius claimed victory because the pontiffs delivered a conditional response: *if* Clodius had not obtained approval from the *populus, then* the land could be returned to Cicero *sine religione* (*Ad Att.* 4.2.3). As Tatum points out, Clodius must have based his defense on the *lex Clodia de exilio Ciceronis*, which had apparently authorized the construction of the shrine to Libertas; this law constituted popular approval, accord-

given by both Livy and Cicero: that anyone seeking to dedicate a
temple needed authorization, from the Senate or tribunes before the
lex Papiria, and from the people afterward.

More interesting than the actual provisions of the *ius publicum
dedicandi* is what was not mentioned in the laws: the oft-repeated claim
that only magistrates could dedicate temples. Mommsen argued that
only certain magistrates—praetors, consuls, censors, dictators, and the
special *duumviri aedi dedicandae*—could dedicate temples; a *privatus* could
never perform this function.[23] While it is true that the *mos maiorum*
may have largely restricted dedications to these particular magistrates,
the laws recorded by both Livy and Cicero merely indicate that the
dedicant had to be approved before the ceremony could properly
take place, and there are several cases which indicate that holding
one of Mommsen's offices was not necessary. In 495, a *primus pilus*
centurion named M. Laetorius was chosen by the people to dedicate
the temple of Mercury, and we have already discussed the shrine to
Concordia dedicated in 304 by the aedile Cn. Flavius.[24] Both stories
as described by Livy seem to have many apocryphal elements, especially as the historian fits them into his description of the Struggle of
the Orders, yet the dedication of Flavius is confirmed by Pliny the
Elder and the tradition of Laetorius' dedication may be genuine as
well. Furthermore, two instances of dedications by *privati* are indis-
putable. M. Marcellus dedicated the temple of Honos and Virtus in
205 which his father had vowed seventeen years earlier, and Cato
the Elder dedicated the shrine of Victoria Virgo in 193, two years
after he himself had vowed it; to the best of our knowledge, neither
man held public office at the time of the dedication.[25] Modern scholars have been forced to assume that both men were appointed *duumvir*,
but Livy does not report that either man held this office, although

---

ing to Clodius, and thus the dedication should stand. Cicero's efforts should therefore be seen as an attempt to show that the law did not constitute approval for the
dedication, which explains why Cicero devoted much of his speech to an attack on
the *lex de exilio*. There is no need to postulate that the *lex Papiria* did not cover
tribunes.

[23] Mommsen, *RS* 2.618–620. This view has been followed by all subsequent scholars. Cf. Willems (1887–1883), 306; Bleicken (1975), 111–112; and Ziolkowski (1992),
222–223.

[24] Laetorius: Livy 2.27. Flavius: Livy 9.46.

[25] Marcellus: Livy 29.11.13. Cato: Livy 35.9.6. It is of course possible that both
men had been elected *duumviri aedi dedicandae* and Livy simply omitted to mention
this fact, but the historian always reported the office held by the dedicant for other
dedications; his silence here is noteworthy.

he customarily does include this fact in his notices.[26] Livy's silence in these cases does seem meaningful therefore, and we should be prepared to accept that it was not actually necessary to be appointed *duumvir* in order to dedicate a temple, so long as one obtained the required approval from the appropriate body.[27] The only legal requirement was that the dedicant be approved by a governmental body, the Senate or the tribunes according to the law of 304 or the people according to the *lex Papiria*.

The legal sources of the Empire, which often draw upon Republican traditions and usage, confirm this picture. Roman law recognized that property might fall into one of many different categories, and some of these categories were based on what we might call an object's religious quality. Thus, *res profanae* are those objects which have no religious connection, but are privately owned and used.[28] A private individual could make a spot *locus religiosus* by burying a body in a spot where he had the right to do so, for instance if he was the owner; burial on public land would not qualify as *religiosus*.[29] Only items dedicated to the gods above under the authority of the Roman people constituted *res sacrae*, the highest of the religious categories. The *Digest* defines *res sacrae* as "those things which have been consecrated by an act of the whole people, not by anyone in his private capacity. Therefore, if someone makes a thing sacred for himself, acting in a private capacity, the thing is not sacred but profane."[30] Again the *Digest* emphasizes that items dedicated by someone acting on his own are not *res sacrae*, because the act lacked public approval. It thus serves to confirm the tradition which we have seen in both Livy and Cicero, that the state had to grant specific approval to an individual before he could dedicate a temple.

The importance of obtaining legal permission to make a proper

---

[26] Cf. 34.53.5–7, where he specifies that Q. Marcius Ralla and C. Servilius held this office in 194; 35.41.8, again involving Ralla, this time in 192; and 36.36.5, when C. Licinius Lucullus dedicated the temple of Juventas. The brevity of the notices can not be an issue in omitting this fact, for the notice in 35.41.8 is as short as possible: *dedicavit Q. Marcius Ralla duumvir.*

[27] These are the only known exceptions to the rule outlined by Mommsen, which at least supports the position that the *mos maiorum* restricted dedications to the upper magistrates and the *duumviri*.

[28] Watson (1968), 9–10.

[29] Watson, (1968), 5–8.

[30] *Dig.* 1.8.6.3: *Sacrae autem res sunt hae, quae publice consecratae sunt, non privatae: si quis ergo privatim sibi constituerit sacrum, sacrum non est, sed profanum.* Watson (p. 10, n. 1) points out that *profanum* is used here simply to mean "not *sacrum*" and not in the technical sense described above. See further Watson (1968), 1–2, 9–10, 21.

dedication is attested epigraphically as well. Two inscriptions indicate that A. Postumius, consul in 180 and censor in 173, obtained
permission by a *lex Plaetoria* to dedicate two altars, one to Verminus
and one to an unknown deity.[31] This *lex Plaetoria* seems to have been
a specific law enabling Postumius to dedicate these altars rather than
a third general law outlining principles for public dedications. By the
terms of the *lex Plaetoria*, Postumius was appointed a *duumvir*, so these
inscriptions also give evidence of the existence of *duumviri* for the
dedication of sacred objects in Rome, a subject to which we now
turn for further discussion.

II. *The Role of* Duumviri Aedi Dedicandae

As with the construction of new temples, a special office existed for
the dedication of temples, the *duumviri aedi dedicandae*. And as with the
duumviri aedi locandae, it is not possible to pinpoint the exact circumstances under which these men were appointed. Ten temples were
dedicated by *duumviri*, not counting the temple of Mars, which was
dedicated by a *duumvir sacris faciundis* in 388.[32] It has been suggested
that *duumviri* were appointed only when "the person who would be
most interested in performing the dedication" was dead or otherwise
unavailable.[33] However the evidence does not lend itself to such a
simple explanation, for we can point to one man who was certainly

---

[31] *ILLRP* 121, 281.

[32] Livy 6.5.8. The use of this office to dedicate a temple is an anomaly, not easily
explained. Since Postumius had been made a *duumvir* to dedicate the temple of
Castor and Pollux one hundred years earlier (Livy 2.42.5), it is impossible to argue
that the Romans had not yet contemplated the creation of a special office to dedicate temples. On the other hand, it is possible that Livy made an error in reference
to the temple of Castor and Pollux; knowing that it was an accepted practice for
sons to be appointed *duumviri* in order to dedicate temples which their fathers had
vowed, the historian may have assumed that when Postumius dedicated this temple,
he must have been appointed *duumvir*, without any actual record of that fact. The
dedication of the temple of Mars by the *duumvir s.f.* T. Quinctius may thus have
been the first step towards the development of a special office for temples. The next
duumviri aedi dedicandae are attested in 216 for the temple of Concordia, although
duumviri aedi locandae are attested in 345 for the temple of Juno Moneta.

[33] Death has been postulated as the reason for the appointment of *duumviri* in
several cases, for example Iuventas and Fortuna Equestris; see Pietilä-Castrén (1987),
62, 66, 81, 88. Mommsen, *RS* 2.621, speaks only of the absence of the person who
would be most interested in the temple without postulating death as a necessary
explanation. By "the person who would be most interested in the temple", Mommsen
seems to mean the vower or a close relative of his.

alive and apparently in Rome, yet was not chosen to dedicate his temple.[34] Furthermore, in none of the instances where *duumviri* were appointed can we state definitively that the man who had vowed the temple was dead or otherwise unavailable at the time of the dedication.[35] As with the *duumviri aedi locandae*, the appointment of *duumviri aedi dedicandae* could occur whenever the Senate felt it desirable.

It seems somewhat odd that the Romans chose *duumviri* to dedicate temples when only one man was need to perform the ceremony. The appointment of two men can probably be traced, as Mommsen suggested, to the principle of collegiality which dominated many Republican offices, e.g. the consulship and the censorship.[36] Furthermore, in several instances there were two temples to be dedicated in a given year, so each of the *duumviri* would have a task to perform. Such was the case with the temples of Venus Erycina and Mens in 215, with Fortuna Primigenia and Vediovis *in insula* in 194, and with Venus Erycina and Pietas in 181.[37] The selection of which *duumvir* would dedicate which temple was self-evident in the first and third of these pairs: Fabius and Otacilius dedicated the temples which they themselves had vowed, and L. Porcius Licinus and M'. Acilius Glabrio dedicated the temples which their fathers had vowed. For the second set, the *duumviri* could have drawn lots for the temples or made a joint decision on the division of responsibilities, as the consuls did for provinces, or the Senate could have specified which temple each was to dedicate.[38]

In four other cases, however, only one temple was dedicated even though two *duumviri* were appointed. For the temple of Concordia, Livy reports the names of both men appointed in 216, but does not indicate which of them actually performed the dedication. In the other three cases, Livy reports only the name of the man who actually dedicated the temple as *duumvir*, although presumably this man did have a colleague. The criteria for which man should perform the

---

[34] L. Furius Purpurio was definitely alive in 194 and 192 when the temples he had vowed to Vediovis were dedicated, because he was a member of the embassy sent to assist Manlius Vulso in 189 (Livy 37.55.7).

[35] M. Marcellus did dedicate the temple of Honos et Virtus in 205 after his father had been killed in battle in 208 (Livy 29.11.13). Interestingly, Marcellus may not have been appointed *duumvir* for this purpose, for this is one of the two instances where Livy does not specify that the dedicant had been appointed to this office.

[36] Mommsen, *RS* 2.622.

[37] Livy 23.31.9, 34.53, 40.34.

[38] Mommsen, *RS* 2.622.

ceremony are again hard to determine, although it appears that a
conscious decision could be taken in favor of one man or the other.
A. Postumius dedicated the temple of Castor and Pollux which his
father had vowed, and it is unlikely that his appointment for this
particular honor was left to chance. The other two instances involved
men who were not related to the vower, so again lots may have
been used to determine who would dedicate the temple, or the Senate may have chosen one or the other. In such instances, the second
duumvir seems to have had no task other than perhaps attending the
ceremony and helping to insure that the ritual was carried out properly. That the names of such men did not survive can hardly be
surprising, given the insignificance of their task; the annalists and
Livy would have been interested in who dedicated the temple, not
who watched the ceremony.

A curious feature of these *duumviri* is that among the generals who
dedicated temples which they had vowed on a campaign several years
earlier, none was appointed a *duumvir* for this purpose. Such men
took advantage of their next magistracy to dedicate their temples.
On the other hand, when their sons dedicated the temple, they were
often appointed *duumviri* for this purpose. Perhaps the office of *duumvir*
was considered a lesser office, more suitable for the introduction of
a young man to public life than for a statesman who had fought
successful campaigns abroad. The majority of the *duumviri aedi dedicandae*
were men at the start of political life, who had held no office before
dedicating the temple.[39] A classic example is again provided by the
Postumii; the son who dedicated the temple as *duumvir* in 484 went
on to attain the consulship and an augurate, and was sent on an

---

[39] Apart from the clearly exceptional case of Fabius Maximus and Titus Otacilius
in 215 (on whom see the following paragraph), only one established statesman might
be included in the ranks of *duumviri aedi dedicandae*: C. Servilius Geminus for the
temple of Vediovis in 194 (Livy 34.53.7). One might try to relate this exception to
factional politics; Scullard (1951) argues that Servilius was an opponent of the Scipios (78–81) and that L. Furius Purpurio, who vowed the temple, was a Scipionic
supporter (93–95). The opponents of Scipio in the Senate might thus have needed
to put forth an established statesman to dedicate the temple in order to overcome
the supporters of Purpurio. However, the picture drawn of factional politics at this
time is often overstated, so one should look for other suggestions as well. For one
possibility, Livy names the *duumvir* only as C. Servilius; the identification as Geminus
has been made by modern scholars, e.g. Broughton (*MRR* 1.346). It is possible that
the Servilius named by Livy was an otherwise undistinguished member of the family, whose career never got off the ground despite his dedication of the temple of
Vediovis.

embassy by the state.[40] Not all *duumviri* went on to such illustrious careers, but the Senate clearly allowed its members to attempt to use the office as a springboard to public life for their sons. This arrangement illustrates one way in which the dedication could be a significant event, and also reveals that the Senate as a body was sufficiently well-disposed towards its magistrates to choose the son as *duumvir*.

Only in one instance were the men who vowed temples appointed *duumviri* for the purpose of dedicating it, and this was clearly an exceptional situation. The temples involved are those of Venus Erycina and Mens, vowed at the outset of the Second Punic War as part of the religious response to Hannibal's invasion. Q. Fabius Maximus and T. Otacilius had vowed these temples in 217 on the order of the Senate following a consultation of the Sibylline Books.[41] Two years later, Fabius asked the Senate to make him a *duumvir* for the purpose of dedicating the temple of Venus Erycina, which he had vowed. The Senate ordered the consul-designate to propose to the people that Fabius be appointed *duumvir* for this purpose, with the result that Fabius and Otacilius dedicated the temples which they had vowed.[42]

Several features stand out as highly unusual in this sequence of events. As mentioned above, these are the only two *duumviri aedi dedicandae* who were already established magistrates, in the sense that both had already achieved at least the praetorship, and in Fabius' case much more besides. In addition, the responsibility for dedicating these temples did not rest on these men personally. As indicated in Chapter Two, vows undertaken on behalf of the state were the state's responsibility to fulfill, not the magistrate who happened to make the vow.[43] For example, the temple of the Magna Mater, which like the temples of Mens and Venus Erycina had been built on the orders of the Sibylline Books, was dedicated by the praetor M. Iunius Brutus, a man who had nothing to do with the original vow.[44] Yet the vows had been made by an individual, and the situation in 215 was desperate; the Romans could not afford to have anything vitiate the fulfillment of these vows and lose the benefits to a technicality, in

---

[40] Broughton, *MRR*, 2.608.
[41] Livy 22.9–10.
[42] Livy 23.30–31.
[43] See Chapter Two, pp. 36–45.
[44] Livy 36.36.3.

this instance that the vow had been fulfilled by a man other than the vower.[45] The urgency of the situation is also evidenced by the completion of both temples within two years and meant that the state did not have the luxury of waiting for Fabius and Otacilius to achieve another office before dedicating the temples. In this situation of the mixed use of procedures, Fabius, though not responsible for the fulfillment of the vows, came forward voluntarily to insure the proper performance of the dedication ceremony. The decision to have Fabius perform the dedication might also be another sign of Fabius' ascendancy in the state after the battle of Cannae had validated his strategy for fighting Hannibal.[46] This incident offers one indication that Romans felt an individual who vowed a temple maintained some responsibility for dedicating the temple, even a temple vowed at the direction of the Senate.[47] It also reveals another significant fact about Roman religion which is often overlooked: the Romans were capable of determining that some vows were more important than others and thus had to be fulfilled in a more punctilious manner.

This incident also reminds us of a crucial fact about the selection of *duumviri*, that the choice of *duumvir* was made by the Senate, even if that choice was subsequently approved by the *populus*.[48] The Senate possessed the power to decide which individual would perform the dedication by utilizing one of three mechanisms: either they appointed the son of the vower as *duumvir*, or they took the dedication away from the vower's family by appointing someone else as *duumvir*, or they did nothing and allowed the vower himself to dedicate the temple when he next attained office. Although the Senate had limited control over the election of men to magistracies, their passive cooperation was required in not advancing another person as *duumvir* to dedicate the temple. By these means the Senate had the

---

[45] Roman religion is well-known for its meticulous insistence on having any religious ceremony carried out precisely and without flaws. Roman history is full of examples of rites, or even elections, being repeated from the start because of a minor flaw in the ceremony. Cf. the example of the resignation of Tiberius Gracchus, cited by Cicero, *ND* 2.10–11.

[46] It is unknown whether Otacilius came forward voluntarily when he saw the example of Fabius, or whether he needed significant persuasion before he agreed to dedicate the temple of Mens. It is extremely unlikely that he was forced to perform the dedication against his will, and as the husband of Fabius' neice his appointment might be yet another indication of the powerful position occupied by Fabius at this moment.

[47] On this point, see further above, pp. 60–61.

[48] Cf. Chapter Four, pp. 148–52.

ability to determine who would reap the benefit of the *gloria* accruing to the man who dedicated the temple.

An apt comparison might be to the prorogation of consuls on campaign. By choosing to prolong a general's command or designating his province to one of the consuls for the coming year, the Senate played a major role in determining the amount of *gloria* that a general was able to win through his military exploits.[49] For instance, the Senate did not prorogue L. Scipio after defeating Antiochus at Magnesia, but assigned Asia as a province to one of the consuls for 189; even after news of the victory was received in Rome the Senate sent out ten commissioners rather than allowing Scipio to settle the affairs of the province before returning to Rome.[50] Certainly this treatment compares unfavorably with that accorded to Flamininus earlier, whatever one may think of the motives for these decisions.[51] On the other hand, the Senate prorogued Scipio's successor in Asia, Manlius Vulso, as well as his colleague in Greece, M. Fulvius Nobilior, in order to finish mopping up their operations against the Galatians and the Aetolians.[52] They were finally recalled in 187, and then only when M. Aemilius Lepidus, a personal *inimicus* of Fulvius, raised a objection in the Senate about their prorogation, claiming that they "ruling as if they were kings in place of Philip and Antiochus."[53] Notice that in the aftermath, Lepidus, who undoubtedly lodged this complaint in part because he wished to succeed to the command in the East, was still sent to Liguria, his original assignment. These episodes reveal clearly that there were heavy political implications over the distribution of provinces, because of the glory and booty that could be won on campaign. While the Senate may not have been able to control the election of consuls, it was clearly able to limit the amount of glory available through the selection of provinces and the decision whether or not to prorogue the current consuls.[54] In the same way, the Senate could decide whether or not to

---

[49] See Jashemski (1950), especially pp. 36–37; and more recently and with more examples and discussion, Kloft (1977), esp. 56–61.

[50] Livy, 37.50.1–8, 37.55.4–7.

[51] Gruen (1984), 217–218, expresses the situation well: "it is hard not to see in this a political defeat for the Scipios, who failed to get the same privilege that had been accorded to Flamininus." Scullard (1951), 133–37, sees this as part of the factional attacks on the Scipios which culminated in the famous trials a few years later.

[52] Livy 38.35.3.

[53] Livy 38.42.

[54] Of course this power was weakened greatly in the Late Republic, when the

appoint *duumviri*, and hence could control the amount of *gloria* obtained by the man who had vowed the temple. An examination of those men who are known to have dedicated temples reveals how this worked in practice, and shows once again how the magistrates and Senate usually cooperated in the introduction of new temples to Rome.

III. *The Identity of Dedicators*

The identity of those men who dedicated temples, when compared with those who vowed them, carries a number of implications for Roman politics and for the addition of cults to the Roman pantheon. We must note at the outset that we know the identity of the dedicator for only a limited number of the temples built during the Republic. Moreover, for some of these temples we do not know which person had originally vowed the temple. Thus, we have of the names of both the vower and the dedicator for only seventeen of the temples which were vowed by generals on campaign, or about one in every four temples.[55] Nonetheless, the results are so striking that we can not simply dismiss them; of these seventeen temples, eleven were dedicated either by the man who had made the vow or by his son. A twelfth was dedicated by a more distant relative, but still a member of the same *gens*, while only five were dedicated by someone with no blood connection. Over seventy percent of the temples were dedicated by the same family which had vowed the temple, a number which can not be ascribed to mere chance, even if the sample size is small. Because of Senatorial control over the choice of dedicators,

---

comitia began to take provincial allocations out of the Senate's hands and to appoint magistrates to long-term commands. This did not prevent the Senate from trying to exercise this control, however; for instance, they assigned the demarcation of forests and woodlands to the consuls of 59, whom they expected to include Caesar, in an attempt to limit his opportunity for self-aggrandizement.

On the issue of controlling elections, see Develin (1985), 105–106, who argues that the Senate effectively controlled the choice of the consuls themselves.

[55] We know the names of both the vower and the dedicator for an additional three temples which were built on orders from the Sibylline Books. I have omitted these from the main study because the involvement of the Sibylline Books means that these temples were state-sponsored and not sprung from individual initiative. They thus tell us little about Senate-magistrate relations in the founding of new temples. For the record, two of these three (Venus Erycina and Mens, but not Ceres, Liber, and Libera) were dedicated by the same man who had been chosen to make the vow.

this fact strongly suggests that the picture of the foundation of new
temples in Rome is not one of magistrates attempting to involve the
state by their vows, nor of the Senate attempting to usurp credit for
the construction of a new temple, but of harmonious cooperation
between the Senate and its magistrates. If the Senate had been dis-
pleased with a magistrate's action in vowing a new temple, they surely
would not have allowed him or his son to make the dedication. By
examining the dedication of these temples in detail we can see this
cooperation between Senate and magistrates more clearly.

Livy's reports on the founding of the temple to Castor and Pollux,
one of the earliest temples in Rome, are nothing if not sparse. Livy
first notes that during the battle of Lake Regillus the dictator
Postumius, "neglecting nothing of either divine or human aid" vowed
a temple to Castor.[56] Livy says nothing more about this temple until
his account of the year 484, when he inserts the following statement:
"The temple of Castor was dedicated in the same year on the Ides
of July; it had been vowed during the Latin war by Postumius the
dictator; his son, made a *duumvir* for this very purpose, dedicated
it."[57] Nothing is said about who built the temple, or who paid for it,
and because this is prior to 304, we can not say that the dedicator
had to be approved by the Senate or the tribunes, let alone the
populus. Nevertheless it is clear that harmony existed between the
Senate and Postumius, for the Senate appointed the dictator's son to
be *duumvir* in order to dedicate the temple. This honor is surely
indicative of the cooperation that existed between the corporate Senate and the family of the Postumii as they introduced the cult of
Castor and Pollux to Rome.

This example is by no means an isolated case. The temple of Salus
provides another excellent example where we can deduce cooperation between the Senate and its magistrates. Livy again provides two
laconic sentences relating to this temple. Under the year 307, he
observes: "In the same year, the [contract for the] temple of Salus
was let by C. Iunius Bubulcus, censor, which he had vowed as consul [in 311] in the war against the Samnites."[58] Then, in 302 after
defeating the Aequi in battle, "he dedicated the temple of Salus as

[56] Livy 2.20.12.
[57] Livy 2.42.5: *Castoris aedes eodem anno idibus Quintilibus dedicata est. Vota erat Latino
bello a Postumio dictatore: filius eius duumvir ad id ipsum creatus dedicavit.*
[58] Livy 9.43.25: *Eodem anno aedes Salutis a C. Iunio Bubulco censore locata est, quam
consul bello Samnitium voverat.*

dictator, which he had vowed as consul and for which he had let
the contract as censor."[59] By 302, of course, dedications had to be
approved by the Senate or the tribunes, but there are other reasons
for adducing Senatorial cooperation. Livy specifies that Bubulcus performed all three of the major tasks involved in erecting a new temple:
vowing, letting the contract, and dedicating it. This is not evidence
of a single man's ability to railroad a new temple through the Senate, but rather the opposite. Four years elapsed between the vow
and the letting the contract for the temple, but the Senate raised no
objections to this delay.[60] We may assume that if Bubulcus had not
been elected censor, the Senate would have made some arrange-
ments for letting the contract, such as appointing *duumviri aedi locandae*,
but they were willing to wait for Bubulcus to try his luck in the
censorial elections. When construction on the temple was completed,
the Senate approved Bubulcus as the person to dedicate the temple.
Our sources do not hint at any conflict between the Senate and
Bubulcus; Livy hints only at the honor paid to Bubulcus by allowing
him to have charge of all three facets of introducing a new temple.

Similar scenarios reappear throughout the Republic. Lucius Papirius
Cursor as consul dedicated a temple to Quirinus in 293 after celebrating a triumph over the Samnites. Livy goes to some length to
refute the notion that it had been vowed during that battle against
the Samnites and insists that it had been vowed by Papirius' father
as dictator and only dedicated by the son.[61] If Livy is correct, then
the temple must have been vowed at least sixteen years prior to its
dedication, one of the longest such gaps between vow and dedication. Yet the Senate did not appoint *duumviri* to speed the fulfillment
of the vow, but the dedication was authorized only when Papirius'
son attained the consulship.[62] As with the Postumii, this father-son
combination reveals cooperation between the family and the Senate.
Two other examples of this father-son combination can be found in
a single year in the early second century. The temple of Pietas, vowed
by M'. Acilius Glabrio, consul, in 191 on the eve of the battle of

---

[59] Livy 10.1.9: *aedem Salutis, quam consul voverat censor locaverat, dictator dedicavit.*

[60] Compare the response to L. Manlius and the temple of Concordia, below pp.
182–83.

[61] Livy 10.46.7: *ab dictatore patre votam filius consul dedicavit exornavitque hostium spoliis.*

[62] As an established member of the Senate, it is more likely that authorization for
Papirius came from the Senate rather than the tribunes, but in any event the Senate's
forbearance in not appointing *duumviri* is significant.

Thermopylae, was dedicated in 181 by his son of the same name, who was made a *duumvir* for this purpose.[63] In the same year the other *duumvir* Lucius Porcius Licinus dedicated a second temple to Venus Erycina, complementing the temple on the Capitoline which had been dedicated in 215. This second temple had been vowed by his father as consul during the Ligurian war.

Five other temples in the early second century were dedicated by the man who had been most responsible for its construction, and this again can be taken as a sign of harmony between the individual and the Senate. In 197, the consul C. Cornelius Cethegus vowed a temple to Juno Sospita in battle against the Gauls; he dedicated it as censor three years later.[64] Also in 194 the urban praetor Gnaeus Domitius dedicated the temple of Faunus, for which he and C. Scribonius had let the contract as aediles in 196.[65] In the following year M. Porcius Cato dedicated a temple to Victoria Virgo which he had vowed two years earlier.[66] Finally one of the censors of 179, Marcus Aemilius Lepidus, dedicated the temples to Juno Regina and Diana, both of which he had vowed eight years previously during his campaign against the Ligurians; he also dedicated the temple of Lares Permarini which had been vowed by his clansman L. Aemilius Regillus.[67] In all these instances, the Senate did not necessarily appoint these men to dedicate the temples; Cato apparently did not even hold office when he dedicated his temple, and the other three were elected to magistracies by the *comitia*. The Senate may not even have approved their authorization, since we do not know the date of the previously discussed *lex Papiria* which gave the right of authorization to the people. Yet the Senate did refrain from appointing *duumviri* to dedicate these temples, and the cooperation between the Senate and its magistrates is nowhere more evident than in 179. M. Aemilius Lepidus requested, and was granted, twenty thousand *asses* to celebrate

---

[63] Livy 40.34.4. The temple of Pietas provides a particularly good example of cooperation between the Senate and the magistrate who vowed the temple, for the elder Glabrio let the contract for the temple *ex senatus consulto*, as we have already noted (Chapter Four, pp. 146–47).

[64] Livy 34.53.3.

[65] Livy 34.53.4. No vow is known for this temple, nor for any of the other temples built by aediles out of their fines. It is clear from Livy that aediles who built temples were associated closely with their temples, just as generals were associated with temples they had vowed while on campaign.

[66] Livy 35.9.6.

[67] Livy 40.52.1–3.

games in conjunction with the dedication of his temples. If allowing
the man who vowed a temple to dedicate it does not signal good
relations between the Senate and that man, then granting him money
to celebrate the dedication with games surely does.

The significance of the Senate's decision *not* to appoint *duumviri*
becomes clearer if we look at the instances where the Senate did
take the honor of the dedication away from the vower's family by
appointing someone else as *duumvir*. We know of only five cases where
our sources specify that individuals from two different families were
responsible for the vow and dedication of the temple. In the first
instance we can see that haste was desirable in the completion of the
temple, but it is difficult to understand why the man who had originally vowed the temple was not given the honor of dedication. In
the year 217, Livy reported that

> it became a matter of religious concern that the contract for the temple
> of Concordia, which the praetor L. Manlius had vowed during a mu-
> tiny in Gaul two years earlier, had not yet been let. Thus C. Pupius
> and K. Quinctius Flamininus, created *duumviri* for this purpose by the
> urban praetor M. Aemilius, let the contract for building the temple on
> the Arx.[68]

In the following year, two other men, Marcus and Caius Atilius,
were made *duumviri* and dedicated the now completed temple.[69] In
this instance it is clear that the nervousness caused by the presence
of Hannibal in Italy and his two victories at Trebia and Trasimene
caused the departure from the standard procedure. Other temples,
such as that of Salus, had gone without contracts for more than two
years without drawing the interest of the urban praetor, but in 217
the populace was afraid that the tardiness in regard to letting the
contract was causing a breach in the *pax deum*. Speed was thus at a
premium; the contract had to be let without delay, and construction
on the temple was completed in only one year. The appointment of
duumviri in this case is entirely unexceptional, but it is surprising that
Manlius was not given the responsibility either for letting the contract or for the dedication. Perhaps he had been killed in the open-

---

[68] Livy 22.33.7–8: *In religionem etiam venit aedem Concordiae, quam per seditionem militarem biennio ante L. Manlius praetor in Gallia vovisset, locatam ad id tempus non esse. Itaque duumviri ad eam rem creati a M. Aemilio praetore urbano C. Pupius et K. Quinctius Flamininus aedem in arce faciendam locaverunt.*

[69] Livy 23.21.7.

ing battle of the Hannibalic War, or perhaps he simply lacked enough friends in the Senate to support him.[70]

The other four temples dedicated by men other than the vower have little in common other than the dates of their dedication, but this fact does suggest some intriguing conclusions. M. Livius Salinator, as consul, vowed a temple to Iuventas in 207 at the battle of Metaurus and as censor three years later let the contract for its construction.[71] However, the temple was not dedicated until 191, when Salinator may well have been dead.[72] Salinator did, however, have a son, Gaius, who actually served as naval praetor in 191 in the campaigns against Antiochus. It is odd that Gaius did not dedicate the temple, especially since he held office in the year in which the temple was dedicated. This may indicate that the family had some strong opponents in the Senate who wished to deprive the family of this honor, or it may simply be that Gaius was already in the East when a decision was taken on the dedication of the temple. Sixteen years had elapsed since the vow had first been uttered, and the Senate may not have wanted to wait for his return. On the other hand, after sixteen years it is difficult to believe that the Senate was suddenly in a hurry to have the temple dedicated immediately rather than waiting another year or two for Gaius to return. The Senate clearly made a conscious choice not to have Gaius Salinator dedicate his father's temple: the temple of Iuventas was dedicated by the *duumvir* C. Licinius Lucullus.

The temple to Fortuna Primigenia, vowed in 204 and dedicated in 194, was also dedicated by a member of a different family from the one which had vowed it. P. Sempronius Tuditanus is said to

---

[70] This Manlius might be the L. Manlius Vulso who ran unsuccesfully for the consulship in 216 (Livy 22.35.1–2; cf *MRR* 1.238 where he is identified as such). This would imply that Manlius was alive, but did lack sufficient support among the aristocracy; for whatever reason he was not felt to be a suitable person either for constructing or dedicating the temple. The reasons may have been related to the message which the temple was supposed to convey; cf. Chapter Four, pp. 154–55 and n. 154.

[71] Livy 36.36.5.

[72] Salinator last appears in the historical record when he served as censor in 204. It would be unusual if a man who had held so many offices up to that point held none for the next thirteen years, and was sent on no embassies. Yet the censorship was the highest office, so perhaps we should not expect to hear more about his career. Salinator held the consulship for the first time in 219; assuming that he held this office between the ages of thirty and forty, he would have been between sixty and seventy in 191. This is certainly towards the upper limit of a Roman life span, but it is not unreasonable to imagine that Salinator lived to such an age.

have vowed the temple as consul at the battle of Croton and let the contract as censor, yet Q. Marcius Ralla was appointed *duumvir* in 194 to dedicate the temple.[73] It is possible, as some have suggested, that he was dead by the time of the dedication, ten years after the vow, but there is no evidence to show whether he was or not.[74] Tuditanus also may not have had a son who was suitable for an official life.[75] Just as with the temple of Iuventas, the Senate selected a member of a different family to dedicate the temple of Fortuna Primigenia.

The two temples to Vediovis, which were vowed by L. Furius Purpurio in 200 and 196, were also dedicated by non-relatives. According to Livy, Purpurio vowed a temple in battle against the Gauls while serving as praetor in 200; this temple was dedicated on the Tiber island by the *duumvir* C. Servilius in 194.[76] While serving as consul in 196, Purpurio vowed another temple, and this temple was dedicated on the Capitoline in 192 by the *duumvir* Q. Marcius Ralla.[77] These two temples have posed innumerable problems for scholars, beginning with the possibility that they may simply be a doublet.[78] Because we have reports of two separate dedications, it seems likely

---

[73] Livy 29.36; 34.53. There are problems with chronology and nomenclature in Livy's account; Tuditanus was censor in 209 and consul in 204, and Livy even calls him P. Sempronius Sophus in one reference, although no such individual is known to have held these offices at this time. See further Chapter Four, pp. 142–43. See also Briscoe (1981), 132–33.

[74] Pietilä-Castrén (1987), 66. We are not entitled to assume that Tuditanus was dead by 194 simply because he did not dedicate this temple. His last known office was an embassy to Greece, Rhodes, and Egypt from 201 to 199.

[75] Suolahti (1963), 321. Other family members, such as brothers, nephews, or cousins, are not known to have been appointed *duumviri aedi dedicandae*. The only temple dedicated by a family member other than a son was the temple of Lares Permarini, dedicated by M. Aemilius Lepidus when he was serving as censor on behalf of his clansman L. Aemilius Regillus (Livy 40.52). The family connection here was not terribly close, but his election to the censorship must have seemed the best opportunity for a relation to dedicate this temple.

[76] Vow: Livy 31.21.12. Dedication: 34.53.7.

[77] Livy 35.41.8. Remains of this temple have been discovered near the *tabularium* of Sulla; cf. Colini (1942).

[78] See Briscoe (1973), 112–14, who gives a clear presentation of the problems involved. In general, I follow his conclusions. The problem is compounded by attempting to determine which god was being honored in each case. The text of Livy when recording the vow of the first temple reads the god as *deoiovi*, which has been interpreted as, or even emended to, Diiovis, i.e. the god Vediovis or Veiovis. However, it could also be read as *deo Iovi*, the god Jupiter, although the inclusion of *deo* seems superfluous. At the dedication Livy's text clearly reads Jupiter, but the *fasti* do not record a temple of Jupiter on the *insula*, but rather a temple to Vediovis. On

that there were two temples, neither of which was dedicated by Purpurio himself. In this instance, however, we have explicit evidence that Purpurio was alive at the time of dedications because he was a member of the embassy sent to assist Manlius Vulso in 189.[79] The decision not to have Purpurio dedicate these temples is undoubtedly related to the controversy which surrounded Purpurio's request to celebrate a triumph, even though he was only a praetor.[80] The request was eventually granted, partly because the consul Aurelius, who was technically Purpurio's superior and who found his chance for military glory preempted by the actions of Purpurio, had not yet returned to Rome. This was a precedent-setting event; Purpurio was the first praetor to celebrate a triumph, and that fact undoubtedly stirred up jealousy and hostility on the part of many senators in addition to Aurelius. This hostility makes it easy to see why Purpurio was denied the right to dedicate the temples which he had vowed. But we should not view this incident in a vacuum; while this treatment of Purpurio may have been partly motivated by personal animosity, it also appears to be part of a larger movement.

As mentioned above, the curious feature about these four temples dedicated by non-relatives is that they were all dedicated in a three-year span, from 194 to 191, even though the vows for building them had been made on distinctly different occasions. For instance, the temple of Iuventas was vowed sixteen years before it was dedicated, and the temple of Fortuna Primigenia ten years prior to its dedication. It can hardly be coincidence that the heavy concentration of non-relative *duumviri* occurred at exactly this time. The years 194–187 saw several decisive victories in the East followed by a series of magnificent triumphs, each more lavish than the one before.[81] These years also witnessed a series of extraordinary political events as the Senate attempted to assert its authority over these individuals and its control over the ever-increasing amounts of money coming to Rome at this time. We should remember that Scipio Nasica's request of money for his games was denied in 191, a rejection that was apparently

---

the other hand, other literary sources recognize only the second temple, which is agreed by all ancient sources and the *fasti* to be for Vediovis.

[79] Livy 37.55.7.

[80] For the debate in the Senate, see Livy 31.48–49.

[81] E.g. Flamininus in 194, Glabrio in 190, Scipio Asiaticus in 189, Nobilior in 187, culminating with Manlius Vulso in 187, the event which Livy held responsible for the introduction of *luxuria* to Rome.

unprecedented.[82] In 187 M'. Acilius Glabrio was accused of not turning in enough booty to the treasury following his triumph two years earlier, and these charges resulted in his eventual withdrawal from the censorship campaign.[83] The trials of the Scipios and the Bacchanalian affair of 186 took place in this period as part of this attempt.[84] The comparison to prorogation raised earlier may also be relevant here, for these are precisely the years when conflict over prorogation looms larger in our sources, including the complaints of Lepidus discussed above.[85]

This period was also an intense time of temple construction, as eight temples were dedicated in just the three years from 194–191. Considering the tenor of these years, it is not surprising to see the Senate attempt to exercise more control in the matter of new temples. One of the eight temples was an aedilician construction, and hence did not pose this problem for the state, but five of the other seven temples were dedicated by men unrelated to the vower.[86] If, as was argued in the previous chapter, the appointment of *duumviri aedi locandae* was a regular occurrence and not as significant for the accumulation of *gloria*, control in the matter of new temples would best be exercised over dedications. Cato serves as the apparent exception which proves the rule; he was allowed to dedicate his own temple in 193, in the midst of this increased supervision by the Senate, because he was already known to be supportive of the collective Senatorial authority and did not have to be used as an example to others.[87]

---

[82] See Chapter Two, pp. 55–60.

[83] Livy 37.57–58. Cf. Gruen, (1990) 70–71 and 134–36, and Shatzman (1972), 191–92. The latter believes the charges were intended only to force Glabrio's withdrawal, but Gruen notes that Fulvius Nobilior and Manlius Vulso also ran into difficulties and thus sees Glabrio as part of the pattern.

[84] The trials of the Scipios are far too complex to be treated in a mere footnote, but it is clear that whatever the Scipios had done and whatever the chronology, charges, and outcome of the "trials", the effect was to put a blot on their record and reduce their influence. See now Gruen (1995). On the Bacchanalian affair, see Gruen (1990), 34–78, and on the problem of commanders and booty more generally see 69–72 and 133–141.

[85] See p. 177.

[86] The temple of Faunus was built by aediles, one of whom, Cn. Domitius, performed the dedication (Livy 34.53). The five temples dedicated by non-relatives include the four we have already discussed dedicated by *duumviri*, and the temple of the Magna Mater, dedicated by the praetor M. Iunius Brutus (Livy 36.36).

[87] C. Cornelius Cethegus was also allowed to dedicate the temple he had vowed to Juno Sospita when he was censor in 194. Again, we can only speculate on the reasons. Perhaps he won approval from the plebs, perhaps since he was already censor the Senate decided to allow him to proceed with the dedication, or perhaps

This campaign to restrain the leading generals of the state may help to explain one other curious feature about the temples dedicated by *duumviri* at this time. The temple to Fortuna Primigenia was dedicated by the *duumvir* Q. Marcius Ralla in 196, the same man who dedicated the second temple of Vediovis two years later. Yet apart from these two offices, Ralla is completely unknown, and there is no obvious reason why he should have been employed twice in three years for the same purpose. We know of no relationship between Ralla and P. Sempronius Tuditanus or Ralla and L. Furius Purpurio which might explain why he dedicated their temples. Nor do we know of any relationship between Tuditanus and Purpurio which might explain why the same man was involved with both of their temples. It seems likely that Ralla's very obscurity provides the clue as to why he was chosen *duumvir* on these two occasions. The Senate may have wanted to give the high-profile dedication ceremony to low-profile men, and thus remove this ceremony entirely from the political arena.

It might be objected that these *duumviri* were appointed in the years 194–191, while the other incidents which reveal the Senate's attempt to rein in its magistrates occurred in the 180's, and that taking the dedication away from the vower can not have had a great effect in controlling magistrates. But that is precisely the point; when the small step of giving the dedication to other men failed to have an effect, more drastic steps were taken. Nasica's request for money was refused, several triumphs were contested, and finally, several generals were accused of various improprieties, real or imagined. By the late 180's, following the death of Africanus and the censorship of Cato, the Senate's campaign to limit the power of its magistrates was apparently over: in 181 sons were again appointed *duumviri* to dedicate temples which their fathers had vowed.[88] As we have already noted, these appointments indicate good relations between the dedicator and the body of the Senate. The Senate must have felt that its actions of the previous fifteen years had sufficiently reestablished its preeminent position.

---

like Cato the Senate decided they did not have to make an example of him. We should also note that this temple was dedicated in 194, at the start of this period of increased Senatorial control; perhaps Cethegus was the last to benefit from the usual cooperation which appertained in these matters.

[88] The temples of Pietas and Venus Erycina: Livy 40.34.4.

IV. *Conclusions*

The examples of individuals dedicating their own temples, or of relatives dedicating those temples, are clearly more numerous than those dedicated by non-relatives. Admittedly, they represent only a fraction of the temples dedicated in Rome during the Republic. For most of the others, our sources fail to specify either who vowed or who dedicated the temple, thus denying us the opportunity to draw conclusions from their identities. Extrapolating from the data we do have would lead to the conclusion that almost three of every four temples were dedicated by the man who vowed it or by his son. The significance of this statistic extends beyond mere confirmation of the conclusion reached in Chapter Two, that vows made by generals on campaign were considered personal vows and hence were usually the responsibility of the general to fulfill. It shows that the Senate and its magistrates were not engaged in a constant struggle over control of erecting new temples in Rome.

The construction of most of the new temples in Rome was produced by a harmonious cooperation between the Senate and its magistrates, and this cooperation took several forms. Individual members of the Senate obviously supported each other's actions, as of course they would be the ones who voted to approve each other as dedicators. This is hardly surprising, as the Senate often functioned as a mutual back-scratching society; support for another's dedication might be a repayment for previous support, or it might be an investment for future support. More interesting are the relations between the Senate as a corporate body and individual magistrates. As we saw in the previous chapter, the Senate usually assumed at least some of the financial burden for the construction of new temples. Yet the Senate still allowed the magistrate who had initially vowed the temple to reap the benefits of making the dedication, and such dedications could be accompanied by games, which increased the opportunity for distinguishing one's family. On the other hand, the actions of Fabius and Otacilius indicate that the benefits did not flow only in one direction. Although they were not responsible for making the dedications, they came forward to insure that the vows would be properly received by the gods, even though they might not receive great personal advantage.[89] On both sides, as a member of the Sen-

---

[89] Certainly Fabius was not remembered for having dedicated the temple of Venus

ate and as an individual magistrate, it was clear that one had certain responsibilities to insure that the system for introducing new cults to Rome continued to function smoothly.

The dedication of new temples also illustrates the Roman religious mentality and how intertwined religion and politics were in Rome. Under normal circumstances, the responsibility for fulfilling personal vows lay with the individual and the responsibility for fulfilling state vows lay with the state; religious affairs and political interests were mutually supportive. Yet it is in extraordinary circumstances that we gain our most revealing glimpses into the Roman mindset. Under the stresses of the Second Punic War, vows took on extraordinary importance, and fulfilling them promptly and properly was of paramount importance. Thus the state took responsibility for fulfilling Manlius' vow of a temple to Concordia, and Fabius Maximus and Titus Otacilius, although not technically responsible, became *duumviri* to ensure that the vows of 217 were scrupulously fulfilled. Twenty-five years later the Senate perceived a threat coming from inside rather than outside, from their own generals rather than from a foreign enemy. In that situation, when Rome's military superiority was unquestioned, strict fulfillment of the vows seemed less important than reining in the magistrates, so the Senate assigned responsibility for fulfilling vows made by one man to other men. No Roman would have seen anything improper in any of this, except perhaps those generals who lost the opportunity to add to their *gloria*. Religious affairs, including the building of new temples, could be modified to suit political interests, and political affairs could be modified to suit religious interests.

Erycina, but for his successful campaigns prior to the Second Punic War and then for his delaying strategy during that war. Otacilius had not yet held the consulship in 215, so he may have hoped to further his political career by performing the dedication (in vain as it turned out, for his election to the consulship in 214 was blocked by Fabius himself).

CONCLUSIONS

The analysis of the various stages involved in erecting a new temple in Rome has brought to light some new aspects of this phenomenon. Although the high degree of cooperation between the Senate and its magistrates ought not to come as a surprise, it does paint a very different picture from the one usually offered for this process. The initiative for most temples, all except the eight built on the orders of the Sibylline Books, rested with the individual, while control of the process still rested largely with the Senate. The Senate approved the vow made by the general on his campaign, the Senate approved funding for the construction of the temple, often by appointing special *duumviri* for this purpose, and the Senate generally allowed the family which had been responsible for vowing the temple to perform the dedication. What we see throughout the Early and Middle Republic is not a series of ambitious generals trumpeting their accomplishments and promoting their electoral hopes by the construction of grandiose religious monuments, but an orderly process in which both sides shared the responsibility and the benefits. The situation changes fundamentally in the Late Republic, and those changes will be discussed below, but throughout temple building remains an integral part of the Roman political as well as religious scene.

Senatorial involvement should in fact alert us to a point which has often been completely overlooked in discussions of temple construction: the benefits which this process brought to the state. A new temple furthered the interests of the state by solidifying the *pax deum*. It offered public recognition of the role of the gods in supporting and protecting the Roman state, and represented a communal giving of thanks for success. The introduction of a new deity in particular made a public statement that this deity had helped the Romans to victory and could therefore be added to the divine forces which championed the Romans' cause. It thus became an integral piece of the argument that the Romans were superior to other nations in their cultivation of the gods and hence deserving of their political hegemony. By supporting the actions of generals who vowed new temples, the Senate was supporting the religious welfare of the state, which helps to account for their willingness to cooperate and participate so fully in the process. Yet the benefits which the state received were not solely religious.

Because the Senate participated actively in the construction of new temples, this process also served to reaffirm its position as the central organ of the Roman government. Since the construction of a new temple furthered the Romans' relations with the gods, the decision by a general to vow a temple indicated his concern for the welfare of the community and allowed the state to share in his glory. By furthering the Romans' relations with the gods, the general acknowledged that the needs of the state were primary and that his own desire to achieve prominence among the ruling elite was a secondary concern. By bringing his vow before the Senate, he acknowledged that the Senate was the locus of dignity, and that he could best achieve his ambitions by working through the Senate. Rather than viewing the individual's decision to vow a temple solely as a statement of self-aggrandizement, we should also see it as a means of publicly linking himself with the best interests of the state in promoting the *pax deum*. Once again the Senate would gladly support the action of an individual in which he voluntarily subordinated himself to the collective interests of the state and to the Senate as guardian of those interests. The erection of a new temple thus simultaneously validated the position of the Romans within the Mediterranean world and the position of the Senate within the Roman state.

An important point which is often overlooked in standard discussions of Roman temple building supports this interpretation. The construction and decoration of temples seems not to have been aimed at future electoral success, which was one of the primary purposes of self-promotion in Rome. The incident of Fulvius Flaccus and the roof tiles from the temple at Croton makes this amply clear. Flaccus had nothing to gain in the electoral arena when he attempted to despoil the sanctuary at Croton; he was holding the censorship at the time and thus had already achieved the pinnacle of Roman magistracies. Even consuls had relatively little to gain, for only a select few could go on to the censorship or a second consulship, and it is evident from a glance at the electoral results that the construction or decoration of a temple had little effect on the outcome of the censorial elections.[1] Such displays would also be likely to have little

---

[1] Cf. Millar (1984), 11. Approximately one-third of those who vowed temples went on to attain the censorship; this is a slightly greater percentage than the one-

effect on how a general was viewed by other members of the ruling elite, and so can hardly have helped in the jockeying for position within the aristocracy. This implies that Roman generals were focused on other aims when they engaged in the construction or decoration of a new temple in Rome.

Given the nature of Roman society, it seems likely that they were more concerned with their place in history. The goal of a Roman aristocrat was not merely to surpass his contemporaries, but to outshine everyone who had preceded him and to set a standard for future generations. The recitation at Roman funerals not just of the deceased's accomplishments but of all his ancestors' accomplishments as well would have fed into this need to leave one's mark in the historical record.[2] For example, Pompey's accomplishments in the East need to be seen not just in the context of his struggle for supremacy with Crassus and Caesar, but also in his attempt to surpass Scipio Africanus, Scipio Asiaticus, Aemilius Paullus, and a host of other Roman luminaries. Flaccus' designs on the temple of Hera Lacinia leave the same impression: he wanted his temple to Fortuna Equestris to be the first in Rome with a marble roof, because it would ensure his place in Roman annals. The means he attempted to use in order to achieve this goal may have been extraordinary, but the goal itself was not.

With the benefit of hindsight, it seems that the episode involving Flaccus and the temple of Fortuna Equestris forms part of the transition into developments of the Late Republic regarding the construction of new temples. One of these developments is the attempt by the general to create a monument which would be closely linked with his name and provide a means of lasting glory. Whereas Flaccus attempted only to roof his temple in marble, within the next fifty years three structures were constructed entirely of marble.[3] The first

---

fifth of all consuls who could reach this office, but elections were affected by many other factors. For instance, Cato's election to the censorship in 184 is not likely to have been affected by his erection of a temple to Victoria Virgo ten years earlier. See also the results of Pietilä-Castrén (1987) listed on 160–161, where the builders of monuments during the period of the Punic Wars are almost equally divided among the "Last Known Member of the Family or the Branch", the "First Consul of the Family or the Branch", and a "Member of a Renowned and Flourishing Family".

[2] In this regard, Wiseman (1985), 3–7, has noted how the epitaphs and *tabulae triumphales* of Roman aristocrats emphasize being the first to accomplish a certain feat; this clearly reflects the historical consciousness of the great Roman leaders.

[3] Cf. Ziolkowski (1988) on these marble constructions.

of these was built around 146 by Q. Caecilius Metellus Macedonicus, shortly followed by a temple to Hercules Victor by L. Mummius in 142 and a temple to Mars by D. Iunius Brutus Callaicus.[4] It is significant that none of these three marble temples appears on any of the surviving copies of the *fasti* and that two of them were built with the general's *manubiae*.[5] These temples are thus diametrically opposed to the normal construction of public temples, which tended to use local limestone and which, as we have seen, were usually financed by the Senate. The message of these temples also stands in opposition to that of state temples: they emphasize the glory and the accomplishments of the individual general rather than the welfare of the state and the primacy of the Senate.[6] In this way these temples foreshadow developments of the Late Republic.

Another aspect of these developments is the increasing reference to temples by the names of their founders. No temple built prior to the latter half of the second century is described in this way, although several earlier secular structures were known by the names of their founders.[7] The building complex of Metellus may be the earliest example of this phenomenon, if in fact it included the construction of new temples.[8] A more definite example comes from the temple of Honos et Virtus erected by Marius following his campaigns against the Cimbri and Teutones. Already in Cicero's time this shrine was referred to as the *aedes Mariana*, and other Roman authors continued to refer to a *monumentum Marianum* or even multiple *monumenta Mariana*.[9]

---

[4] There is some question as to whether the complex built by Metellus included temples or just a portico surrounding two pre-existing temples; cf. Vell. Pat. 1.11.3–7; Vitruvius, 3.2.5; Pliny, *NH* 36.24 and 36.35; and Festus, 363. For modern discussions, see Boyd (1953); Morgan (1971); and Richardson (1976), 61, and (1992), 221. The temples of Mummius and Brutus are more certain; see *ILS* 20; Nepos, *apud* Priscian 8.18; and Val. Max. 8.14.2.

[5] Although there is an entry in the *fasti* for Jupiter Stator on 5 September which could be related to a temple built by Metellus, there is no corresponding opening for another temple to Juno Regina after the one built by M. Aemilius Lepidus in 179, and it seems highly unlikely that Metellus built two temples but had state sanction for only one. As noted in Chapter Four, p. 135, it is doubtful that the entry for Mars Invictus on the Venusine *fasti* for May 14 refers to the temple of Iunius Brutus.

[6] In this regard one should note the great difficulty which Metellus had in securing the consulship in 143 despite the construction of his temple; cf. *De Vir. Ill.* 61.3; Val. Max. 7.5.4; Livy *Ep. Oxy.* 52. He clearly reaped little political benefit from his temple foundation, and may even have roused opposition by his extravagance.

[7] E.g. the Columna Minucia and the Columna Maenia, or the more famous Basilica Porcia and Basilica Sempronia.

[8] Cf. above, n. 4, and Pliny, *NH* 36.40.

[9] Cicero, *Sest.* 116; *Planc.* 78; *De Div.* 1.59; Vitruvius 3.2.5, 7. *praef.* 17; Val. Max. 1.7.5, 2.5.6, 4.4.8.

194   CONCLUSION

This temple, like the preceding temples of Mummius and Iunius
Brutus, was built using the *manubiae* of the victorious general, confirming the connection between the use of the general's booty and
the emphasis which the monument placed on the individual.[10] But
Marius is merely the best-known example of this trend; numerous
other temples built in the Late Republic or in the early Empire also
bore the names of their founders. For instance, Pompey the Great
built a temple to Hercules which was known as the *aedes Pompi*, and
the divinity in question could actually be called Hercules Pompeianus.[11]
Nor was this practice embraced only by the great military leaders
who challenged the predominant role of the Senate; the staunch
conservative Domitius Ahenobarbus, the proconsul of 49 who was
appointed to replace Caesar in Gaul, built a shrine containing a
famous statue of Neptune which Pliny the Elder called the *delubrum
Domitii*.[12] Later examples include the temple of Apollo Sosianus, built
by the consul of 32 and dated either just before or just after the
battle of Actium, a temple to Diana rebuilt by L. Cornificius in the
reign of Augustus and henceforth called Diana Cornificiana, and
an *aedes Seiani* built by Tiberius' notorious praetorian prefect.[13] Significantly most of these temples were private shrines or rededications
of existing buildings; as such they provided ample scope for self-
aggrandizement without needing the close involvement of the Senate.
It is therefore not surprising that these temples focused attention on
the individual rather than the state, but at the same time they are
not characteristic of additions to the state cult during the Republic.
Rather they are indicative of trends which reached their culmination
in the Principate of Augustus.

One of these trends, clearly visible in the politics of the Late
Republic, is an increasing emphasis on the individual and these temples
show how this trend also becomes evident in religion.[14] A curious
feature of religion in the Late Republic is a noticeable dropoff in the

---

[10] *ILS* 59 reveals that Marius' temple was constructed out of *manubiae* taken from
the Cimbri and Teutones.

[11] *aedes Pompi*; Pliny, *NH* 34.57; Hercules Pompeianus: Vitruvius 3.3.5.

[12] Pliny, *NH* 36.26. Another temple to a goddess known as Diana Planciana was
probably dedicated around the same time, if it was erected by the aedile of 54. Cf.
Panciera (1970–71), esp. 125–134.

[13] Apollo Sosianus: Pliny, *NH* 13.53. Diana Cornificiana: Suet. *Aug.* 29.5; cf. *CIL*
6.4305. *Aedes Seiani*: Pliny, *NH* 36.163.

[14] See the comments of Hopkins and Burton (1984), 80–81, for other aspects of
this trend.

number of state temples dedicated, even while the hum of building activity described above continues unabated. After the construction of the portico of Metellus in the 140's, either with or without new temples, only one state temple can be said for certain to have been built following a general's vow in battle, although three others may have been.[15] Even if one counts the uncertain cases, the total of four temples spread over a ninety-year period is the slowest rate of construction since generals began vowing temples in the fourth century. During this time the Romans continued to engage in frequent warfare against foreign foes and continued to expand the borders of their dominion, so opportunities continued to exist for Roman generals to vow new temples. This should not be taken as an indication that religion was unimportant or in decline during the Late Republic as has so often been argued.[16] That generals continued to erect temples, albeit in a different fashion, indicates that religion continued to be very important, but as political behavior changed with the individual becoming increasingly prominent, religious behavior changed in the same way. Given the close relationship between religion and politics at Rome, this development should come as no surprise; as the one changed, the other was bound to change along with it. Temples emphasizing the importance of the state gave way to temples emphasizing the importance of the individual.

This point corroborates the interpretation offered in this study on the message conveyed by the construction of new state temples. If the purpose of erecting a new temple was to glorify the general's name, then it is hard to understand the fact that additions to the state pantheon came to a virtual standstill in the Late Republic; the great military leaders of the first century should have built more temples, which would have provided them with more opportunities to promote their own ambitions. On the other hand, if the participation of

---

[15] The temple of Fortuna Huiusce Diei vowed by Q. Lutatius Catulus at the battle of Vercellae in 101 was certainly a state temple, and the temple of Honos et Virtus built by Marius following the same campaign seems likely; the *fasti* are inconclusive on this point. The temple of Hercules Victor dedicated by L. Mummius in 142 does not appear anywhere on the state calendars, while the temples to Ops Opifera by L. Caecilius Metellus Delmeticus (Pliny, *HN* 11.174) and to Pietas in the Circus Flaminius (Cicero, *De Div.* 1.98, Obsequens 54) may be rededications. Cf. Richardson (1992). The temple to Venus Verticordia was erected in 114 following a consultation of the Sibylline Books and not by virtue of a general's vow.

[16] See e.g. Taylor (1949). Numerous recent studies have effectively debunked the notion that religion was in decline in the Late Republic. See in particular Liebeschuetz (1979), 1–54; Wardman (1982), 22–62; Beard & Crawford (1985), 25–40.

the individual Roman general in the construction of a state temple served to confirm the central importance of the state and of the Senate in directing the affairs of state, it is not at all surprising that these figures chose not to become involved in this process, but concerned themselves with monuments which would enhance their own stature. One of the defining characteristics of the Late Republic is a shift in emphasis from the interests of the republic to the interests of the individual, a feature clearly reflected in the power struggles of the various military leaders as they ignored the wishes of the Senate and even the dictates of the *comitia* to pursue their own goals. In this regard, the construction of a state temple did not serve as an effective means for a general like Marius or Sulla to promote his ambitions because it focused attention on the interests of the state. Therefore fewer state temples were dedicated, and more shrines which were connected more intimately with the individual himself, as indicated by the phenomenon of naming the temple after the general who built it.

These new concerns can be seen very clearly in the last two temples built prior to 44 B.C.E. which were part of the state religious system. In 55, Pompey the Great dedicated a temple to Venus Victrix, a goddess with whom he claimed a special connection. Yet this dedication differed markedly from the usual construction by a victorious general, for Pompey dedicated the temple as part of a larger complex which was dominated by the erection of the first permanent stone theater in Rome. Although Pompey argued that he had merely built a temple and underneath "placed steps for watching games", already in the third century C.E. Tertullian criticized Pompey for using the temple merely as a means for avoiding censure, since the Senate had habitually refused to allow the construction of a stone temple in Rome.[17] Modern scholars have generally agreed that the temple was a secondary feature, and certainly the plan of the complex lends support to this notion, as the theater dwarfs the small temple at the top.[18] This complex was certainly intended to focus attention on Pompey himself, and not on the community; it included numerous

---

[17] Tertullian, *De Spect.* 10.5
[18] Cf. Hanson (1959), 45, for remarks on modern scholars who have almost entirely ignored the temple in their discussions of this complex. Although Hanson himself does not disregard the temple in such a cavalier fashion, he too notes (47) that one cannot deny "the personal and political motives which governed the founding of Pompey's theater."

statues, including fourteen representations of the nations conquered by Pompey, and was laid out in a Hellenistic-style garden rather than following the Italian tradition.[19] J. Hanson, in his detailed analysis of this complex, even points out how in the Hellenistic world the construction of a temple may be connected with ruler cult; if so, Pompey would have preceded Caesar in angling for divine honors.[20] Whatever the significance of the various aspects of this complex, Pompey could certainly lay claim to constructing the first stone theater in Rome, and a marble theater at that. The attention drawn by the theater would have overshadowed any conception about the primacy of the state conveyed by the construction of the adjoining temple.

Caesar responded to Pompey's building project with one of his own, the Forum Julium, which also included the construction of a new state temple, to Venus Genetrix. The timing of this project and Caesar's choice of deity makes it very clear that he was more concerned with personal aims than with the religious needs of the community. Caesar began to make plans for the construction of this forum in 54, only a year after the dedication of Pompey's theater, and according to Appian, the temple was originally vowed to Venus Victrix, the chief goddess of Pompey's complex.[21] Thus these actions were originally directed specifically against Pompey; Caesar appropriated Pompey's special divinity just before the critical battle, almost in the manner of an *evocatio*. After Caesar proved triumphant, his aims changed, for when the temple was finally dedicated in 46, the goddess was called Venus Genetrix.[22] This was clearly intended to enhance Caesar's own stature and to promote a new conception of himself; the goddess was not merely the ancestor of the Roman people, but more importantly the ancestor of the Julian clan. She was thus a private family goddess whom Caesar raised to the level of a state goddess in order to confer a divine aura on himself and his family.[23] Certainly the actions of Caesar in constructing a forum and a temple

---

[19] For the statues, cf. Pliny *NH* 7.34, 36.41. On the Hellenistic aspects of the garden, cf. Grimal (1943), 183–88.

[20] Hanson (1959), 53–55.

[21] Construction plans: Cicero, *Ad Att.* 4.16.8, where it is clear that Cicero is one of the agents whom Caesar has retained to buy land for his project. The first mention of the temple is its vowing at the battle of Pharsalus (Appian, *BC* 2.68), but some scholars feel that Caesar must have decided to include a temple before this date. Cf. Anderson (1984) 41; Weinstock (1971) 79–82.

[22] Dio 43.22.2.

[23] Cf. the comments of Weinstock (1971), 84–85.

closely associated with his family set a precedent which was subsequently followed by many of the emperors.[24] This temple should be viewed not so much as the last Republican state temple, but rather as the first Imperial building project.

The process of constructing new temples thus not only reveals critical elements of the Republican system of government, but it also reflects the shift in the Late Republic which culminated in the establishment of the Augustan principate. Fundamentally, the Republic depended on the cooperation of a highly competitive group of nobles. The construction of new temples illustrates one way in which that cooperation operated: individual Roman generals vowed the majority of these temples on their campaigns, while their peers sitting in the Senate accepted the vow on behalf of the state and provided political and financial support for the vower. By this means nobles might seek glory for themselves and still promote the overall interests of the state: relations with the gods would be solidified and relations among the aristocracy would be maintained. Therefore, rather than viewing the erection of new temples as primarily an exercise in individual self-aggrandizement, the erection of new temples should be seen as the product of a symbiotic relationship between the Senate and its magistrates, in which both sides contributed and both sides benefited. In the Late Republic, as competitive urges came to the fore and eventually outweighed the need for cooperation, the inseparable connection of religion with politics in Roman society ensured that the result would be reflected not only in the political structure of the Roman state, but in its religious structures as well.

---

[24] Thus Anderson (1984) quite rightly begins his study of the Imperial fora with the Forum Iulium. Cf. also Kyrieleis (1990), 432; Weinstock (1971), 82.

STATE TEMPLES INTRODUCED IN ROME, 509–55 B.C.E.

DEITY	DATE	CIRCUMSTANCES	VOWER	$ SOURCE	DEDICATOR
Saturn	501–493	N. R.	N. R.	N. R.	N.R.
Mercury	495	N. R.	N. R.	N. R.	centurion
Ceres, Liber/a	493	DROUGHT, WAR (Latins)	dictator	booty (Sen.)	consul
Castor & Pollux	484	WAR (Latins: Lake Regillus)	dictator	N. R.	duumvir (son)
Dius Fidius	466	N. R.	Tarquin	N. R.	consul
Apollo	431	PLAGUE	Senate?	N. R.	consul
Mater Matuta	396	WAR (Veii)	dictator	N. R.	N. R.
Juno Regina (II)	392	WAR (Etruscans)	dictator	N. R.	N. R.
Mars	388	WAR (Gauls)	N. R.	N. R.	duumvir s.f.
Juno Lucina	375	N. R.	N. R.	N. R.	N. R.
Juno Moneta	344	WAR (Aurunci)	dictator	duumviri	N. R.
Concordia (I)	304	reconciling Orders	aedile	fines	curule aedile
Salus	302	WAR (Samnites)	consul	N. R.	dictator (self)
Vica Pota	4th c.	N. R.	N. R.	N. R.	N. R.
Bellona	296	WAR (Samnites/Etruscans)	consul	N. R.	N. R.
Jupiter Victor	295	WAR (Samnites)	consul	N. R.	N. R.
Venus Obsequens	295	N. R.	aedile	fines	N. R.
Victoria	294	WAR (Samnites)	aedile	fines	consul (self)
Jupiter Stator	294	WAR (Samnites)	consul	duumviri	N. R.

Appendix 1 (cont.)

DEITY	DATE	CIRCUMSTANCES	VOWER	$ SOURCE	DEDICATOR
Quirinus	293	WAR (Samnites)	dictator	N. R.	consul (son)
Fors Fortuna	293	WAR (Samnites/Etruscans)	consul	booty	N. R.
Aesculapius	291	PLAGUE	N. R.	Senate	N. R.
Summanus	278	lightning hits statue	N. R.	N. R.	N. R.
Consus	273?	WAR (Samnites et al.)	consul?	N. R.	N. R.
Tellus	268*	earthquake in WAR (Picenes)	consul?	N. R.	N. R.
Pales	267*	WAR (Salentini)	consul?	N. R.	N. R.
Vortumnus	264*	WAR (Volsinii)	consul?	N. R.	N. R.
Janus	260?*	WAR (1st Punic)	consul?	N. R.	N. R.
Tempestates	259*	surviving storm at sea	consul	N. R.	N. R.
Spes	258?*	WAR (1st Punic)	consul?	N. R.	N. R.
Fides	249?*	WAR (1st Punic)	dictator?	N. R.	N. R.
Minerva Capta	241*	captured in WAR?	N. R.	N. R.	N. R.
Flora	241/238	DROUGHT	aediles	Senate	N. R.
Honos	233*	WAR (Ligurians)	consul	N. R.	N. R.
Hercules Custos	3rd c.	N. R.	N. R.	N. R.	N. R.
Hercules Victor	3rd c.	N. R.	N. R.	N. R.	N. R.
Feronia	> 217	N. R.	N. R.	N. R.	N. R.
Vulcan	> 214	N. R.	N. R.	N. R.	N. R.
Concordia (II)	216	mutiny in Gaul	praetor	duumviri	duumviri
Mens	215	WAR (2nd Punic: post-Trasimene)	praetor	Senate	duumvir (self)
Venus Erycina (I)	215	WAR (2nd Punic: post-Trasimene)	dictator	Senate	duumvir (self)
Honos et Virtus	205	WAR (Gauls)/WAR (Syracuse)	consul	N. R.	son (no office)

Appendix 1 (*cont.*)

DEITY	DATE	CIRCUMSTANCES	VOWER	$ SOURCE	DEDICATOR
Vediovis (I)	194	WAR (Gauls)	praetor	N. R.	duumvir
Juno Sospita	194	WAR (Gauls)	consul	N. R.	censor (self)
Faunus	194	N. R.	aediles	fines	praetor (self)
Fortuna Primigenia	194	WAR (2nd Punic)	consul	N. R.	duumvir
Victoria Virgo	193	WAR (Spain)	consul	N. R.	self (no office)
Vediovis (II)	192	WAR (Gauls & Ligurians)	consul	N. R.	duumvir
Magna Mater	191	WAR (2nd Punic)	N. R.	Senate	praetor
Iuventas (II)	191	WAR (2nd Punic: Metaurus)	consul	N. R.	duumvir
Ops	> 186	N. R.	N. R.	N. R.	N. R.
Luna	> 182	N. R.	N. R.	N. R.	N. R.
Venus Erycina (II)	181	WAR (Ligurians)	consul	N. R.	duumvir (son)
Pietas	181	WAR (Antiochus: Thermopylae)	consul	Senate?	duumvir (son)
Hercules Musarum	179?	WAR (Ambracia)	consul?	booty? cens.?	N. R.
Lares Permarini	179	WAR (Antiochus)	praetor	N. R.	censor (gens)
Diana (II)	179	WAR (Ligurians)	consul	N. R.	censor (self)
Juno Regina (III)	179	WAR (Ligurians)	consul	N. R.	censor (self)
Sol et Luna	> 174	N. R.	N. R.	N. R.	N. R.
Fortuna Equestris	173	WAR (Celtiberians)	propraetor	duumviri	censor (self)
Castor/Pollux (II)	173–46	N. R.	N. R.	N. R.	N. R.
Penates	> 167	N. R.	N. R.	N. R.	N. R.
Jupiter Stator (II)	146	WAR (Macedonians)	praetor	N. R.	N. R.
Mars Invictus	138*?	WAR (Lusitanians)	consul	booty	N. R.
Jupiter Fulgur	2nd c.	N. R.	N. R.	N. R.	N. R.

Appendix 1 (*cont.*)

DEITY	DATE	CIRCUMSTANCES	VOWER	$ SOURCE	DEDICATOR
Ops Opifera	2nd c.	N. R.	consul?	N. R.	N. R.
Venus Verticordia	114	atoning for Vestals' unchastity	N. R.	Senate	N. R.
Lares V . . .	> 106	N. R.	N. R.	N. R.	N. R.
Fortuna H. Diei	101	WAR (Cimbri & Teutones)	proconsul	N. R.	N. R.
Pietas	> 91	N. R.	N. R.	N. R.	N. R.

Notes:
N. R. = not recorded
> [date] = terminus ante quem
* indicates the date when the temple was vowed, since the dedication is unknown
? means there is no direct attestation for this item, but it seems probable based on other evidence

APPENDIX TWO

KNOWN SIBYLLINE CONSULTATIONS, 509–83 B.C.E.

REFERENCE	DATE	REASON or PRODIGY	RESPONSE
Dion. Hal. 6.17, 6.94	496	drought	propitiation for Ceres (temple)
Livy 4.21.5	436	pestilence, earthquakes	*obsecratio* (*duumviris praeeuntibus*)
Livy 4.25.3	433	pestilence	many things (? Temple of Apollo?)
Livy 5.13.5	399	harsh summer after severe winter	*lectisternium*
Livy 5.50	390	Gallic sack	rites of purification
Livy 7.2	364	pestilence	*lectisternium*
Dion. Hal. 14, fr. 11	362	chasm in Forum (Lacus Curtius)	sacrifice item of greatest value [Marcus Curtius]
Livy 7.27.1	346	pestilence	*lectisternium*
Livy 7.28.6-8	344	shower of stones, eclipse	appointment of dictator *causa feriae—supplicatio*
Livy 10.31	295	pestilence, showers of stones, lightning	not reported
Livy 10.47	293	pestilence	summons to Aesculapius, *supplicatio* in interim
Augustine, *CD* 3.17; Oros. 4.5	272?	pestilence	restoration of shrines
V. M. 2.4.5; Livy ep. 49; et al.	249	pestilence	*Ludi Saeculares*

Appendix 2 (cont.)

REFERENCE	DATE	REASON or PRODIGY	RESPONSE
Vell. 1.14; Pliny *NH* 18.286	241/238	drought	temple & games to Flora
Dio 12, fr. 50	228	not reported	"Beware of Gauls when thunderbolt hits Capitol"
Zon. 8.19; Plut. *Marc* 3	225	not reported	Greek and Gaul pair buried alive
Livy 21.62	218	many: lightning hits temple, shower of stones, animal prodigies, phantom ships & men, lots shrink	*lustratio, lectisternium* to Iuventas, sacrifice to Genius populi Romani, *supplicatio* to Hercules, vow by praetor
Livy 22.1	217 (after Trebia)	many: mysterious fires, blood omens, sun & moon prodigies, sweating statues, lots shrink and one falls out by itself	gifts to Jupiter, Juno & Minerva, sacrifices to Juno Regina & Juno Sospita, matrons give to Juno Regina & celebrate *lectisternium*, freedwomen give to Feronia
Livy 22.9.8	217	neglect of Flaminius (pretext after Trasimene)	vow to Mars, temples for Venus Erycina & Mens, Ludi Magni, *ver sacrum, supplicatio, lectisternium*
Livy 22.36	216	many: stone showers, blood flowing, lightning	not reported
Livy 22.57	216	many, and especially the unchastity of 2 Vestals	Greek & Gaul pairs buried alive

Appendix 2 (*cont.*)

REFERENCE	DATE	REASON or PRODIGY	RESPONSE
Livy 25.12	212	verifying *carmen Marciana*	*Ludi Apollini*
Livy 27.37	207	hermaphrodite	sacrifice & procession to Juno Regina (Aventine)
Livy 29.10	205	shower of stones	summons of Magna Mater to drive out Hannibal
Livy 31.12.9	200	many: hermaphrodites, monstrous animals, lightning	same as 207, plus hymn, offering to Juno Regina
Livy 34.55	193	repeated earthquakes	*supplicatio* with garlands
Livy 35.9	193	many: floods, showers of stones, lightning, wasps	*novemdiale, supplicatio, lustratio*
Livy 36.37.4	191	stone showers, temple hit by lightning	fast for Ceres, *novemdiale, supplicatio*, sacrifices
Livy 37.3	190	many: lightning, shower of earth, mule foaling	*supplicatio*, sacrifices by noble youths at night
Livy 38.35	189	not reported	statue of Hercules erected in his temple
Livy 38.36	188	eclipse	three-day *supplicatio*
Livy 38.44	187	pestilence	three-day *supplicatio*
Livy 39.46	183	rain of blood	*supplicatio*
Livy 40.19	181	pestilence, blood showers, spears shaking	*supplicatio* and *feriae* in all Italy
Livy 40.37	180	pestilence	*supplicatio*, both in city and country, with garlands

Appendix 2 (cont.)

REFERENCE	DATE	REASON or PRODIGY	RESPONSE
Livy 40.45	179	many: unusual storms, mule with 3 feet	sacrifice, *supplicatio*
Livy 41.21.10	174	pestilence, other prodigies	*supplicatio*, vow to have *feriae* & *supplicatio*
Livy 42.2.3	173	many: shower of stones, clouds of locusts, UFO(?)	sacrifices, two *supplicationes*, *feriae*
Livy 42.20	172	lightning destroys columna Aemilia	*lustratio*, *supplicatio*, sacrifice & games for Jove
Livy 43.13	169	meteor, animal prodigies, rain of stones & blood	sacrifice, *supplicatio*, garlands
Livy 45.16	167	temple hit by lightning, meteors, blood from hearth	*supplicatio*, sacrifice of fifty goats in forum
Obs. 13	165	pestilence, famine	*supplicatio*, *lustratio*?
Livy ep. oxy. 54; Front. 7	143	"other reasons"	opposition to Aqua Marcia and Anio
Obs. 21	143	[prodigies], defeat by Salassi	when fighting Gauls, OK (*fas*) to sacrifice in their land
Obs. 22	142	pestilence, famine	*supplicatio* (*per decemviros*)
D.S. 34.10; Cic. *Verr.* 2.49	133	prodigies after death of Tiberius Gracchus	embassy to Sicily
Phlegon (*FGH* 257 f 36 X)	125	hermaphrodite	hermaphrodite expiation (hymn, etc)

Appendix 2 (cont.)

REFERENCE	DATE	REASON or PRODIGY	RESPONSE
Obs. 35	118	earthquake, rain of milk, swarm of bees	sacrifices
Obs. 37; V. M. 8.15; et al.	114	unchastity of 3 Vestals	temple to Venus Verticordia
Obs. 40	108	burning bird & owl	sacrifice on island Cimolus by freeborn children
Obs. 44	102	many: shower of stones, spears shaking	ash of victims scattered at sea, 9-day *supplicatio*
Pliny *NH* 2.100; 3.123	100	burning shield in sky (?)	foundation of Eporedia
Gran. Lic. 35.1–2 (Crin. p. 13)	87	not reported	peace & tranquility when Cinna & six tribunes banished

THE SIBYLLINE ORACLE RECORDED BY PHLEGON OF TRALLES[1]

⟨Μ⟩ οἶραν ὀπισθομα ⟨θῶν τίνῳ ἔ⟩ φυ πᾶς εἰς τόπον ἐλθ ⟨εῖν⟩,   1α
῞Ο σσα τέρα ⟨τε⟩ καὶ ὅσσα παθήματα δαίμονος Αἴσης   1
᾽Ι στὸς ἐμὸς λύσει, τάδῳ ἐνὶ φρεσὶν αἵ κε νοήσῃς
᾽Ρ ώμῃι ἐῇι πίσυνος. καί τοί ποτέ φημι γυναῖκα
᾽Α νδρόγυνον τέξεσθαι ἔχοντά περ ἄρσενα πάντα
Ν ηπίαχαί θῷ ὅσα θηλύτεραι φαίνουσι γυναῖκες.   5
Ο ὐκ ἔτι δὴ κρύψω, θυσίας δέ τοι ἐξαγορεύσω
Π ροφρονέως Δήμητρι καὶ ἁγνῇι Περσεφονείῃι.
᾽Ι στῶι δῷ αὐτὴ ἄνασσα θεά, τὰ μὲν αἵ κε πίθηαι,
Σ εμνοτάτῃι Δήμητρι καὶ ἁγνῇι Περσεφονείῃι·
Θ ησαυρὸν μὲν πρῶτα νομίσματος εἰς ἓν ἀθροίσας,   10
῞Ο ττι θέλεις ἀπὸ παμφύλων πόλεων τε καὶ αὐτῶν,
Μ ητρὶ Κόρης Δήμητρι κέλευ θυσίαν προτίθεσθαι.
Α ὐταρ δημοσίαι κέλομαί σε τρὶς ἐννέα ταύρους

Φ ανὰς ἠυκέρους θυέμεν λευκότριχας, αἵ κεν
῾Υ μετέραι γνώμῃι κάλλει προφερέστατι ὦσιν.   15
Π αῖδας ὅσας πάρας εἶπα κέλευ ᾽Αχαιστὶ τάδῳ ἔρδειν
᾽Α θανάτην βασίλισσαν ἐπευχομένας θυέεσσιν
Σ εμνῶς καὶ καθαρῶς· τότε δὴ μετέπειτα δεχέσθω
῎Ε μπεδῳ ἀφῷ ὑμετέρων ἀλόχων ἱερῷ, αὐτὰρ ἐπῷ αὐτοῖς
᾽Ι στῶι ἐμῶι πίσυνοι λαμπρὸν φάος αἵδε φερόντων   20
Σ εμνοτάτῃι Δήμητρι. τὸ δεύτερον αὖτε λαβοῦσαι
Τ ρὶς τόσα, νήφαλα πάντα, πυρὸς μαλεροῖο τιθέντων
῞Ο σσαι ἐπισταμένως θυσίαν γραῖαι προτίθενται.
Π ροφρονέως δῷ ἄλλαι Πλουτωνίδι τόσσα λαβοῦσαι
῞Ο σσαι ἐν ἡλικίῃι νεοθηλέα θυμὸν ἔχουσιν,   25
Ν ηπιαχοί, σεμνὴν Πλουτωνίδα παντοδίδακτον

---

[1] The text is copied exactly as it appears in F. Jacoby, *Die Fragmente der Griechischen Historiker*, vol. 2B, (Berlin, 1929).

Ἐ ν πάτραι εὐχέσθων μίμνειν πολέμου κρατέοντος,
Λ ήθην ⟨δῷ⟩ Ἕλλήνεσσι πεσεῖν πόλεώς τε καὶ αὐτῆς·
Θ ησαυρὸν δὲ κόροι καὶ παρθένοι ἔνθα φερόντων

B

Ἰ στῶι θειοπαγεῖ, καὶ ὑφάσματα ποικίλα σεμνή   30
Π λουτωνὶς κοσμείσθω, ὅπως σχέσις ᾗσι κακοῖσι.
Π ροφρονέως δῷ ὅτι κάλλιστον καὶ εὐκτὸν ἐπῷ αἶαν
Ὥ ς θνητοῖσιν ἰδέσθαι ἐπέπλετο, καὶ τὸ φέρεσθαι
Ἰ στῶι σύμμικτον δῶρον βασιληίδι κούρηι.
Α ὐτὰρ ὅτῷ ἂν Δήμητρι καὶ ἀγνῆι Περσεφονείηι,   35
Γ αίας ὑμετέρας ἀπερυκέμεναι ζυγὸν αἰεί,
Α ἰδωνεῖ Πλούτωνι βοὸς κυανότριχος αἷμα
Λ αμπροῖς εἵμασι κοσμητοὺς μετὰ ποιμένος ὅστις
Λ ήματι ᾧ πίσυνος βοὸς ἄρταμος αὐτὸς ὅδῷ ἔσται,
Ὅ σσοι τῷ ἄλλοι ὁμοῦ πίσυνοι κατὰ πατρίδῷ ἔασι·   40
Μ ὴ γὰρ ἀπιστόφιλος θυσίαισιν ἀνὴρ παρεπέσθω,
Ἔ ξω δῷ, ἔνθα νομιστὸν ἐπέπλετο φωτὶ τάδῷ ἔρδειν
Ν ηπίστωι καὶ ἄδαιτον ἔχειν θυσίαν. κατὰ δῷ αὐτήν,
Ὅ στις ἂν ἡμετέρων χρησμῶν ἴδρις ἐς τόδῷ ἵκηται,
Σ εμνὸν Φοῖβον ἄνακτα μετελθέτω ἐν θυσίαισι   45
Π ροφρονέως βωμοῖς ἔπι πίονα μηρία καύσας
Α ἰγῶν πανλευκῶν νεάτην· ἀτὰρ οἴδατε πάντες,
Λ ισσέσθω Φοῖβον Παιήονα κρᾶτα πυκάσσας
Ἰ κτήρ, ἐσπίπτοντος ὅπως λύσις ᾗσι κακοῖο.
Ν οστήσας δῷ ἀπὸ τοῦ βασιληίδα πότνιαν Ἥρην   50
Ἀ ργὴν βοῦν θύων πατρίοισι νόμοισι κατῷ αἶσαν·
Ὑ μνεῖν ⟨δῷ⟩ αἵ κε γένει προφερέστεραι ὦσῷ ἐνὶ λαοῖς

Κ αὶ νήσων ναέται τὴν ἀντιπάλων ὅτῷ ἂν αἶαν
Ο ὐ δόλωι, ἀλλὰ βίαι Κυμαίδα πρόφρονες αὖτε
Ν άσσωνται, σεμνῆς βασιληίδος οἵδε τιθέντων   55
Ἐ ν πατρίοισι νόμοις Ἥρας ξόανόν τε καὶ οἶκον.
Ἵ ξει δῷ, ἂν μύθοισιν ἐμοῖς τάδε πάντα πίθηαι
Σ εμνοτάτην βασίλισσαν ἐπελθὼν ἐν θυσίαισιν   58
Ν ήφαλα †κεν ῥέξας, ὅσαι ἡμέραι εἴσῷ ἐνιαυτοῦ,   59
Ἐ ν πολλῶι χρόνωι αὖ τόδῷ ἐφῷ ὕστερον, οὐκ ἐτῷ ἐπῷ αὐτοῖς, 60
Ὅ ς κε τάδε ῥέξηι, κείνου κράτος ἔσσεται αἰεί·   61
Ν ηφαλίμων ἀρνῶν τε ταμὼν χθονίοις τάδε ῥέξον.

Ἦ μος ἂν ἤδη ἔχηις μεγάλῴ Ἥρης οἰκίῴ ἀπάντηι,
Ξ εστά θῴ ὅτῴ ἂν ξόανῴ ἦισι καὶ τἆλλῴ ὅσῴ ἔλεξα, σάφῴ ἴ⟨σθι⟩,
Ἐ ν πετάλοισιν ἐμοῖς (ὑπὸ κερκίδος ἀμφὶ καλύπτραν
Ἱ μέρτῴ ὅσσῴ ἔβαλον γλαυκῆς ἐλάας πολυκάρπου
Ἀ γλαὰ φύλλα λαβοῦσα) λύσιν κακοῦ· ἦμος ἂν ἔλθηι
Ὕ μμι χρόνος μάλα κεῖνος, ἐν ὧι ποτε τἆλλα νεόγνῴ ἦι,
Τ ρὼς δῆτῴ ἐκλύσει σε κακῶν, ἅμα δῴ Ἑλλάδος ἐκ γῆς.
Α ὐτὰρ σοῦ μεταβᾶσαν ἐποτρύνεις ἀγορεῦσαι

LIST OF KNOWN *DUUMVIRI*

DUUMVIRI AEDI LOCANDAE

NAME(S) OF DUUMVIR	YEAR	TEMPLE	RELATION TO VOWER
not reported	345	Juno Moneta	not reported
C. Pupius	217	Concordia	none
K. Quinctius Flamininus			
M'. Acilius Glabrio	190	Pietas	same man
not reported	180	Fortuna Equestris	not reported

DUUMVIRI AEDI DEDICANDAE

NAME(S) OF DUUMVIR	YEAR	TEMPLE	RELATION TO VOWER
A. Postumius Albus	484	Castor & Pollux	son
M. Atilius	216	Concordia	none
C. Atilius			
Q. Fabius Maximus	215	Venus Erycina (I)	same man
T. Otacilius	215	Mens	same man
Q. Marcius Ralla	194	Fortuna Primigenia	none
C. Servilius (Geminus?)[1]	194	Vediovis (I)	none
Q. Marcius Ralla	192	Vediovis (II)	none
C. Licinius Lucullus[2]	191	Iuventas (II)	none
M'. Acilius Glabrio	181	Pietas	son
L. Porcius Licinus	181	Venus Erycina (II)	son

Note: T. Quinctius dedicated the temple of Mars in 388 as *duumvir sacris faciundis*.

---

[1] Some identify this man as the consul of 203, who was both a pontiff and a *decemvir sacris faciundis*

[2] Lucullus was also a member of the *tresviri epulones*.

BIBLIOGRAPHY

Alföldi, A. *Early Rome and the Latins.* (Ann Arbor, 1965).

Altheim, F. *A History of Roman Religion.* (London, 1938).

Anderson, J. C. *The Historical Topography of the Imperial Fora.* Collection Latomus 182 (Bruxelles, 1984).

Anderson, R. D., Parsons, P. J. and Nisbet, R. G. M. "Elegiacs by Gallus from Qasr Ibrîm." *JRS* 69 (1979), 125–155.

Appel, G. *De Romanorum Precationibus.* Religionsgeschichtliche Versuche und Vorarbeiten 7 (Giesen, 1909).

Astin, A. E. *Scipio Aemilianus.* (Oxford, 1967).

———. *Cato the Censor.* (Oxford, 1978).

Aust, E. *De Aedibus Sacris Populi Romani.* (Diss. Marpurgi Cattorum, 1889).

Axtell, H. *The Deification of Abstract Ideas in Roman Literature and Inscriptions.* (Chicago, 1907).

Badian, E. *Foreign Clientelae.* (Oxford, 1958).

———. *Roman Imperialism in the Late Republic.* (2nd ed.) (Ithaca, 1971).

———. *Publicans and Sinners: Private Enterprise in the Service of the Roman Republic.* (Oxford, 1972).

Bailey, C. *Phases in the Religion of Ancient Rome.* (Oxford, 1932).

Bakker, J. T. *Living and Working with the Gods.* (Amsterdam, 1994).

Bardon, H. "La Naissance D'un Temple." *REL* 33 (1955), 166–182.

Barton, I. M. (ed.) *Roman Public Buildings.* (Exeter, 1989).

Basanoff, V. *Evocatio. Etude d'un rituel militaire romain.* (Paris, 1947).

Bayet, J. *Les origines de l'Hercule romain.* (Paris, 1926).

———. *Histoire politique et psychologique de la religion romaine.* 2nd edition. (Paris, 1969).

Beard, M. "Religion." in the *Cambridge Ancient History*, Vol. 9. 2nd edition. (Cambridge, 1994), 729–768.

Beard, M, and Crawford, M. *Rome in the Late Republic.* (Ithaca, 1985).

Beard, M, and North, J. (eds.) *Pagan Priests. Religion and Power in the Ancient World.* (Ithaca, 1990).

Bilz, K. *Die Politik des P. Cornelius Scipio Aemilianus.* (Stuttgart, 1935).

Bitto, I. "Venus Erycina e Mens." *ArchStor Messinese* 28 (1977), 121–133.

Bleicken, J. *Lex Publica. Gesetz und Recht in der römischen Republik.* (Berlin, 1975).

Bloch, G. and Carcopino, J. *Des Gracques à Sulla.* 3rd edition. (Paris, 1952).

Bloch, R. *Les prodiges dans l'antiquité classique.* (Paris, 1963).

———. *Les Origines des Rome.* (Paris, 1967).

Bömer, F. "Kybele in Rom: Die Geschichte ihres Kultes als politisches Phänomen." *Römisches Mitteilungen* 71 (1964), 130–151.

Bona, F. "Sul concetto di 'Manubiae' e sulla responsabilità del magistrato in ordine alla praeda." *SDHI* 26 (1960), 106–175.

Bouché-Leclerq, A. *Histoire de la divination dans l'antiquité.* (Paris, 1879–1888).

———. *Manuel des Institutions Romaines.* (Paris, 1931).

Boyancé, P. *Études sur la Religion Romaine.* (Paris, 1972).

Boyd, M. J. "The Porticoes of Metellus and Octavia and Their Two Temples." *PBSR* 21 (1953), 152–159.

Bremer, J. "The Legend of Cybele's Arrival in Rome." in *Studies in Hellenistic Religions* (M. J. Vermaseren, ed.), (*EPRO* 78, Leiden, 1979), 9–22.

Briscoe, J. *A Commentary on Livy Books XXXI–XXXIII.* (Oxford, 1973).

——. *A Commentary on Livy Books XXXIV–XXXVII.* (Oxford, 1981).
Broughton, T. R. S. *The Magistrates of the Roman Republic.* (Cleveland, 1951–52).
Brunt, P. A. *Italian Manpower, 225 B.C.–A.D. 14.* (Oxford, 1971).
——. *"Laus Imperii."* in *Imperialism in the Ancient World* (P.D.A. Garnsey and C.R. Whitaker, eds.) (Cambridge, 1978), 159–191.
——. *The Fall of the Roman Republic and Related Essays.* (Oxford, 1988).
Burkert, W. *Greek Religion.* (Cambridge, MA, 1985).
Burton, P. "The Summoning of the Magna Mater to Rome (205 B.C.)" *Historia* 45 (1996), 36–63.
Calabi Limentani, I. "I Fornices di Stertinio e di Scipione nel racconto di Livio." *CISA* 8 (1982), 123–135.
Carney, T. F. "The Aims of Roman Military and Foreign Policy in the last Quarter of the Third Century B.C." *PACA* 1 (1958), 19–26.
Cassola, F. *I Gruppi Politici Romani del III Secolo a. C.* (Trieste, 1962).
Castagnioli, F. "L'Introduzione del Culto dei Dioscuri nel Lazio." *SR* 31 (1983), 3–12.
Catalano, P. "Aspetti spaziali del sisteme giuridico-religioso romano. Mundus, templum, urbs, ager, Latium, Italia." *ANRW* 16.1 (Berlin, 1978), 440–553.
Champeaux, J. *Fortuna. Recherches sur le culte de la Fortune à Rome et dans le monde romain des origines à la mort de César. Vol. I: Fortuna dans la religion archaïque.* (Paris, 1982).
——. *Fortuna. Recherches sur le culte de la Fortune à Rome et dans le monde romain des origines à la mort de César. Vol. II: Les transformations de Fortuna sous la Règpublique.* (Paris, 1987).
Coarelli, F. "La Porta Trionfale e la Via dei Trionfi." *DArch* 2 (1968), 55–103.
——. "Il sepolcro degli Scipioni." *DArch* 6 (1972), 36–106.
——. "Public Building in Rome between the Second Punic War and Sulla." *PBSR* 45 (1977), 1–19.
Cohee, P. *"Instauratio Sacrorum."* *Hermes* 122 (1994), 451–468.
Colini, A. M. *"Aedes Veiovis inter Arcem et Capitolium."* *BullCom* 70 (1942), 5–56.
Cornell, T. "Some Observations on the *Crimen Incesti.*" in *Le délit religieux dans la cité antique.* (Rome, 1981), 27–37.
Crawford, M. *The Roman Republic.* (Atlantich Highlands, 1978).
Daremberg, C. and Saglio, E. *Dictionnaire des Antiquitès Grecques et Romaines.* (Paris, 1877–1919).
De Martino, F. *Storia della costituzione Romana.* Volume II. (Naples, 1954).
De Ruggiero, E. *Lo stato e le opere pubbliche in Roma antica.* (Torino, 1925).
De Sanctis, G. *Storia dei Romani.* (Torino, 1907–1923).
Degrassi, A. *Inscriptiones Italiae XIII.ii. Fasti Anni Numani et Iuliani.* (Rome, 1963).
Degrassi, D. "Il culto di Esculapio in Italia centrale durante il periodo repubblicano." in *Fregellae 2. Il Santuario di Esculapio* (F. Coarelli, ed.), (Rome, 1986), 145–152.
Develin, R. "Prorogation of Imperium before the Hannibalic War." *Latomus* 34 (1975), 716–722.
——. "Religion and Politics at Rome during the Third Century B.C." *Journal of Religious History* 10 (1978), 3–21.
——. *Patterns in Office-Holding, 366–49 B.C.* Collection Latomus 161 (Bruxelles, 1979).
——. *The Practice of Politics at Rome, 366–167 B.C.* Collection Latomus 188 (Bruxelles, 1985).
Diels, H. *Sibyllinsiche Blätter.* (Berlin, 1890).
Dorey, T. A. (ed.) *Livy.* (London, 1971).
Douglas, E. M. "Juno Sospita and Lanuvium." *JRS* 3 (1913), 63–72.
Drews, R. "Pontiffs, Prodigies, and the Disappearance of the *Annales Maximi.*" *CP* 83 (1988), 289–299.
Dumézil, G. *Archaic Roman Religion.* (Chicago, 1970).
Earl, D. C. *The Moral and Poltical Tradition of Rome.* (Ithaca, 1967).

Eck, W. "Senatorial Self-Representation: Developments in the Augustan Period." in *Caesar Augustus: Seven Aspects* (F. Millar and E. Segal, eds.), (Oxford, 1984).

Eckstein, A. "Human Sacrifice and Fear of Military Disaster in Republican Rome." *AJAH* 7 (1982), 69–95.

——. *Senate and General. Individual Decision Making and Roman Foreign Relations, 264–194 B.C.* (Berkeley, 1987).

Epstein, D. *Personal Enmity in Roman Politics, 218–43 B.C.* (London, 1987).

Erkell, H. "Ludi saeculares und ludi Latini saeculares. Ein Beitrag zur römischen Theaterkunde und Religionsgeschichte." *Eranos* 67 (1969), 166–174.

Fears, J. R. "The Cult of Virtues and Roman Imperial Ideology." *ANRW* 17.2 (Berlin, 1981), 827–948.

Fowler, W. Warde. *The Roman Festivals.* (London, 1889).

——. *The Religious Experience of the Roman People.* (London, 1922).

Frank, T. *Roman Buildings of the Republic. An Attempt to date Them from Their Materials.* (Rome, 1924).

——. *An Economic Survey of Ancient Rome. Vol. I: The Republic.* (Baltimore, 1933).

Frier, B. *Libri Annales Pontificum Maximorum: The Origins of the Annalistic Tradition.* (Rome, 1979).

Fritz, K. von. *The Theory of the Mixed Constitution in Antiquity.* (New York, 1954).

Gabba, E. *Dionysius and the History of Archaic Rome.* (Berkeley, 1991).

Gagé, J. *Recherches sur Les Jeux Séculaires.* (Paris, 1934).

——. *Apollon Romaine.* (Paris, 1955).

Galinsky, G. K. *Aeneas, Sicily, and Rome.* (Princeton, 1969).

Gargola, D. J. *Lands, Laws, and Gods: Magistrates and Ceremony in the Regulation of Public Lands in Republican Rome.* (Chapel Hill, 1995).

Garland, R. *Introducing New Gods.* (Ithaca, 1992).

Garnsey, P. D. A. *Famine and Food Supply in the Graeco-Roman World.* (Cambridge, 1988).

Gérard, J. "Legende et politique autour de la Mère des Dieux." *REL* 58 (1981), 153–175.

Giovannini, A. *Consulare Imperium.* (Basel, 1983).

Girard, J.-L. "Minerva Capta: Entre Rom et Faleries." *REL* 67 (1989), 163–169.

Goar, R. J. *Cicero and the State Religion.* (Amsterdam, 1972).

Gordon, A. E. "The Cults of Aricia." *University of California Publications in Classical Archaeology* 2 (1934), 1–20.

——. "The Cults of Lanuvium." *University of California Publications in Classical Archaeology* 2 (1938), 21–58.

Graillot, H. *Le Culte de Cybèle, mère des dieux, a Rome et dans l'empire romaine.* (Paris, 1912).

Grimal, P. *Les jardins Romains. À la fin de la Republique et aux deux primeirs siècles de l'Empire.* (Paris, 1943).

Gruen, E. S. *The Hellenistic World and the Coming of Rome.* (Berkeley and Los Angeles, 1984).

——. *Studies in Greek Culture and Roman Policy.* (Leiden, 1990).

——. *Culture and National Identity in Republican Rome.* (Ithaca, 1992).

——. "The 'Fall' of the Scipios." in *Leaders and Masses in the Roman World. Studies in Honor of Zvi Yavetz* (I. Malkin and Z. W. Rubinsohn, eds.), (Leiden, 1995), 59–90.

Halkin, L. *La Supplication d'Action de Graces chez les Romains.* (Paris, 1953).

Hall, A. "New Light on the Capture of Isaura Vetus by P. Servilius Vatia." in *Akten des VI. Internationalen Kongresses fur Griechische und Lateinische Epigraphik* (Munich, 1972), 568–571.

Hanson, J. *Roman Theater Temples.* (Princeton, 1959).

Harris, W. V. *War and Imperialism in Republican Rome.* (Oxford, 1979).

——. *Ancient Literacy.* (Cambridge, 1989).

Hayne, L. "The First Cerealia." *Antiquite Classique* 60 (1991), 130–38.

Hickson, F. *Roman Prayer Language. Livy and the Aeneid of Virgil.* (Stuttgart, 1993).

Hoffmann, W. *Wandel und Herkunft der Sibyllinischen Bücher in Rom.* (Diss. Leipzig, 1933).

——. *Rom und die Griechische Welt im 4. Jahrhundert.* Philologus Supplement 27 (1934).

Hopkins, K. *Conquerors and Slaves.* Sociological Studies in Roman History, Vol. I. (Cambridge, 1978).

——. *Death and Renewal.* Sociological Studies in Roman History, Vol. II. (Cambridge, 1984).

Jashemski, W. *The Origins and History of the Proconsular and the Propraetorian Imperium to 27 B.C.* (Chicago, 1950).

Jocelyn, H. D. "The Roman Nobility and the Religion of the Republican State." *Journal of Religious History* 4 (1966), 89–104.

Jolowicz, H. F. and Nicholas, B. *Historical Introduction to the Study of Roman Law.* (3rd ed.) (Cambridge, 1972).

Jones, A. H. M. *The Greek City from Alexander to Justinian.* (Oxford, 1966).

Kajanto, I. *God and Fate in Livy.* (Turku, 1957).

Keaveney, A. "Sulla Augur." *AJAH* 7 (1982), 150–171.

——. "Sulla and the Gods." in *Studies in Latin Literature and Roman History* III. Collection Latomus 180 (Bruxelles, 1983), 44–79.

Kienast, D. "Rom und die Venus vom Eryx." *Hermes* 93 (1965), 478–489.

——. *Augustus, Prinzeps und Monarch.* (Darmstadt, 1982).

Kierdorf, W. "*Funus* und *Consecratio*: Zu Terminologie und Ablauf der römischen Kaiserapotheose." *Chiron* 16 (1986), 43–70.

Kloft, H. *Prorogation und ausserordentliche Imperien 326–81 v. Chr.* (Hain, 1977).

Köves-Zulauf, T. *Reden und Schwegen. Römische Religion bei Plinius Maior.* (Munich, 1972).

Kyrieleis, H. "Bemerkungen zue Vorgeschichteder Kaiserfora." in *Hellenismus in Mittelitalien* (ed. P. Zanker). (Gottingen, 1990), 431–438.

Lahusen, G. *Untersuchungen zur Ehrenstatue in rom. literarische und epigraphische Zeugnisse.* (Rome, 1983).

Lake, Agnes K. "The Supplicatio and Graecus Ritus." in *Quantulacumque. Studies Presented to Kirsopp Lake* (London, 1937), 243–251.

Laqueur, R. "Über das Wesen des Römischen Triumphs." *Hermes* 44 (1909), 215–245.

Latte, K. *Römische Religionsgeschichte.* (Munich, 1960).

Le Bonniec, H. *Le culte de Cérès à Rome des origines à la fin de république.* (Paris, 1958).

Le Gall, J. "Evocatio." in *Mélanges Heurgon* (Paris, 1976), 519–524.

Liebeschuetz, J. "The Religious Position of Livy's History." *JRS* 57 (1967), 45–55.

——. *Continuity and Change in Roman Religion.* (Oxford, 1979).

Linderski, J. "Cicero and Roman Divination." *PP* 37 (1982), 12–38.

——. "The *Libri Reconditi*." *HSCP* 89 (1985), 207–234.

——. "The Augural Law." *ANRW* II.16.3, (Berlin, 1986), 2146–2312.

——. "Roman Religion in Livy." in *Livius. Aspekte Seines Werkes.* Xenia. Konstanzer Althistorische Vorträge und Forschungen 31 (1993), 53–70.

Lippold, A. *Consules. Untersuchungen zur Geschichte des Römischen Konsulates von 264 bis 201 v. Chr.* (Bonn, 1963).

Luce, T. J. *Livy. The Composition of His History.* (Princeton, 1977).

Lugli, G. *Roma Antica. Il Centro Monumentale.* (Rome, 1946).

MacBain, B. *Prodigy and Expiation: A Study in Religion and Politics in Republican Rome.* Collection Latomus 177 (Bruxelles, 1982).

Magdelain, A. *Recherches sur L' "Imperium", la loi curiate, et les auspices d'investiture.* (Paris, 1968).

Marquardt, J. *Römische Staatsverwaltung.* (Leipzig, 1881–1885).

——. *De l'organisation financière chez les romains.* in *Manuel des antiquités romaines*, vol. 10. (Paris, 1888).

Marsh, F. B. *The Founding of the Roman Empire.* (Austin, 1922).
Martina, M. "Aedes Herculis Musarum." *DArch* ser. 2, vol. 3 (1981), 49–68.
Mello, M. *Mens Bona.* (Naples, 1968).
Meslin, M. *La fête des kalendes de janvier dans l'empire romain.* Collection Latomus 115 (Bruxelles, 1970).
Michels, A. K. *The Calendar of the Roman Republic.* (Princeton, 1967).
Millar, F. "The Political Character of the Classical Roman Republic, 200–151 B.C." *JRS* 74 (1984), 1–19.
Momigliano, A. "Camillus and Concord." *CQ* 36 (1942), 111–120.
Mommsen, T. *Römisches Staatsrecht.* (Leipzig, 1887–1888).
———. *Römisches Strafrecht.* (Leipzig, 1899).
Montanari, E. "Mens." *Religion e Civiltá* 2 (1976), 173–235.
Morgan, M. G. "The Portico of Metellus: A Reconsideration." *Hermes* 99 (1971), 480–505.
———. "Villa Publica and Magna Mater." *Klio* 55 (1973a), 215 245.
———. " 'Metellus Pontifex' and Ops Opifera: A Note on Pliny *Naturalis Historia* 11.174." *Phoenix* 27 (1973b), 35–41.
———. "The Introduction of the Aqua Marcia into Rome, 144–140 B.C." *Philologus* 122 (1978), 25–58.
———. "Politics, Religion, and the Games in Rome, 200–150 B.C." *Philologus* 134 (1990), 14–36.
Moxon, I. S., Smart, J. D., and Woodman, A. J., eds. *Past Perspectives: Studies in Greek and Roman Historical Writing.* (Cambridge, 1986).
Münzer, F. *Römische Adelsparteien und Adelsfamilien.* (Stuttgart, 1920).
Musial, D. "Sur le Culte d'Esculape à Rome et en Italie." *DHA* 16 (1990), 231–238.
Musumeci, F. "Statuae in Publico positae." *SDHI* 44 (1978), 191–203.
Niccolini, G. *I Fasti dei tribuni della plebe.* (Milano, 1934).
Nicolet, C. *The World of the Citizen in Republican Rome.* Trans. by P. S. Falla. (Berkeley, 1980).
Nisbet, R. G. *M. Tulli Ciceronis "De Domo Sua ad Pontifices" Oratio.* (Oxford, 1939).
Nock, A. D. "A Feature of Roman Religion." *HTR* 32 (1939), 83–96, reprinted in *Essays on Religion and the Ancient World* (Oxford, 1986), 481–492.
North, J. A. "Conservatism and Change in Roman Religion." *PBSR* 44 (1976), 1–12.
———. "Religious Toleration in Republican Rome." *PCPS* 25 (1979), 85–103.
———. "Novelty and Choice in Roman Religion." *JRS* 70 (1980), 186–191.
———. "Religion and Politics, from Republic to Principate." *JRS* 76 (1986), 251–258.
———. "Religion in Republican Rome." in *Cambridge Ancient History*, Vol. 7.2 (2nd ed.). (Cambridge, 1989), 573–624.
Ogilvie, R. M. *A Commentary on Livy Books 1–5.* (Oxford, 1965).
———. *The Romans and Their Gods in the Age of Augustus.* (London, 1969).
———. *Early Rome and the Etruscans.* (Sussex, 1976).
Packard, D. W. *A Concordance to Livy.* (Cambridge, MA, 1968).
Palmer, R. E. A. "The Censors of 312 B.C. and the State Religion." *Historia* 14 (1965), 293–324.
———. *The Archaic Community of the Romans.* (Cambridge, 1970).
———. *Roman Religion and Roman Empire: Five Essays.* (Philadelphia, 1974a).
———. "Roman Shrines of Female Chastity from the Caste Struggle to the Papacy of Innocent I." *RSA* 4 (1974b), 113–159.
———. "C. Verres' Legacy of charm and love to the city of Rome: a new document." *RPAA* 51–52 (1978–1979, 1979–1980), 111–136.
———. "A New Fragment of Livy Throws Light on the Roman Postumii and Latin Gabii." *Athenaeum* 78 (1990a), 5–18.

———. "Studies of the Northern Campus Martius in Ancient Rome." *Trans. Amer. Phil. Soc.* 80 (1990b), 1–64.

Panciera, S. "Nuovi documenti epigrafici per lo topografia di Roma antica." *RPAA* 43 (1970–1971), 109–134.

Pape, M. *Griechische Kunstwerke aus Kriegsbeute und ihre öffentliche Aufstellung in Rom.* (Diss. Hamburg, 1975).

Parke, H. W. *Sibyls and Sibylline Prophecy in Classical Antiquity.* (B. C. McGing, ed.) (London, 1988).

Perret, J. *Les origines de la légende troyenne de Rome (231–81).* (Paris, 1942).

Pietilä-Castrén, L. "New Men and the Greek War Booty in the Second Century B.C." *Arctos* 16 (1982), 121–144.

———. *Magnificentia Publica: The Victory Monuments of the Roman Generals in the Era of the Punic Wars.* (Helsinki, 1987).

Pighi, J. B. *De Ludis Saecularibus populi romani quiritium.* (Amsterdam, 1965).

Platner, S. B. and Ashby, T. *A Topographical Dictionary of Ancient Rome.* (London, 1929).

Quinn-Schofield, W. K. "*Ludi, Romani magnique varie appellati.*" *Latomus* 26 (1967), 96–103.

Radke, G. *Zur Entwicklung der Gottesvorstellung und der Gottesverehrung in Rom.* (Darmstadt, 1987).

———. "Nouveaux points de vue sur la mentalitè religeuse des Romains." *Kernos* 4 (1991), 31–46.

Rawson, E. "Prodigy Lists and the Use of the *Annales Maximi*." *CQ* 21 (1971), 158–169 = *Roman Culture and Society* (Oxford, 1991), 1–15.

———. "Scipio, Laelius, Furius and the Ancestral Religion." *JRS* 63 (1973), 161–174 = *Roman Culture and Society* (Oxford, 1991), 80–101.

———. "Religion and Politics in the Late Second Century B.C. at Rome." *Phoenix* 28 (1974), 193–212 = *Roman Culture and Society* (Oxford, 1991), 149–168.

———. "The Antiquarian Tradition: Spoils and Representations of Foreign Armor." in *Staat und Staatlichkeit in der frühen römischen Republik* (W. Eder, ed.) (Stuttgart, 1990), 157–173 = *Roman Culture and Society* (Oxford, 1991), 582–598.

Richardson, J. S. "The Triumph, the Praetors, and the Senate in the Early Second Century B.C." *JRS* 65 (1975), 50–63.

Richardson, L. Jr. "The Evolution of the Porticus Octaviae." *AJA* 80 (1976), 57–64.

———. "Hercules Musarum and the Porticus Philippi in Rome." *AJA* 81 (1977), 355–361.

———. "Honos et Virtus and the Sacra Via." *AJA* 82 (1978), 240–246.

———. *A New Topographical Dictionary of Ancient Rome.* (Baltimore, 1992).

Rizzo, G. E. *Monete greche della Sicilia.* (Rome, 1946).

Robinson, O. F. *Ancient Rome. City Planning and Administration.* (London, 1992).

Roesch, P. "Le Culte d'Asclepios à Rome." in *Médecins et Médecine dans l'Antiquité* (G. Sabbah, ed.), (Saint-Etienne, 1982), 171–179.

Rohde, G. *Die Bedeutung der Tempelgründungen im Staatsleben der Römer.* (Marburg, 1932).

Rollin, J. *Untersuchungen zur Rechtfragen romischer Bildnisse.* Bonn 1979).

Rose, H. J. *Ancient Roman Religion.* (London, 1949).

Rosenstein, N. "*Imperatores Victi*: The Case of C. Hostilius Mancinus." *CA* 5 (1986), 230–252.

———. *Imperatores Victi. Military Defeat and Aristocratic Competition in the Middle and Late Republic.* (Berkeley, 1990).

Rotondi, G. *Leges Publicae Populi Romani.* (Milan, 1912).

Rüpke, J. "Livius, Priesternamen und die Annales maximi." *Klio* 75 (1993), 155–179.

Salmon, E. T. *Samnium and the Samnites.* (Cambridge, 1967).

Scheid, J. "Le délit religieux dans la Rome tardo-républicaine." in *Le délit religieux dans la cité antique.* (Rome, 1981), 117–171.

———. *Religion et piete à Rome.* (Paris, 1985).

——. *Romulus et Ses Frères. Le Collège des Frères Arvales, Modèle du Culte Public Dans la Rome des Empereurs*. (Paris, 1990).

Schilling, R. *La religion romaine de Venus, depuis les origines jusqu' au temps d'Auguste*. (Paris, 1954).

——. "The Roman Religion." in *Historia Religionum*, Vol. I (C. J. Bleeker, G. Widengren eds.), (Leiden, 1969), 442–494.

——. *Rites, Cultes, Dieux de Rome*. (Paris, 1979).

Schlag, U. *Regnum in Senatu: Das Wirken römischer Staatsmänner von 200 bis 191 v. Chr.* (Stuttgart, 1968).

Schleussner, B. *Die Legaten der römischen Republik: Decem Legati und ständige Hilfsgesandte*. (Munich, 1978).

Scullard, H. H. *Roman Politics, 220–150*. (Oxford, 1951.)

——. "Scipio Aemilianus and Roman Politics." *JRS* 50 (1960), 59–74.

——. *Scipio Africanus: Soldier and Statesman*. (London, 1970).

——. *A History of the Roman World: 753–146 B.C.* (London, 1980).

——. *Festivals and Ceremonies of the Roman Republic*. (Ithaca, NY, 1981).

Seguin, R. "La religion de Scipion l'Africain." *Latomus* 33 (1974), 3–21.

Shatzman, I. "The Roman General's Authority Over Booty." *Historia* 21 (1972), 177–205.

——. *Senatorial Wealth and Roman Politics*. (Brussels, 1975).

Shields, E. L. *Juno: A Study in Early Roman Religion*. Smith College Studies 7 (1926).

Shipley, F. W. "A Chronology of the Building Operations in Rome from the Death of Caesar to the Death of Augustus." *MAAR* 9 (1931), 7–60.

Simms, R. *Foreign Religious Cults in Athens in the Fifth and Fourth Centuries B.C.* (Diss., U. of Virginia, 1985).

Spaeth, B. "The Goddess Ceres and the Death of Tiberius Gracchus." *Historia* 39, (1990), 182–195.

——. *The Roman Goddess Ceres*. (Austin, 1996).

Stambaugh, J. E. "The Functions of Roman Temples." *ANRW* 16.1 (Berlin, 1978), 554–608.

Staveley, E. S. "The Political Aims of Appius Claudius Caecus." *Historia* 8 (1959), 410–433.

Stehle, E. "Venus, Cybele and the Sabine Women: The Roman Construction of Female Sexuality." *Helios* 16 (1989), 143–164.

Strong, D. E. "The Administration of Public Building in Rome during the Late Republic and Early Empire." *BICS* 15 (1968), 97–109.

Suolahti, J. *The Roman Censors. A Study on Social Structure*. (Helsinki, 1963).

Szemler, G. J. *The Priests of the Roman Republic*. Collection Latomus 127 (Bruxelles, 1972).

Tamm, B. "Le Temple des Muses à Rome." *Opuscula Romana* 3 (1961), 157–167.

Tatum, W. J. "The *Lex Papiria de Dedicationibus*." *CPh* 88 (1993), 319–328.

Taylor, L. R. "New Light on the History of the Secular Games." *AJP* 55, (1934), 101–120.

——. *Party Politics in the Age of Caesar*. (Berkeley, 1949).

Thomas, G. "Magna Mater and Attis." *ANRW* II.17.3 (Berlin, 1984), 1499–1535.

Toher, M. "Augustus and the Evolution of Roman Historiography." in *Between Republic and Empire: Interpretations of Augustus and His Principate* (K. Raaflaub and M. Toher, eds.). (Berkeley, 1990), 139–154.

Toynbee, A. J. *Hannibal's Legacy*. (London, 1965).

Turlan, J. "L'obligation *ex-voto*." *RD* 33 (1955), 504–536.

Van Doren, M. "Peregrina Sacra. Offizielle Kultübertragungen im alten Rom." *Historia* 3 (1955), 488–497.

Vanggaard, J. H. *The Flamen. A Study in the History and Sociology of Roman Religion*. (Copenhagen, 1988).

Vermaseren, M. J. *Cybele and Attis: The Myth and the Cult*. (London, 1977).

Versnel, H. *Triumphus. An Inquiry into the Origin, Development and Meaning of the Roman Triumph.* (Leiden, 1970).
——. "Two types of Roman *devotio.*" *Mnemosyne* s. IV 29 (1976), 365–410.
Veyne, P. *Bread and Circuses.* (London, 1990).
Vogel, K. H. "Zur rechtlichen Behandlung der römischen Kriegsgewinne." *ZSS* 66 (1948), 394–423.
Wagenvoort, H. *Roman Dynamism.* (Oxford, 1947).
——. "The Origin of the Ludi Saeculares." *Meded. Kon. Ned. Akad. v. Wetensch. afd. Lett. N.R.* 14, no. 4 (1951), reprinted in *Studies in Roman Literature, Culture and Religion*, (Leiden, 1956), 193–232.
Wallace-Hadrill, A. "Roman Arches and Greek Honours: The Language of Power at Rome." *PCPS* 36 (1990), 143–181.
Walsh, P. G. *Livy: His Historical Aims and Methods.* (Cambridge, 1961).
Wardman, A. *Religion and Statecraft Among the Romans.* (Baltimore, 1982).
Watson, A. *The Law of Property in the Late Roman Republic.* (Oxford, 1968).
——. *The State, Law and Religion: Pagan Rome.* (Athens, GA, 1992).
Weigel, R. D. "The Duplication of Temples of Juno Regina in Rome." *AncSoc* 13–14 (1982–83), 179–192.
Weinstock, S. "*Ludi Tarentini* und *ludi saeculares.*" *Glotta* 21 (1933), 40–52.
——. "Two Archaic Inscriptions from Latium." *JRS* 50 (1960), 112–118.
——. "Victor and Invictus." *HTR* 50 (1957), 211–247.
——. *Divus Julius.* (Oxford, 1971).
Weissenborn, W. and Müller, H. *Titi Livi ab urbe condita libri.* (Berlin, 1880–1911).
Willems, P. *Le Sénat de la République Romaine et ses attributions.* (Louvain, 1878–1883).
Wiseman, T. P. *Clio's Cosmetics.* (Leicester, 1979).
——. ed. *Roman Political Life 90 B.C.–A.D. 69.* (Exeter, 1985).
——. "Monuments and the Roman Annalists." in *Past Perspectives: Studies in Greek and Roman Historical Writing* (I. S. Moxon, J. D. Smart, and A. J. Woodman, eds.). (Cambridge, 1986), 87–101.
——. "*Conspicui Postes Tectaque Digna Deo*: The Public Image of Aristocratic and Imperial Houses in the Late Republic and Early Empire." in *L'Urbs: Espace urbain et histoire.* CEFR 98 (Rome, 1987), 393–413.
——. *Historiography and Imagination.* (Exeter, 1994).
Wissowa, G. *Religion und Kultus der Römer.* (Munich, 1902).
Wuilleumier, P. "Tarente et Le Tarentum." *REL* 10 (1932), 127–146.
——. "Tarente et Le *Tarentum.*" *REL* 16 (1938), 139–145.
Zanker, P. *The Power of Images in the Age of Augustus.* (Ann Arbor, 1988).
Ziolkowski, A. "Mummius' Temple of Hercules Victor and the Round Temple on the Tiber." *Phoenix* 42 (1988), 309–333.
——. *The Temples of Mid-Republican Rome and Their Historical and Topographical Context.* (Rome, 1992).
——. "Between Geese and the Auguraculum: The Origin of the Cult of Juno on the Arx." *CP* 88 (1993), 206–219.

INDEX

M'. Acilius Glabrio (cos 191)   42–49,
  128, 146–47, 158, 180, 186
M'. Acilius Glabrio (cos suff. 154)   173
acrostic poetry   80
aedes, definition of   11
aedes Seiani   194
aediles   19, 26, 70, 112, 127, 128,
  134, 141, 143–144, 147, 163, 165,
  169–70, 181
    aedilician temple building   135,
      186
M. Aemilius Lepidus   72, 138, 141,
  155, 177, 181, 186
L. Aemilius Paullus   192
M. Aemilius Paullus   141
L. Aemilius Regillus   70, 128, 131,
  181
M. Aemilius (Regillus?)   43, 154
Aeneas   14, 108
Aequi   179
Aesculapius   23, 24, 34, 61, 93, 97,
  99, 100, 101, 106, 107, 114, 120
Alban Mount   39, 66–67
Antiochus III (king of Syria)   42, 128,
  146, 177, 183
Aphrodite   103
Apollo   22–23, 53, 74
    Republican temple of   14, 22, 53
    Augustan temple of   76, 98
    Apollo Medicus   22
    Apollo Sosianus   194
    and Sibylline Books   78, 97–98
Apulia   107
Aqua Marcia   83, 91
Aquilonia   52
Ara Maxima   14, 66
Aricia   15
aristocracy
    and direction of religious affairs
      90, 103, 113, 115, 166, 168
    competition among   1–2, 4, 8,
      50, 66, 130, 162, 192
    cooperation among   3, 9, 75, 198
Arval Brethren   47, 101
Asia Minor   160
C. Asinius Pollio   130
M. and C. Atilius (aediles)   182

M. Atilius (or Acilius) (*duumvir*)   81
M. Atilius Regulus   32, 55
Attalus I (king of Pergamon)   110–11
augurs   77, 112, 149, 164–65, 174
Augustus   78, 98, 130, 148, 194
    Augustan Principate   3, 130,
      194, 198
Aulus Gellius   117–19
C. Aurelius Cotta   185
auspices   31, 37, 39, 52, 60, 64
Aventine hill   15, 25, 63, 112

Bacchanalia   186
Bellona   28, 29, 48
Bona Dea   167
booty   8, 30, 53, 59–60, 74,
  117–19, 121–29, 134, 136, 152,
  177, 186, 194

L. Caecilius Metellus Delmaticus   134
Q. Caecilius Metellus Macedonicus
  193
M. Caelius Rufus   70
Cannae   176
Capitoline hill   14, 36, 38–39, 41, 71,
  76, 83–84, 102, 109, 181, 184
    Capitoline Jupiter   24, 78
    Capitoline triad   63
carmen Marciana   87
Carthage   15, 127, 128
Sp. Carvilius Maximus   64, 123, 130,
  135, 145, 147
Castor and Pollux   14, 25, 30
    temple of   22, 104, 111, 134,
      148, 159, 174, 179
Caudine Forks, treaty of   51, 53, 60
Celtiberians   29, 139, 156
censors
    and dedications   169–70
    and public contracts   140
    and temple contracts   142–44,
      147, 153, 155, 158–59
    and quinquennial vows   37–38
Ceres   24, 92, 93, 98
    Cerealia   26
Ceres, Liber and Libera   49, 97,
  100–101

temple of 6, 25–26, 44, 98, 104, 111
Christianity 14
Circus Maximus 26, 71
A. Claudius Caecus 28–29, 35, 48–49
A. Claudius Sabinus 124
M. Claudius Marcellus (cos 222) 131–32, 136
M. Claudius Marcellus (cos 196) 136, 170
P. Clodius Pulcher 166
comitia 41, 148, 150, 151, 181, 196
Concordia 102
    temple of (ded. 304) 127, 163–65, 170
    temple of (ded. 216) 148, 150, 152, 154, 173, 182, 189
consuls
    and contracts 140, 145–47
    and dedications 163–64, 170
    and temples 31–32, 68, 160, 191
    and vows 36–41, 49, 55
Consus, temple of 24
    Q. Marcius Coriolanus 26, 27
C. Cornelius Cethegus 63, 67, 129, 145, 181
P. Cornelius Scipio Aemilianus 37
L. Cornelius Scipio Asiaticus 57–58, 69, 128–29, 177, 192
P. Cornelius Scipio Africanus 69, 71, 157, 187, 192
    attack against 57–58, 186
C. Cornelius Scipio Barbatus 163–164
P. Cornelius Scipio Nasica 56, 58–61, 69, 74, 157, 185
L. Cornelius Sulla Felix 3, 79, 196
L. Cornificius 194
Corsica 131
Croton, battle of 64, 184
Croton, temple of Hera Lacinia at 139, 191
Cumae 77 n. 1, 79 n. 10
cura urbis 141
Cybele see Magna Mater

Damophilos 101
daps 94
decemviri sacris faciundis 73, 79–85, 89, 91, 96–97, 112, 115, 165
P. Decius Mus 30
dedicatio 141
Delphi 92

Demeter and Kore 100
devotio 30, 35 n. 1
Diana 22
    temple of (ded. by Servius Tullius) 15
    temple of (ded. 179) 72, 181
    Diana Cornificiana 194
dictator
    clavi figendae causa 24
    feriarum constituendarum causa 94
    and temple contracts 144–45, 147, 153
    and temple dedications 170, 179–80
dies natalis 102, 135
Digest 171
Dionysius of Halicarnassus 86, 100
Cn. Domitius Ahenobarbus 181
L. Domitius Ahenobarbus 194
drought 20, 21, 24–26, 37, 78, 101
C. Duilius 71
duumviri aedi dedicandae 64, 148–150, 164, 170, 172–76, 178, 181–82, 184, 189
duumviri aedi locandae 141, 146–47, 149–155, 158–159, 172–173, 180, 186, 190
duumviri navales 150
duumviri sacris faciundis 22, 25, 81, 98, 172

Enna 92
Q. Ennius 65
Epidaurus 23, 99, 106
epulum Iovis 94
Erythrae 77 n. 1, 79
Eryx 99, 108
Etruscans 14, 28, 48, 63, 77, 91, 106, 145
Evander (Arcadian king) 14, 103, 104
evocatio 15, 29 n. 59, 62, 63, 144, 145, 197

Q. Fabius Maximus Verrucosus (Cunctator) 112, 149, 173, 175–76, 188–89
famine 13, 20, 25, 82, 111
fanum 55
fasti 5, 19, 135, 193
    fasti Venusini 135
Faunus, temple of 144, 181
Felicitas, temple of 131, 135
ficus Ruminalis 141
Fidenates 22

Fides 62
  temple of 102
flamen Floralis 101
flamen Martialis 149
C. Flaminius 39, 49, 154
Cn. Flavius 163, 170
Flora, temple of 25–6, 97, 101–2, 144
  Floralia 26
Fons, temple of 130
  Fontinalia 135
foreign elements in Roman religion
  91, 95, 114
    foreign deities 11, 13, 29, 33,
    61–64, 93, 99, 114
fornices 71, 130
Fors Fortuna, temple of (ded. by
  Servius Tullius) 22
Fors Fortuna, temple of (ded. 293)
  31, 123, 127, 130, 135, 145, 147
Fortuna Equestris 14 n. 8, 29–30,
  148
    temple of 27, 138, 148, 151–52,
    155, 192
Fortuna Muliebris 27–28
  temple of 26
Fortuna Primigenia 14 n. 8, 64
  temple of 142, 146, 173, 183,
    185, 187
Forum Romanum 22
Forum Boarium 64, 71
Forum Holitorium 48, 63, 145
Forum Julium 197
Fregellae, Asclepium at 107 n. 113
Frontinus 83
Q. Fulvius Flaccus 29, 60–61, 129,
  138–39, 151–52, 155, 191–92
M. Fulvius Nobilior 6, 65–66,
  132–33, 137–39, 155, 177
L. Furius Camillus 151–53
M. Furius Camillus 44–45, 53–54,
  56, 62, 74, 86, 87, 144, 152
M. Furius Crassipes 73
L. Furius Purpurio 129, 146, 155,
  184–85, 187

games 8, 16, 29–30, 87, 92, 138,
  151–152, 157–158, 162, 182, 185,
  188, 196
    see also *ludi*
Gauls 63, 86–87, 129, 146, 150, 160,
  181–84, 194
gloria 2, 66–68, 70–71, 73, 75, 116,
  161–62, 177–78, 186, 189
Gorgasos 101

Greece 43, 47, 62, 65, 137, 160, 177
Greek elements in Roman religion
  93, 103, 113
    Greek gods 14, 97–99, 104, 115
    Greek rituals 14, 66, 94–97
      Graecus ritus 93, 96, 104
    innovations ascribed to Greek
      influence 93–96, 98–101
Greek culture 34, 65, 107, 114–15
Greek hexameter poetry 113, 115

Hannibal 20, 64, 85–86, 94, 96,
  99, 102, 108, 110, 151, 154–55,
  175–76, 182
haruspices 96, 165
Hellenistic world 23, 80, 197
Hera Lacinia, temple of 139, 156,
  191–92
Hercules 103–4, 120
    Hercules Custos, temple of 97,
    103–4
    Hercules Musarum 65
      temple of 6, 132, 137
    Hercules Pompeianus 194
    Hercules Victor, temple of 193
    see also Ara Maxima
hermaphrodite 82, 88, 89
Honos and Virtus, temple of (ded. 205)
  130–31, 136, 170
Honos and Virtus, temple of (ded. by
  Marius) 130, 193
C. Hostilius Mancinus 51 n. 57, 52
  n. 59

Ilipa 59
imperator 163–64
Imperial arches 71
imperium 35–6, 46–49, 59–61, 146,
  158, 168–69
inimicus 138, 159, 177
instauratio 16
Isis 5, 12 n. 4
C. Iulius Caesar 3, 130, 192, 194,
  199–98
D. Iunius Brutus Callaicus 131, 135,
  193–94
M. Iunius Brutus 175
C. Iunius Bubulcus 142, 146, 179–80
ius publicum dedicandi 163–71
Iuventas 95
  temple of 142, 146, 183–85

Janus 22, 101
Juno 14, 101

Juno Moneta, temple of 147, 151–53
Juno of Veii 15, 53, 144
 Juno Regina, temple of (ded. 392) 15, 53, 62, 144
Juno Regina, temple of (ded. 179) 72, 181
Juno Sospita 63–64
 temple of 63, 145, 181
Jupiter 101
 Jupiter Feretrius, temple of 22
 Jupiter Latiaris 39
 Jupiter Optimus Maximus 14, 29, 138
  temple of 21–22, 39, 76–77, 79, 81, 98, 101
 Jupiter Stator, temple of (vowed by Romulus) 22, 55
  Jupiter Stator, temple of (vowed 294) 55, 74, 158
  Jupiter Stator, temple of (2nd century?) 73
 Jupiter Victor 30, 62, 65
  temple of 29
Juturna, spring of 22

M. Laetorius 170
Lake Regillus, battle of 22, 26, 30, 104, 111, 179
Lake Trasimene, battle of 20, 39, 49, 99, 102, 182
Lanuvium 64
Lares Permarini, temple of 70, 131, 181
Latin festival 39–40
Latin League 15, 64
Lavinium 104
lectisternium 23, 92–95, 98
P. Lentulus Sura 93 n. 55
lex Domitia 149
lex Ogulnia 164
lex Papiria 166–71
lex Plaetoria 172
Libertas, shrine of (ded. by Clodius) 166
Licinia (Vestal Virgin) 167
C. Licinius Lucullus 183
L. Licinius Lucullus 120–21, 131, 135
Liguria 129, 160, 177, 181
C. Livius Salinator 183
M. Livius Salinator 142, 146, 183
locatio 139, 141, 144, 158, 161
Lucania 107
Luceria, battle of 55

C. Lucretius Gallus 120
ludi 44, 69–71, 94, 138
 Ludi Apollinares 41, 87
 Ludi Magni 41–45, 47, 94
 Ludi Saeculares 79
 Ludi Scenici 23, 95
Luna, temple of 19
Lusitanians 56, 59, 69
lustratio 92, 94
lustrum 37–38
Q. Lutatius Cerco 64

Magna Graecia 24, 106–107
Magna Mater (Cybele) 62, 93, 99–100, 105, 109–11
 temple of 91, 97, 99, 109, 143, 175
Magnesia, battle of 177
Cn. Manlius Vulso 177, 185
L. Manlius 152, 155–55, 182, 189
manubiae 4, 8, 56, 116–40, 145, 156, 159–61, 193–94
 manubial building theory 116, 124, 127–31, 134, 140, 160–161
Q. Marcius Ralla 64, 184, 187
Q. Marcius Rex 84
C. Marius 2, 3, 131, 193, 194, 196
Mars 24
 temple of 172
 Mars Invictus, temple of 131, 135, 193
Mater Matuta, temple of 45, 54
Mens, temple of 20, 97, 102, 112, 149, 151, 173, 175
Mercury 97, 98,
 temple of 164, 170
Metaurus, battle of 96, 99, 109, 142, 183
Minerva 14, 24, 133
Q. Minucius Thermus 67, 129
monumentum 126, 137
Mt. Ida 110
mos maiorum 50, 65, 117, 122, 163, 164, 170
L. Mummius 193–94
L. Munatius Plancus 130
Muses 138
mutiny 20, 58, 69, 150, 154, 157, 182
Mylae, battle of 71

Neptune 194
nobilis 32

Nortia (Volsinian goddess) 12 n. 4
novemdiale sacrum 89, 94, 105, 109
novus homo 32
Nuncupatio Votorum 47

obsecratio 22
Cn. Octavius 71
M. Octavius 92
Q. Ogulnius 99, 141
T. Otacilius 149, 173, 175–76, 188–89

Palatine hill 78, 99, 166
Pales, temple of 32
Pallor and Pavor, temple of 22
Q. Papirius 166
L. Papirius Cursor 30–31, 52, 123, 135, 180
Cn. Papirius Maso 130, 135
patricians 32
    patrician-plebeian relations 165
pax deum 4, 7, 12, 16–17, 20–21, 24–27, 33, 35, 47, 55, 58, 60, 68, 86–87, 90, 92, 147, 182, 190–191
Peace of Phoenice 110
peculatus 122
pecunia censoria 133
Penates 14
Pessinus 99
Philip V (king of Macedon) 96, 110, 111, 177
Phlegon of Tralles 80 n. 14
Phrygia 62, 99
Picenes 32
Pietas, temple of 48, 146, 148, 173, 180
plague 13, 20–24, 33, 37, 41, 82, 87–88, 95, 98
plebeians 25, 32, 111–12, 115, 123–24, 164–69
Pliny the Elder 16, 102, 120, 132–33
politics, and religion 18, 162, 189, 195, 198
    political factors in religious decisions 7, 84, 105, 159
    political implications of religious decisions 4, 33, 91–92, 114
    see also *inimicus*
Cn. Pompeius Strabo 124
Cn. Pompeius Magnus 2–3, 125, 133–34, 192, 194, 196–97
pontifex maximus 42–43, 149, 163, 165–66
pontiffs 42, 53, 55, 73–74, 87, 89, 96, 164–67

populus 5, 54, 163, 176, 179
C. Porcius Cato 85
M. Porcius Cato 67–69, 118, 170, 181, 186–87
L. Porcius Licinus (*duumvir*) 173, 181
portents 20
porticoes 130
    portico of Metellus 195
A. Postumius Albinus 172
Sp. Postumius Albinus 51–52
A. Postumius Albus 25, 30, 44, 49, 78, 100, 111, 159, 174, 179
A. Postumius Albus Regillensis 159, 174, 179
praeda 117–121, 123, 125–26
Praeneste 64
praetors
    and contracts 140
    and dedications 170
    and temples 31,
    and vows 36, 38
priestly colleges 8, 81, 165
prodigies 4, 16, 19–21, 23, 33, 44–45, 82, 86–91, 96–97, 105, 109, 113
prorogation 72, 177, 186
Pseudo-Asconius 118, 119
Ptolemy Auletes (king of Egypt) 80
pulvinaria 42
C. Pupius 150, 154, 182
Pyrrhus (king of Epirus) 20–21, 107–8

K. Quinctius Flamininus 150, 154, 182
T. Quinctius Flamininus 128, 177
Quirinus, temple of 123, 135–136, 180

res sacra 166, 171
Romulus 103

Sabines 95
sacra publica vs. *sacra privata* 5
Sallentini 32
Salus, temple of 142, 146, 179, 182
Samnites 28, 48, 52, 106, 107, 123, 158, 179, 180
Saturn, temple of 22
C. Scribonius Curio 181
Secession of the Plebs 111–12
Ti. Sempronius Gracchus 86, 92
P. Sempronius Sophus 32
P. Sempronius Tuditanus 64, 142, 146, 183, 187

Senate
  and *duumviri* 149–52, 158, 173, 176–78
  and magistrates' vows 36, 41–45, 48–49, 53–62, 175
  and peace treaties 50–53
  guardian of Roman religion 4, 64, 92–93, 113–15, 165–66, 168
  control of Sibylline Books 81–85, 89–91, 97, 113
  initiating new temples 105–6, 116
  involvement with temple building 5, 61, 116, 143, 146–48, 156–61, 178–82, 188–89, 190–91
  reassertion of authority 50, 59–61, 68, 185–87
senatus consultum 42, 45, 49–50, 57–58, 121–22, 143–44, 146, 167
Sentinum, battle of 29, 106, 127
C. Servilius 174 n. 39, 184
Servius Tullius 15, 64
shower of stones 21, 89
Sibylline Books 7, 20, 23, 25–26, 28, 41, 43–45, 47, 62, 76–116, 142–44, 147, 149, 175, 190
Sicily 99, 108, 109, 114, 132
solutio 37–38
Spain 29, 55, 58, 68, 69, 71, 129, 156, 157
Spes, temple of 102
spoils 59, 117, 119, 121–22, 124, 127–28, 131, 135–37, 160
L. Stertinius 71, 129
Struggle of the Orders 111, 165, 170
Summanus, temple of 21
supplicatio 17, 42, 92–96
Syracuse 136

Tarentum 106–7
Tarquinius Superbus 21, 76–77, 80, 114
Tellus, temple of 32
templum, definition of 11
Tertullian 196
theoxenia 94
Thermopylae, battle of 48, 146, 181
Tiber island 184
tithe, of spoils 30, 39, 53–54, 74, 144
Titus Tatius 101
Trebia, battle of 20, 86, 90, 95, 99, 182

tribuni militum 148
tribuni plebis 112, 163, 165–67, 169, 171, 179
tripudium 52
triumph 32, 38, 41, 59, 66, 67, 72, 124, 180, 185, 186, 187
triumphator 137
Troy 14, 108
M. Tullius Cicero 16, 17, 95, 102, 119, 132, 134, 166–168, 193
Tusculum 104

Uni (Etruscan goddess) 63

Vediovis, temple of *in insula* 146, 173, 184
Vediovis, temple of *in Capitolio* 184, 187
Veii 15, 44, 53, 62, 144
Velabrum 135
Venus Obsequens, temple of 127
Venus Erycina 62, 93, 100, 108–10, 114
  temple of *in Capitolio* 20, 97, 99–100, 102, 149, 151, 173, 175
  temple of *extra portam Collinam* 103, 148, 173, 181
Venus Genetrix, temple of 197
Venus Verticordia, temple of 21, 97, 102–3, 112
Venus Victrix, temple of 196–197
Venusia 107
ver sacrum 43–44, 47 n. 42, 94
Verminus 172
C. Verres 134
Vesta 101
  temple of 22
Vestal Virgins 21, 88, 103, 112, 167
Victoria 102
  temple of 99, 127
Victoria Virgo, temple of 131, 170, 181
Virgil 17
virtus 69
Virtus 62
  see also Honos and Virtus
Vitruvius 101
Volscians 24, 26
Volsinians 15
Vortumnus (Volsinian god) 12 n. 4
vota nuncupata 38, 46, 47
vota privata 60–61, 162
vota publica 36, 41, 46 n. 38, 60–61

wars
  and *supplicationes* 96
  and vows 4–5, 7, 20, 28–33, 35,
    45, 48–49, 53–57, 68–69,
    128–129, 190
  Cimbric 3, 131, 193
  Latin 30, 179
  Ligurian 72, 181
  First Macedonian 110
  Third Macedonian 71
  First Punic 20, 99, 102, 108
  Second Punic 31, 85–87, 90,
    99, 108–9, 127–28, 175, 183,
    189
  Second Samnite 106, 142, 179
  Third Samnite 23–24, 34, 55,
    106–7
  Volscian 24–25, 78